Back

TO THE

USER

CREATING

USER-FOCUSED

WEB SITES

New Riders

Tammy Sachs & Gary McClain, Ph. D.

Back to the User: Creating User-Focused Web Sites

Copyright © 2002 by New Riders Publishing

International Standard Book Number: 0-7357-1118-6

Library of Congress Catalog Card Number: 00-112191

Printed in the United States of America

First Printing: January 2002

06 05 04 03 02   7 6 5 4 3 2 1

Interpretation of the printing code: The rightmost double-digit number is the year of the book's printing; the rightmost single-digit number is the number of the book's printing. For example, the printing code 02-1 shows that the first printing of the book occurred in 2002.

Trademarks

Warning and Disclaimer

Publisher
David Dwyer

Associate Publisher
Stephanie Wall

Executive Editor
Steve Weiss

Product Marketing Manager
Kathy Malmloff

Managing Editor
Sarah Kearns

Acquisitions Editor
Leah Williams

Development Editor
John Rahm

Project Editor
Michael Thurston

Copy Editor
Audra McFarland

Technical Editors
Mark Emanuelson
Keith Instone

Publicist
Susan Nixon

Cover Designer
Aren Howell

Interior Designer
Kim Scott
www.bumpy.com

Compositor
Kim Scott

Cartoonist
Frank Sergi II

Indexer
Angie Bess

Table of Contents

Introduction   xxi

Part I   The View from 30,000 Feet

1   Why Your Web Site? For That Matter, Why Our Book?   3

How to Engage Target Users in the Development Process   5
   Learning to Think Like Your Users   6
Who Are We, Anyway? We Thought You Would Never Ask   8
How We Organized This Book   10

2   Use Research, Make It Actionable, Then Act on It While It's Hot   13

Why Do Research Anyway?   14
The Benefits of Web Development Research
 "What's My ROI?"   15
   Benefit 1: Generating Consensus   16
   Benefit 2: Learning to Think Like Your Target User   18
   Benefit 3: Research Saves Time and Money   19
   Benefit 4: Research Helps to "Sell It Up the Line"   20
   Benefit 5: Launching with Confidence   22
I've Bought into the Idea, Now Tell Me What I Need to Know
 to Make Research Pay for Itself   22
   Lesson 1: Research Before You Spend Big Bucks   23
   Lesson 2: Bring the Whole Team into the Process   24
   Lesson 3: Do Rapid Prototyping Not Paper Prototyping   25
   Lesson 4: Don't Treat Test Participants Like Lab Rats   26
   Lesson 5: Interview People Who Would or Do Actually Use
     Your Site   28
   Lesson 6: Don't Confuse "Can They Use It?" with
     "Will They Want To?"   29

Part II   Attracting Visitors to Your Site, at Least Long Enough to See What You Have to Offer

3   Your Homepage Is a 30-Second Window of Opportunity: Don't Be Shy!   33

Show Them What You Have to Offer   34
Strut Your Credentials, Particularly Where They Matter   37
Don't Have Credentials? Beg and Borrow (But Don't Steal) 'Em!   39
Use Your Real Estate Wisely   41
Make Sure Your Design Is in Service to Your Concept   44
Your Homepage Should Serve Your Strategic Goals   45
The More the Merrier
 Figure Out Who Your Customers Are and Welcome Them   49

Tell the Truth Up-Front
Bad News Is Worse in the Check-Out Aisle!   51
A Few Hard Questions   52

4   Understanding How Users "Bucket" Your Space
Better Use Their Language, Because They Are Not There to Join Your Company   **53**

And This Site Would Be About...?   54
I Love Your Org Chart... Too Bad I'm Not Looking for a Job   54
What Fascinating Categories You Have! Each One a Mystery
Unto Itself   58
I Know the Web Is a Creative Place, But You're Losing Me   60
From Russia with Love and the Limited "Role"
Russian Dolls and Rollovers   60
I Don't Want to Put Myself in That Category Either, and Don't
Call *Me* a Baby-Boomer!   63
Confronting the Unfamiliar: Start by Looking Outside
Your Organization   66
Just Because Every Department *Wants* a Button on the
Homepage Doesn't Mean They Need One   69
And Don't Forget to Ask: "Are We Offering What Target Users
Want and Expect?"   71
The View from 30,000 Feet   72
A Few Hard Questions   72

5   It's Okay to Be Different: Just Make Sure People Know What You Offer   **73**

Loved the Show, But Save It for Broadway
May I Please See My Checking Account Balance Now?   74
Knock It Off, Picasso! Art Is for the Walls   77
Designers Work in Mysterious Ways
Iconography Is Only Compelling in Church   82
Bells and Whistles Can Sink Your Anchors   84
Go Iconoclastic! But Navigate at Your Own Risk   86
Make Sure the Site Is in Sync with the Brand   88
The View from 30,000 Feet   89
A Few Hard Questions   90

6   People Don't Read: Don't Make Them!   **91**

If They Want to Read a Novel, They'll Buy One   92
Let Your Pictures Do the Talking   95
Pictures Don't Have to Say a Thousand Words, But They Need
to Say Something That Makes Sense   96
An Image Can Be Worth a Thousand Words... But Not If It Whispers   97

Images Often Work Harder Than Words   99
People Are Just as Literal with Words   100
First Things First
   Begin with Important Features   101
Tell People—Briefly—What You Want Them to Do   103
Save People from the Garden Path   104
If Your Mom Can't Read It, the Print's Too Small!   106
The View from 30,000 Feet   107
A Few Hard Questions   108

7   Just Because the Competition Does It That Way, Doesn't Mean It's Right   109

Jump Off the Bandwagon!   110
Model Online Processes After Offline People
   Design with Logic That Is Easy to Follow   111
Don't Reinvent the Wheel Online, Either!   113
Call Us Crazy, But We Think the Left Nav Bar Should Be Left
   Where It Is   114
People Just Want to Go Home! Don't Count on Your Logo to
   Get Them There   116
Two Kids, a Dog, and a Split Level   116
The View from 30,000 Feet   118
A Few Hard Questions   119

Part III   Making Sure They "Stick" Around
**   *Your Day-to-Day Challenge to Enhance User Experience***

8   A Frustrated User Is No User at All: Don't Let Him Leave Your Site!   123

Hitting the Wall
   Strategies for Recovery   124
Death by Frustration
   Who Will Save the Day?   126
The Customer Is Always Right
   Rules of Thumb for Managing Error Conditions   129
Users Aren't Programmers: Don't Assume They Know What
   You're Talking About   131
   1. How and When to Back Up   132
   2. How to Manipulate Windows   133
   3. How to Enlarge or Shrink an Image   134
   4. How and Why to Add a Plug-In/Upgrade Your Browser   134
Absolute Power Is a Good Thing
   Don't Mess with the User's Control   135
The View from 30,000 Feet   136
A Few Hard Questions   136

9   Adventures in Downloading
"…But Do I Have To?!"   **137**

   Plug-Ins!!! Plug-Ins???   137

   So You're Ready to See My Site? Not So Fast, Mr. User   138

   Download a Plug-In? The Only Thing I'm Downloading Is
      Confusion! What Does This Stuff *Do*, Anyway?   139

   Another Burning Question: "Why Should I?!"   141

   Help, I'm Lost! And Where's That Download?   143

   Déjà Vu All Over Again
      The Same Concerns to the Power of 10   145

   A Download Kind of Crowd? Finding a Starting Point   147

   Branding a Download and Downloading a Brand
      Be Consistent!   149

   The View from 30,000 Feet   149

   A Few Hard Questions   150

10   When I Need Your Assistance, Believe Me, I'll Ask!
Getting Information, Directions, Help, or Anything Else   **151**

   Thanks for the Great Directions, But I Already Know How
      to Do That   152

   Next Steps
      Can I Please Have a Hint?   154

   By the Way, What's in It for Me?   156

   I'm Not Going into That Room Until You Turn a Light On   161

   It's 10:00 P.M.: Do You Know Where Your Users Are (and
      Vice Versa)?   162

   Searching and Advanced Searching
      *I Know There's a Quicker Way to Get There, But I
      Want the Scenic Route*   166

   I Don't Have Time for "War and Peace"
      Notes on the Content Pages   167

   Thanks! Just When I'm Starting to Have Fun, You Tell Me It's Illegal   171

   Is It an Ad or Is It Information
      If It's Not Useful, It's Pollution   173

   The View from 30,000 Feet   174

   A Few Hard Questions   174

11   Hieroglyphics Are Only Interesting When You Are Visiting the Pyramids
Icons and Language   **175**

   Offline Metaphors Don't Always Translate Well to the Web   176

   Each and Every Icon or Button Can Have One—and Only
      One—Meaning   179

   "What's Clickable?" Is NOT a Trick Question   180

The Many Sides of Online Meaning   181

If Your Icons Need a Legend, You're in Trouble   182

The Design of a Site Is in and of Itself a Metaphor   184

The Web Is About Putting Control in the Hands of the User   185

The View from 30,000 Feet   186

The Hard Questions   186

Part IV   Zeroing In
Site Design and Navigation

12   Give the People What They Want (and More), or They'll Find Someone Who Can!   **189**

Content: You Know, That Stuff You Usually Have to Read   190

Oh Yeah? Says Who?   190

A Simple Rule of Thumb: Why Is It Here?   192

Established Brands
I Trust You, But Don't Disappoint Me   192

The Double-Edged Sword
Do I Want Content from This Brand?   195

New Brands
Why Should I Believe What You Have to Say?   198

Third-Party Content
A Judicious Solution   199

Is the Hype Machine in Operation?
*Overcoming User Skepticism of Articles and
"Objective" Viewpoints*   201

But I'm a Commerce Site, Right? Do I Even *Need* Content?   203

Providing Product Information and Reviews
First, the Challenge   203

And Now the Opportunity   204

Another Solution
Content as Community Through User-Generated Content   206

Are Other Users Always Credible?   208

Delivering Content
The Power of Letting the User Opt In   209

The View from 30,000 Feet   210

A Few Hard Questions   210

13   Functionality
Don't Just Lie There, Give Me Some Interaction   **211**

People Like to Play Games, Even When They're Not on a Game Site   212

The Dell Configurator
The First Lesson in the Value of Interactive Features   213

Self-Tests
Why Do You Think Horoscopes Are So Popular?   215

Self-Tests Can Also Help You Connect Prospects to Your Products   216

Interactive Tools
Another Variation of the Self-Test   218

Polls Also Pull Them in, as Long as the Results Are Instant   219

Screensavers and Other "Give-Aways" Also Invite Return Visits
and Build Your Brand   221

The View from 30,000 Feet   222

A Few Hard Questions   222

14   Whiz! Bang! Boom!
Graphics in Service to Content and Functionality   **223**

The First Rule: The Web Is a Visual Medium
Users Want Some Color   224

Users Expect Consistent Use of Graphics and Color Throughout
the Site   224

Users Don't Want to be Delayed by Graphics   226

A Guiding Principle: If It's Not Needed, Get Rid of It   228

Lose the Clutter: White Space Works   230

Another Big Question: Is This Little Picture Actually FOR Anything?   231

A Final Caution: Are You Sure the User Is in Control of
the Experience?   233

The View from 30,000 Feet   234

A Few Hard Questions   234

15   Search
When to Keep Them in Your Playpen and When to Open Them Up to the Universe   **235**

Don't Assume Search and Browse Are Mutually Exclusive   236
Search Engine Jocks   236
Browsers   237
Browser/Searcher Combos   237
The Only Consistency Is Inconsistency   237

Lose the Boolean Logic
Nobody But Statisticians Cares About Probability   238

Spelling
Don't Be So Picky—This Isn't English Class   240

You Say Tomato, I Say...   242

Was That "Lemon" Candy, Candles, or Body Lotion?
Understand How Your Users Want to Search   243

Advanced Search
Your Last Resort...   245

Beware Multiple Fields
Relationships Are Assumed Where They May Not Exist   247

Inside the Playpen or the Whole Web?   249

Search Results
How Much Is Too Much?   251

The View from 30,000 Feet   253

A Few Hard Questions   253

16   Navigation
You Know You're in Trouble When Users Look for Your Site Map   **255**

Let Your Homepage Be Your Guide   256

Be Persistent in Your Navigation   259

A Trail of Bread Crumbs   261

The Customer Is Always Right
"Invalid Entry" Is Not an Option   262

This Isn't Print
Use Anchor Links to Provide Quick Access to Multiple Choices   264

Silos Are for Hay, Not Web Sites
Don't Make People Go Back to Go Forward   264

Use Images to Show People the Way   266

Offer Critical Instructions in Such a Way That They Cannot
Be Missed   266

Don't Force People to Commit Before They Are Ready   267

Scroll at Your Own Risk!   268

The View from 30,000 Feet   269

A Few Hard Questions   270

17   E-Commerce
If They Can't Find It, They Won't Buy It   **271**

Understand Current Buying Behavior   272

Don't Assume a Standard Approach to Shopping in Your Category   274

Use Shopping Metaphors That Make Sense   275

People Want to Know What They're Buying
Use Pictures and Descriptions   277

Track with the Buying Process   279

Offer Incentives   281

Can I Take It Back?
Life Is Mysterious Enough...   283

Use the Fulfillment Process to Cross-Sell   285

Shipping and Handling? Don't Try to Hide It   287

Stay Consistent with Your Brand   289

The View from 30,000 Feet   291

A Few Hard Questions   291

Part V   Back to the 30,000-Foot View
Your Site and Your Brand

18   The Challenges of Transferring an Established Brand to the Web
Top 10 Considerations   **295**

Users Expect Your Site to Look Like You   296

Your Site Should Be Organized, Just Like You   299

What Language Do You Use with Customers? Use the Same on
  Your Web Site   300

Sweat the Details (Down to the Last Tool)   301

Sweating More of the Details
  Don't Forget Site Quality   302

The E-Commerce Question: "How Does the Web Fit with My
  Other Channels?"   303

Account Access
  Encouraging Repeat Visits   304

Don't Disenfranchise Your Customers
  Make Service and Technical Support Useful   305

Consider Adding Premium Services for High-Value Customers   307

Leverage Your Marketing Messages, But Don't Make Your Site
  a Commercial   308

The View from 30,000 Feet   309

A Few Hard Questions   309

19   Business-to-Business
Challenges and Opportunities   **311**

Understand How Your Customers Do Business   312

Remember, Company Rules Exist for a Reason   314

Your Client List Is Your Credibility   315

People Stick to Their Own Kind: Make Sure They Know You
  Are One of Them   317

What's in It for Me?
  Look for Allies Before Attacking a Market   319

Don't Forget That Your Customers Have Customers   320

Leverage Your Brand and Stick to Your Core Competencies   321

Be Careful Who You Set Your Sights On   322

Know the Difference Between End Users and Decision Makers   323

The View from 30,000 Feet   324

A Few Hard Questions   324

Part VI   And the View from Outer Space
Staying Ahead of (or at Least Keeping Up With) the
Speed of Technology

20   Step Out of the Shadows and into Their Shoes
The Power of Listening   **327**

Why Listen? Isn't the Answer Already Obvious?   328

The User Dialogue Establishes the Foundation for Your Site   328
Is It Time for a Revamp? Only Your Users Really Know   329
What Do They Want Next? Anticipating the Curve   330

Checking the Oil: Creating an Ongoing Dialogue   331

You Can't Test in a Vacuum
New Features Versus the Whole Site   332

No Matter How Sophisticated Your Site, Don't Underestimate
the Role of the Offline World   333

21   Just When You Think You Know Everything, It Changes   **335**

Adoption Patterns Do Not Remain Consistent   336

User Needs Grow, and Sites Grow with Them   336

The Role of a Function Can Shift and Mature   338
Chat   338
Online Bidding   338
Message Boards   338
Online Calculators and Worksheets   339
Video/Audio   339
E-Commerce   339

Morphing: First Web Sites, Then Complementary Technologies   340

Parting Words in the Form of a Reminder   341

Appendix   A Crash Course in Web Development Research   **343**

Which Method Do I Use?   344

Focus Groups: What They Are and What They Do   344
Some Rules of Thumb   345
How to Structure a Focus Group   345
How to Make the Results of Focus Group Research Actionable   346

User Experience Research: What It Is and How You Do It   347
Some Rules of Thumb   348
Structuring a User Experience Interview   350
Making User Experience Testing Actionable   351

Index   **353**

About the Authors

Tammy Sachs is President of Sachs Insights, which was founded in 1987. The driving idea behind Sachs Insights was to establish a qualitative research consultancy that brings a user focus to the development of software, web sites, and other interactive products and services. Tammy heads a team of consultants and researchers that help corporate and agency clients integrate research into the product development process, thereby bringing successful, intuitive web sites and software to market. Prior to founding SI, Tammy was a product developer at Citicorp and was responsible for the design, research, and implementation of an interactive home banking product. She has also held a senior planning and research position at Ogilvy & Mather. Tammy attended Wesleyan University, graduating magna cum laude with a B.A. in Psychology and Theater. She also holds an M.B.A. in Marketing from NYU's Stern School of Business.

Gary R. McClain, Ph.D., is Director of Research at Sachs Insights and has more than 10 years experience as a qualitative researcher, focus group moderator, and user experience tester. Gary has also been employed as a strategic planner at Ogilvy-One, working primarily on the IBM account and with the interactive group. He has experience in Systems Design and User Training, which included the development of instructor-led and computer-based training courses at Infodata Systems and Martin Marietta Data Systems. He has held marketing management positions at Information Builders and Sterling Software (formerly VM Software). Additionally, he has written and edited numerous information technology books and two self-help books. He has done graduate work in Clinical Psychology and Education, with a focus on adult development and learning, and he holds a Ph.D. from the University of Michigan.

Dedications

About the Tech Editors

Mark Emanuelson is manager of service provider market development for Cisco Systems covering Europe, Middle East, and Africa. Prior to his current role he led strategic initiatives in Internet marketing and e-commerce development. He has been a university lecturer on Internet project management and marketing. Mark started his career in Silicon Valley where he earned his MBA from Santa Clara University. This native-born Californian now enjoys living with his wife and two-year-old daughter in the United Kingdom.

Keith Instone is an information architect with the User Experience team for ibm.com. He previously worked for Argus Associates, where he provided web usability and information architect consulting for clients such as American Express Financial Advisors, Egreetings.com, Ernst & Young, LookSmart, and Weather.com (The Weather Channel). He was an early adopter of user-centered design practices to the web, including marketing-oriented user testing, navigation inspection, and card sorting. He is the curator of Usable Web, the leading directory of web usability links. You can see what he is up to now at http://keith.instone.org/.

Acknowledgments

More than anyone, Tammy thanks her co-author, Gary McClain, for collaborating so easily and sharing his broad experience as a writer with her.

Gary feels the same way about Tammy. Her drive and enthusiasm were a constant inspiration.

The folks at New Riders—Steve Weiss, Leah Williams, Chris Nelson, and John Rahm—have encouraged us and offered wonderful guidance throughout the process. Our agent, David Fugate of Waterside Productions, believed so strongly in the concept behind the book that he fought long and hard both to maintain our core idea and to offer many ways to enhance it.

We'd like to thank our editor at Sachs Insights, Liam Murphy, who is himself an accomplished author, for painstakingly polishing each chapter, as well as giving us an extra push when it was needed (often) to stay on schedule.

Gary's team of researchers generously shared their stories and ideas from interviewing thousands of research participants and working closely with developers, marketers, and other stakeholders in a myriad of online ventures. They include Lisa Northrop, Mark Safire, Paris Patton, Kathleen Hoski, Susan Warshauer, Katie Guillory, and Jon Helfgot.

Robert Miner, our Managing Director at Sachs Insights, contributed the title and a number of key insights that are woven into the book.

Juliette Quinlan helped immeasurably with administrative support, as did Brian Wallace.

Importantly, we want to thank wonderful clients that have allowed us to partner with them and share their vision to create powerful, compelling, and intuitive web sites, software, video games, and interactive voice response systems.

Tammy wants to thank Eugene Sachs for sparking her initial curiosity about the way people think, learn, and process information; Pat Doyle for introducing her to the world of advertising and marketing; and Doug Newman for teaching her how to collaborate with teams that included the diverse perspectives of marketing and technology.

Last, Tammy thanks her parents, Norma and Jerry Kessler, for encouraging her dream to write and publish this book!

And as always, Gary says: "Thanks, Mom!"

A Message from New Riders

As the reader of this book, you are our most important critic and commentator. We value your opinion and want to know what we're doing right, what we could do better, in what areas you'd like to see us publish, and any other words of wisdom you're willing to pass our way.

As Executive Editor at New Riders, I welcome your comments. You can fax, email, or write me directly to let me know what you did or didn't like about this book—as well as what we can do to make our books better. When you write, please be sure to include this book's title, ISBN, and author, as well as your name and phone or fax number. I will carefully review your comments and share them with the authors and editors who worked on the book.

Please note that I cannot help you with technical problems related to the topic of this book, and that due to the high volume of email I receive, I might not be able to reply to every message. Thanks.

Email: steve.weiss@newriders.com
Fax: 317-581-4663
Mail: Steve Weiss
          Executive Editor
          New Riders Publishing
          201 West 103rd Street
          Indianapolis, IN 46290 USA

Visit Our Web Site: www.newriders.com

On our Web site, you'll find information about our other books, the authors we partner with, book updates and file downloads, promotions, discussion boards for online interaction with other users and with technology experts, and a calendar of trade shows and other professional events with which we'll be involved. We hope to see you around.

Email Us from Our Web Site

Go to www.newriders.com and click on the Contact Us link if you

- Have comments or questions about this book.
- Want to report errors that you have found in this book.
- Have a book proposal or are interested in writing for New Riders.
- Would like us to send you one of our author kits.

- Are an expert in a computer topic or technology and are interested in being a reviewer or technical editor.
- Want to find a distributor for our titles in your area.
- Are an educator/instructor who wants to preview New Riders books for classroom use. In the body/comments area, include your name, school, department, address, phone number, office days/hours, text currently in use, and enrollment in your department, along with your request for either desk/examination copies or additional information.

Introduction

We often marvel to each other about how, in the world of the web, time passes more like in "dog years" than "human years." Yet, with seven dog years equal to one human year, even this metaphor doesn't quite do justice to the rapid progression of web adoption. Some days, we feel like web adoption more closely approximates the speed of light.

The yardstick of user expectation is constantly raised. First, a handful of leading-edge users tested the water by buying online. Soon after that, more and more of the users we talked to—even brand new users—were not only buying online but making their first forays onto the web with this purpose in mind. Over a relatively short period of time, web sites evolved from being "online brochures" to offering sophisticated services like account access, resumé submission, and customer service.

The role of the web has emerged as a means for companies to build their brands through enhancing relationships with their customers and prospects. As web sites have evolved, the stakes have also gotten higher.

Companies have discovered that the opportunity goes hand-in-hand with the responsibility. Users are demanding sites that are not only easy to use but also offer function and content that add value—not just amusement—to their lives. They are judging companies by the "intuitiveness" of their web sites.

The brand is the experience.

Although web adoption has grown by leaps and bounds, users are still real people. Not all users think and perceive alike. They bring offline perceptions and experiences to the web—different decision-making processes, terminology, and brand imagery and varying levels of web-savviness. All of these unique people come to the same web site expecting to have their needs and expectations met, as well as their time (or lack of time) respected.

Companies, in turn, have learned the keys to meeting these demands. In a nutshell, here's how:

- Talk with users.
- Listen to them.
- Make them part of the development team.

Since the early '90s, we have helped companies better understand their audiences by bringing users into our user experience lab. Once there, web site developers and marketers sat tooth by jowl with users of all shapes, sizes, and sophistication levels as they experienced web sites in various stages of development or talked about their expectations, wants, and needs in focus groups. Through the one-way mirror, developers, marketers, and company executives, representing companies ranging from Fortune 100 corporations to start-ups, along with educational institutions and non-profit organizations, watched this process.

In our roles as researcher and consultant, we have found ourselves providing the "voice of the user," helping the development and marketing teams take this invaluable user input and turn it into recommendations and strategy. Our clients have learned that the user's input is invaluable. After all, real people will be using their sites, so why not make those people part of the team?

This doesn't mean that clients always like what they hear. User feedback is often met with sighs of relief; but it is just as often met with expressions of shock or gritted teeth. However, our clients recognize the risk of not having their users help guide the next stage of development. All the best intentions and hard work still aren't enough if customers and prospects can't or won't use their site.

So, what have we learned during these years in the user experience lab?

We've learned a lot about what does and doesn't work in web sites. Brand imagery. Navigation. Nomenclature. Organization. Users have taught us through their comments, as well as their expressions of delight and frustration. Our clients have also taught us much as we worked with them on taking user feedback and struggling with how to reflect it in their sites. It's been a fascinating and exciting process.

Back to the User is about what we've learned: It contains strategic insights that we have gained, practical tips on what to do and what to avoid, and some guidance on how to bring your own users into the development process. While there is no "cookie cutter" formula for making a perfect web site, we have a lot of ideas about what does work, and it is our intention that you will be able to, in turn, use what we have learned to help streamline your own development and marketing efforts, as well as avoid some of the pitfalls that we have encountered.

But most of all, we hope that, throughout the process of building your web site and as you continue to enhance your site in the future, you'll remember to listen to the most important voice of all: the voice of *your* user.

PART I

The View from 30,000 Feet

1   Why Your Web Site?
    For That Matter, Why Our Book?   3

2   Use Research, Make It Actionable, Then Act
    on It While It's Hot   13

CHAPTER ONE

Why Your Web Site?

For That Matter, Why Our Book?

In this book, we will investigate and advocate the role of user experience testing in web site development. User experience, for our purposes, refers to the perceptions and reactions that users have when they visit your site—their thoughts and feelings, cognition and emotion, which ultimately affect whether or not they return.

The first, most obvious question is "Why do it all?" The answer is both complicated and simple. In today's competitive marketplace, cyberspace is increasingly cluttered, indeed littered, with the remains of failed dot-coms—grim reminders that attracting and *maintaining* a presence among users is crucial for both short-term corporate survival (the "honeymoon" period) and long-term viability. It is our view that, ultimately, it is the user who will decide whether any given web site is a success or a failure. Paradoxically, many companies that create web sites do so in a vacuum, failing to ask the very people they seek to serve just what a site should offer, let alone how they would like the site to work. In this book, we spend a lot of time talking about such issues and providing examples. Here are some of the main problems we run into:

- Homepages that don't announce what the site is all about or who it is designed for.

- Sites that frequently don't appeal to their intended target audience.

- Sites that, at the outset, require the user to upgrade their browser, do complex downloads, or understand technical terms and acronyms in order to use the site.

- Great business models that are poorly executed so users can't find information or transact easily.

- Poor concepts that somehow find their way onto sites—when they should have found their way back to the cyberspace drawing board!

Figure 1.1
Here are a few examples of sites that ultimately failed, for various reasons.

Back to the User: Creating User-Focused Web Sites is based on our extensive, first-hand knowledge of user experience testing in New York City, across the USA, and around the world. We have spoken to and observed thousands of web users—both consumers and professionals—in focus groups and user-experience interviews. By so doing, we have helped our clients launch web sites and other interactive services that target users have a need for and are able to intuitively use.

Over the course of our work, we have identified problems common to all web sites, and also a wide variety of site-specific conundrums (be they e-commerce or business-to-business sites) that occur when a user's perspective is not considered. The intent of this book is to share our collective learning with our readers and, in so doing, help companies large and small to conceive and build web sites that create powerful relationships between the companies and their users.

How to Engage Target Users in the Development Process

While marketing research and the ubiquitous focus group have been around for many decades, relatively little is known about how to effectively adapt research techniques to the development of web sites. In part, this is because the Internet is a new and evolving organism: Those who use it have little choice but to be flexible and always ready to adapt their online practices at an exponential speed. Keep in mind, for example, that web sites began as marketing platforms or "online brochures." Over time, many companies began offering core business applications online. Consequently, user-centered design is critical.

Exacerbating this decidedly unfriendly pace, there has also been a gaping disconnect among the various professionals who must be orchestrated in order to proceed with the development process. The people who conceive of and build web sites come together from many different worlds: designers, programmers, marketers, retailers, librarians, cognitive psychologists, and others. Many clients we encounter do not have traditional marketing backgrounds and are unfamiliar with marketing research and what is actually involved in identifying the target market. The broader concern many developers have is how to bring target users into site development in a timely and cost-effective manner.

Therefore, the first goal of this book is to provide a systematic approach to understanding web site development from the proverbial "Day One"—when the site is still at an early conceptual stage or is the rudimentary basis of a business plan. We provide examples of how a wide variety of dot-com initiatives both large and small, as well as "pure plays" and established brands, have used focus groups and user experience testing to validate and evolve their concepts and shape a powerful, intuitive user experience into a viable online brand.

A second objective is to empower all those who participate in web initiatives (from the CEO to the programmer) with the confidence to determine how the target user can mold the development of a web site. The book will demystify the steps and terminology associated with this research and make its purpose and impact crystal clear, so that decision-makers will be able to effectively assess how and when to use development research to create and launch their site. Basically, developers need to ensure that decisions are based on true user needs instead of opinions of what the user needs.

Learning to Think Like Your Users

The broadest goal of this book is to share the collective wisdom we've gained from conducting tens of thousands of focus groups and user experience interviews about what does and does not work in building a web site. We believe that the primary lesson learned by this research is straightforward in theory, however difficult it might be to implement in practice: To be successful, web site developers must shift their thinking from that of business strategists, technologists, or marketers to that of *users*. As we have said, this is easier said than done. While we are all web users, web development team members are not necessarily representative users of their own sites. But companies must accomplish it, we hold, if the development process is to be successful over the long run, in the eyes of its users.

Broadly, *Creating User-Focused Web Sites* explores the following issues:

- Determining if the underlying idea for a web site actually grabs the interest of its intended audience.

- Deciding what online expectations target users have of a brand, and whether these differ from offline perceptions.

- Understanding who a company's target audience is, what the user's needs are, and—by extension—what *your* site can offer that competing sites cannot.

- Focusing on the language and logic target users bring to the table—so that your site doesn't resemble an "org chart," marketing plan, or technical manual.

Although no two sites are the same, many lessons can be learned from other companies' experiences about which "landmines" to avoid when you're trying to create a web site that people will want to use. We offer some guiding principles that are intended to shape the thinking of those who build sites and sharpen the judgment of those who commission them.

Finally, *Creating User-Focused Web Sites* is both practical and action-oriented. As such, it is written for members of all the "camps" involved in web site development. Thus, developers, marketers, and executives can all acquire an understanding of how to connect with that most critical lynchpin in the design process: the user. More explicitly, our book is intended for:

- Senior management of large or small companies who are about to build or rebuild a web site

- Web designers, developers, and information architects

- Web marketers and consultants

- Advertising agency "creatives," planners, and account executives

- Anyone else in an organization who is involved in creating the group's web site

Who *Are* We, Anyway? We Thought You Would Never Ask

Collectively, we are *Sachs Insights*. SI was founded in 1987 to serve the needs of marketers and product developers. Our goal is to bring target users into the development process early on and in a meaningful way so that our clients can launch web sites and other interactive services that consumers want and can use intuitively. If you are developing interactive services, we feel that it is essential for you to tackle issues of both marketability (appeal, positioning/ pricing, competitive differentiation, and so on) and usability (navigation and intuitiveness of language and logic).

Our experience with web site development research spans such categories as children's education and entertainment, financial services, travel, technology products and services, customer service applications, small business, vertical market applications, and e-commerce. In addition to web sites, we have supported the development of desktop software, CD-ROMs, interactive voice response systems, and interactive television program guides.

Figure 1.2

Sachs Insights is a customer experience consultancy.

More specifically, we, the authors, are Tammy Sachs, President of SI, and Gary McClain, SI Director of Research. In 1988, Tammy left her position as product developer for Citicorp, where she was responsible for designing and implementing interactive home banking products, to establish a qualitative research consultancy. Her ambition was to bring a user focus to the development of software, web sites, and other interactive products and services. Today, she heads a team of consultants and researchers who help corporate and agency clients integrate research into the product development process in order to create powerful, salient online brands and effective, user-friendly experiences.

Sharing Tammy's vision has been Gary McClain, Director of Research at SI. Prior to coming to work with Sachs Insights, Gary had acquired ten years of experience as a qualitative researcher, conducting focus groups and usability testing. He was employed as a strategic planner at OgilvyOne, working primarily on the IBM account. He also has experience in systems design and user training (which included the development of instructor-led and computer-based training courses) at Infodata Systems and Martin Marietta Data Systems, and he has written and edited numerous information technology-related books and two self-help books.

We believe that our years of hands-on experience with user testing have given us unique "insight," if you will, into the importance of qualitative research in developing web sites that work for people. Throughout the chapters that follow, a refrain to which we will frequently return is that the power of the user experience cannot be gleaned through standard quantitative methods alone because these fail to ascertain what users really want and expect from web sites. We have found the response of users in testing to be variously enthusiastic, heated, and searching. Frequently, the responses to testing confound, rather than confirm, the most deeply held perceptions of developers—a fact which, more than any other, has accentuated and justified the need for research. But seeing is believing, and in this book we will share our vision with you.

How We Organized This Book

Throughout the text, we will refer to a "30,000-foot view." Basically, this expresses our sense of the holistic view that users have of a given web site, a view that incorporates navigation, design, organization, content, functionality, and branding. As developers or marketers, you could easily focus on only one or two of these considerations and lose sight of the "bigger picture." It is not uncommon, for example, to focus too closely on design and miss opportunities to offer functionality that target users really want. Likewise, developers often focus exclusively on the nuts and bolts of their site and pay less attention to the brand the site was being designed for in the first place.

We have learned the valuable lesson that users have the "30,000-foot view," even if developers don't. Intuitively, users sense when something is missing, and they simply move on. Accordingly, we

The Big Picture.

devote our research to helping our clients attain the 30,000-foot view. In each chapter, we will give you some of our thoughts on how you can maintain that view while developing and marketing your site.

Creating User-Focused Web Sites is presented in six broad sections that examine, in sequence, the following topics:

● The role of user experience research in building successful web sites.

● How to attract visitors to one's web site in the first place.

● How to enhance the users' experience once they are there.

● How to engage processes of design (or re-design) and navigation to make using your web site an intuitive and powerful experience.

● The relationship between branding and web site design.

● Keeping up with technology and innovation in the fast-paced world of Internet commerce.

CHAPTER TWO

Use Research, Make It Actionable, Then Act on It While It's Hot

In Chapter 1, "Why Your Web Site?," we discussed the importance of research as a tool for understanding the expectations, perceptions, and ultimately the experiences of users. Because of the emphasis on research, and because it is through conducting research that we have formed our own thoughts and opinions on web site creation, this seems like a good place to provide our thoughts on how we define and conduct web-related research.

The guiding principal of this chapter may be summed up in the following phrase:

> *The cost of research is high, but the cost of failure is higher.*

With this in mind, this chapter focuses on the benefits of doing research and some of the guiding principles behind how to effectively integrate research into the development process. It is not intended to be a primer on how to conduct research. That would deserve a book unto itself. However, for those interested in learning how to plan, design, and/or manage research throughout the web development process, refer to the Appendix, "A Crash Course in Web Development Research."

Why Do Research Anyway?

After all, the web is constantly changing, and anything you launch today might well be history six months from now. How can you justify the cost of doing research and, moreover, the time you invest in it? How can consumers judge the potential of a new idea or concept? What answers will research provide and how can this feedback be channeled into the development process?

These are just some of the concerns developers express when faced with the question of whether—and how—to bring target users (customers, prospects, and so on) into the development process. Given tight budgets and even tighter timetables, many web development teams question the need to do research. Some lack the expertise or resources to figure out when, how, and what to test, let alone how to integrate results into the site. But developers must ask themselves what research is worth.

Such questions are made even more critical with the failure of many ill-conceived dot-coms, as well as web-based applications on more established sites. More than ever, investors are looking for evidence that there is a "business there;" that if you build an e-commerce web site, customers will come. Similarly, corporate sponsors want reassurance that new web-based initiatives will provide a return on investment and will serve to enhance (and, of course, in no way damage) their existing brands.

The Benefits of Web Development Research
"What's My ROI?"

One of the most exciting aspects of our industry is that it brings together people from so many disciplines—design, marketing, technology, and others. When this "meeting of the minds" goes well, the outcome is a smooth development process and a site that offers a powerful online experience. When it does not go well, what results is a great deal of frustration, lost time, wasted money, and conflicting beliefs and expectations. Indeed, seeing and hearing real people respond to a concept or a prototype is a deeply compelling reason to do qualitative research (using focus groups, interviews, and user experience labs) precisely because of the consensus that observing research generates among diverse members of the team. This section outlines the five most significant benefits, which we have found to be pillars of successful web site development.

Benefit 1: Generating Consensus

It is perhaps an inevitable aspect of human nature that we project our thoughts, values, expectations, and assumptions onto others. Likewise, various players in web site development make this leap when anticipating the needs of their customers. Programmers assume that users share their technological prowess. Marketing people assume that customers respond to ads, promotions, and quizzes. Designers often think that customers appreciate and understand the subtleties of their illustrations, color palettes, and iconography. Hence, if I like Flash, they'll like it. If I hate to register, they will. If I like to personalize a site, they will, too. If I can complete the purchase path with ease, so will they. If those icons make sense to me, they'll make sense to others as well.

In other words, the diverse development team may *itself* be in disarray when it comes to deciding how to proceed with a site. To this we respond, "Enter the user!" (also known as the end user, target user, prospect, investor, or customer). These are the people you most expect to benefit from your site. They may be people who currently buy your product or use your service. They may be people you want to invest in your company or people you want to attract as employees.

One of the beautiful aspects of research is that it incorporates this completely neutral party into the development team. Like other members of the team, consumers are important stakeholders. The outcome of the site—its ease of use and its value—matters to them. And, like developers, consumers come with their own preconceived expectations and experiences that influence how they navigate and what features and pathways interest them. However, unlike other members of the team, customers do not view the site from a professional vantage point, but as users. And it is this perspective that makes their input so important. Bringing target customers into the development process through research serves to:

- Quickly resolve differences of opinion among team members

- Answer questions that are troubling and or dividing the team

- Create a unified perspective—that of the customer

And yet, the way in which consumers are brought into this process is far from apparent. Making the decision to include consumers in the research team is one thing, but setting about the task raises a host of new questions and challenges, the most immediate being "What is the best way to make use of consumer input in web site development?" We suggest that any effective strategy for integrating customer input involves, first and foremost, learning to *think* like a consumer.

Benefit 2: Learning to Think Like Your Target User

There is nothing more painful than watching a team of mostly twenty-something males sit around trying to predict what kind of educational games would engage a preschooler; or better yet, what would enhance the online shopping experience of women purchasing cosmetics. We've observed similarly tortured teams as they attempted to figure out what the optimal online customer service experience would be for first time PC buyers. How about trying to determine what moms want from an online disposable diaper site and what small business owners want in a portal targeted to them?

Our point is that it is really difficult, if not impossible, to truly place oneself in someone else's shoes—be that someone a teen, an entrepreneur, a mom, a pet owner, or an accountant. Yet, the paradox is that most web development entails doing just that, because it involves building an online experience that will be rewarding for a group of users whose needs and expectations are likely very different from those of the developers themselves. Keep in mind here that once a site is live, your users will be totally on their own—sitting in their offices, living rooms, or kitchens—and representing a wide range of backgrounds and levels of sophistication. Doesn't this raise the bar for usability?

In contrast to the efforts of developers who merely imagine user-response, we have observed something very interesting about development teams that watch a few well-conducted focus groups and/or user experience labs: They begin to think and speak like customers. Gone are their *assumptions* about the following issues:

- Who they think customers are, and what they want in a site experience.

- What content or features they seek.

- What expectations they have of the brand online.

- What language and logic they use.

- What will draw them to the site—and what will keep them there.

Over time, bringing target users into the development process accomplishes a transformation in the perspective of developers, marketers, and designers. Through interaction with and observation of real-world users, developers undergo a metamorphosis in perspective: They come to view a site through the eyes of the consumer. What is so powerful (and exciting) about this transformation (besides the fact that it creates consensus among the team) is that it is *actionable*, and can be put in the service of all future web site development.

Herein lies the value of research. It holds out the promise of becoming completely immersed in the way target users think, speak, "bucket," and "label" the features developers want to offer them. Moreover, participating in the research process gives developers a window into what customers themselves want (and don't want) from a particular site or brand. To reiterate, the cumulative impact of this immersion is a gradual transformation from thinking like a developer/marketer to thinking like a user. And the impact of this transformation is felt far after the research is over.

Benefit 3: Research Saves Time and Money

Perhaps the strongest complaint or frustration that developers experience is where to start, when their instincts are telling them to "get it all done at once." As one CEO of a financial services site put it, "Do I create the content first, select the features, or develop the high-level architecture? And, which of the three audiences we serve do I start with?" These are typical questions that plague development teams and needlessly slow down their efforts. Time certainly means money, but it also means a delay in getting to market.

It stands to reason that the acts of gaining team consensus and learning to think like a user will shorten the development cycle and mitigate those painful "forks in the road" and "simultaneous development paths," where a lot of money is spent and time wasted. These obstacles tend to be minimized when users are present to perform the following functions:

- Select among multiple creative approaches.

- Prioritize which functionality and content hold the most promise.

- Kill ideas that are not consumer driven.

- Identify ideas and occasionally "killer apps" that can add tremendous value.

The organic way that the development process unfolds when users are in essence "development partners" runs exponentially faster than when developers are left on their own to intuit (or simply guess) what users would want. In short, having users present impacts the development process in ways such as these:

- It generates a higher level of confidence among the team that they are on the right track. This creates a level of excitement that serves as a catalyst.

- It serves to prioritize the development of features and content based on their appeal and value to users.

And both of these save time and money. 'Nuff said.

Benefit 4: Research Helps to "Sell It Up the Line"

One of the most difficult and time-intensive aspects of the development process is getting buy-in from stakeholders and investors at key junctures in the development process. The challenge is getting the attention of this audience and having them buy into your concept—both financially and in their "gut." To this end, there is nothing more compelling than *seeing* real users talk about the concept with enthusiasm and actually use a prototype of the site with ease and interest. There are two benefits to this:

- Even if research uncovers major flaws in the concept or in the execution of the site, it can also identify powerful fixes.

- Seeing this process unfold is typically very comforting to investors.

As we do throughout the book, we will illustrate this point with an example from our own research. One client, a senior Internet strategist at a major bank, put it this way: "The first $100,000 in funding that I get for a new initiative, I spend building a compelling prototype that I can put on the desks of senior management so they can kick the tires. The next $100,000 I spend on research to explore the concept, get reactions to the prototype, and determine who is the most likely target user." He felt that without a tangible product and observable reaction to it, he'd get bogged down in strategy decks and quantitative assessments of the marketplace and the opportunity—none of which would serve to capture the interest and imagination of stakeholders.

Benefit 5: Launching with Confidence

Another significant reward for doing user research is the palpable sense of confidence that developers have when they believe the web site they have built truly matches the user's needs and expectations. To the extent that it does, the site will live up to the goals that you have set for it, building and supporting the brand and delivering its key functionality. These goals, by the way, need to have been clearly communicated to everyone on the team; exploring the viability of these goals and then affirming them or learning that they may be unrealistic, are a reason for conducting initial research. If developers feel certain that their web site concept generates strong interest among users and that users can intuitively navigate to successfully get information and transact as intended, they'll be far less likely to face unpleasant surprises at launch.

This is not to imply that a compelling and intuitive site experience automatically leads to marketplace success. Obviously, a host of other factors—from the caprice of timing to good marketing and PR—impact how well a site is received in and by the marketplace.

However, research *can* ensure that the most powerful rendition of the initial concept is the one brought to market and, in so doing, that each user's experience is as intuitive and compelling as possible. In today's marketplace, this is not optional, but the required price of entry. Why? Because users are quick to recall a bad experience, and they tend, just as quickly, to share it with others.

I've Bought into the Idea, Now Tell Me What I Need to Know to Make Research Pay for Itself

What follows are some of the most critical lessons we've learned from wearing a variety of hats in the research industry (notably, that of research vendor, web development agency, and "client"). Learning from these lessons can help you get the most value out of the research dollars you spend.

Lesson 1: Research Before You Spend Big Bucks

The idea here is that we all get emotionally vested in our "concept" of how a site should look and work, who it will appeal to, and how it should be positioned or branded. The earlier target users are brought into the act of development, the less emotionally attached the team is to a particular set of ideas, and the more open they are to hearing from users. This is especially true if these two things can be said:

- Users voice thoughts that vary considerably from the team's way of thinking. It may be necessary to go back to the drawing board at that point and come up with new concepts based on direction provided in the research.

- The concept is truly unique and does not just follow a roadmap based on competitive activity. In other words, nobody else is doing it, so you are working in uncharted territory.

One of our first dot-com clients came to us with the idea of creating a site where consumers could air their complaints about poor customer service to marketers (currently, numerous sites offer this opportunity). The concept for the site derived from terrible customer service which the founders had had with a particular company.

In order to determine if this idea was one that would fly on the web, this start-up company chose to implement focus groups before they designed the first screen. Before they had even selected a name for the site, they sought to discover the following things:

- What kinds of people would want to post their complaints on the web?

- What kinds of complaints would those people choose to post?

- What action or satisfaction would they wish to receive in return for their posting?

- What functionality would it take to get users to visit, register, and return?

The founders learned that people did, in fact, respond very well to the idea of posting complaints, but for very different reasons than they themselves had. For example, some didn't expect a response;

they simply wanted the opportunity to vent. Learning who their target audience was and what drove the audience's interest subsequently enabled the developers to create a successful site and build functionality that addressed the needs of their audience.

As this example attests, the earlier research is done, the less dependent the team will be on *their own* assumptions about

- Who the site is for

- Why they will come

- What they will do on the site

- How they will experience the site

And, the earlier the team has answers to these questions, the more fluid and organic the development process will be. Learning can be used to guide the evolution of concepts and these can be explored in further research.

Lesson 2: Bring the Whole Team into the Process

When developing a web site, it is very exciting to witness designers and programmers observing focus groups or usability testing firsthand. Together they see:

- The birth of great ideas for new features

- The emergence of solutions to difficult navigation and design problems

- More than occasionally, the death throes of flawed concepts and approaches

For instance, after observing a designer's furrowed brow and rapt attentiveness following 32 hours of usability testing across four cities, the marketing director commented, "It must be really hard for you to listen to users critique your site hour after hour." To which the designer replied, "Are you kidding?! I'm a designer, and I'm building a site for IT Directors. I rack my brain trying to think like these guys and imagine what makes them tick. *Now* I know."

Like the designer in this example, the best way to get your money's worth from research is to make sure that the *whole* team takes

part, actively or passively, in the research. If you are managing the process, ask the team what problems are puzzling them that they want addressed, and also make sure the research is done at a time and place they can attend.

Of course, the refrain that we'll echo time and again in this text is that even the best design and development teams do better work in partnership with users.

Lesson 3: Do Rapid Prototyping Not Paper Prototyping

We are not proponents of paper prototyping; rather, we believe that people should experience a site in the medium for which it was intended. Although we have occasionally conducted research with paper prototypes, we don't feel that this experience provides users with enough context to effectively react to a concept. Basically, being on the web is multi-faceted, and part of the experience is interacting with a computer, using the mouse to explore the page, and so on. Paper prototypes don't allow for that interaction.

It is relatively cheap and easy to mock up screens so users can experience what the development team has intended. A prototype can be very simple, such as *wireframes* (basic schematic diagrams of web pages depicting the major elements of each page) without color, with pathways that are incomplete, or a transactional path in which only one or two items can actually be placed in the shopping cart. The idea is to simulate a "real" experience so the users' reactions will be as genuine as possible. The most powerful way we've seen to build a site is to create a prototype that can be rapidly morphed based on user feedback.

It is nothing short of painful to conduct two or three consecutive days of user experience testing with a static prototype that reveals the same findings time and again. In contrast, rapid prototyping lends an enormous energy to user experience testing, and the process can lead to powerful new ideas and fixes that, because they are quickly implemented, shorten the time spent getting the product to market. In short, using a flexible, malleable prototype yields a responsive and rapidly evolving site that is optimized for its intended audience.

Lesson 4: Don't Treat Test Participants Like Lab Rats

We've found that technology is something that most everyone is afraid of on some level at one time or another. Bring a "newbie" or IT Director into a usability lab and both are likely to stutter the same halting apology: "I'm sorry, but I can't figure that out. Give me a few minutes to use the site, and I'm sure I can work it out."

The bottom line is that we all entertain the sneaking suspicion that technology is, in fact, smarter than we are, and that if we experience difficulties using it, the problem (or "fault") is our burden to shoulder. We hear this most often from women and from those who didn't grow up using the Internet. Hence, the goal of usability testing is to make test participants as comfortable as possible and the testing scenario as natural as possible. To this end, follow these guidelines:

- Don't call test participants "subjects"—a word that frequently conjures images of lab rats and cages.

- Make eye contact and talk to participants during testing; don't take notes while they are talking. We are also opposed to practices that attempt to quantify the human experience, for instance, the use of eye tracking, stop watches, or line scales.

- Make the lab environment as natural and home-like as possible—comfortable chairs, warm colors, food and drink, a friendly greeting. (We also conduct ethnographic research, interviewing people in their own homes, in cabs, or wherever they use technology, but not generally for web site user experience testing).

- Let participants know "they are testing the site; the site is not testing them." Basically, we encourage people to act on their first impulse and not to worry about being evaluated.

- Don't make them bellow their responses or take directions from a piped in "voice of God." These are not natural behaviors.

- Treat the test participant as your partner, and encourage him to vocalize his experiences as he clicks a button or selects a path (especially if he experiences difficulty with navigation). What words or cues could make it intuitive for him and better meet his needs?

Lesson 5: Interview People Who Would or Do Actually Use Your Site

A great deal of usability testing, as currently practiced, is done among friends, family, and or temps. Although a tight budget is often cited as one reason for this (and it is arguable that some testing is better than none), this approach is highly problematic.

Friends and family lack objectivity for one, and they are not necessarily the type of folks who are prospects for your site. Actually, they seldom bear more than a passing resemblance to your target audience.

We encourage clients to think long and hard about who their target audience(s) are and how to define them demographically (for example, by employing variables such as their annual income), attitudinally (do they consider themselves to be "wine lovers"?), and behaviorally (are they frequent e-commerce users?). If your site sells perfume, information obtained by interviewing those who never buy perfume, not even as a gift, can be worse than useless because it wastes precious time and money. The vital question of "can they use it?" is, therefore, intertwined with the question of "will they use it?" Which brings us to the next point.

Lesson 6: Don't Confuse "Can They Use It?" with "Will They Want To?"

Many traditional testing strategies are designed to quantify aspects of the user experience, and they tend to pose questions like this:

- How long does it take for a user to complete a task?

- Do users rate the "task" as easy to use or intuitive?

- What quantitative assessments can be made about the paths people travel?

We think the real goal of user experience testing should be to discover the following truths (from the very people to whom a site is targeted):

- Can they use it? And what corrections can be made to language and navigation to enhance the usage experience?

- Moreover, will they use it?

The second of these questions is of equal import, for many reasons:

- If the site does not offer more than current on- or offline sources, users are likely to leave the site.

- If the homepage does not do a better job than other available sources, they will also leave the site.

- If the site, and the homepage in particular, do not support the brand and the brand's goals, the site will not meet the company's objectives.

When designing user experience research, it is important to address issues of usability and marketability, and this critical issue is addressed in the Appendix. Let's start by visiting the first critical window on the user experience: the homepage.

PART II

Attracting Visitors to Your Site, at Least Long Enough to See What You Have to Offer

3 Your Homepage is a 30-Second Window of Opportunity: Don't Be Shy!   33

4 Understanding How Users "Bucket" Your Space *Better Use Their Language, Because They Are Not There to Join Your Company*   53

5 It's Okay to be Different: Just Make Sure People Know What You Offer   73

6 People Don't Read: Don't Make Them!   91

7 Just Because the Competition Does It That Way, Doesn't Mean It's Right   109

Your Homepage Is a 30-Second Window of Opportunity: Don't Be Shy!

Channel surfing is an art on the World Wide Web. Users move from one site to the next at what seems like the speed of sound, barely waiting for a homepage to load before deciding whether it's really a place they want to hang around and explore. If they don't see what they're looking for on the homepage (or at any rate how to get to what they want), they won't stick around looking for long. The key to developing a successful homepage is to discover and use messages, words, features, and images that will capture the attention and interest of your audience. In this chapter, you will explore some of the insights we have learned from user experience testing regarding how to make the homepage as intuitive and "friendly" a space as possible.

Show Them What You Have to Offer

One of the biggest challenges of conducting business on the web is establishing a presence for a product or service for which there is no precedent. If people have no conceptual model for what a site provides, this challenge is all the greater: Users need to be educated about what is being offered. More importantly, they still need to be sold on the products and services. In other words, developers must be certain that what they are selling is clear and compelling to users, given the limited real estate on the homepage and the even more limited "window" you have to get their attention.

On this matter, we believe that the following insight speaks for itself. A new site offered consumers the ability to send email and greeting cards with video clips included. In order to do this, the user was required to use a web cam to record her video (of, say, a family portrait, new dog, or college reunion), and then she had to download software from the company's site that would permit the video to be included in the email or electronic card. These clips could thereafter be stored on the company's site for future use.

So far, so good. However, when testing the first version of the site, we learned that most people (including the technologically sophisticated) didn't know what a web cam was, much less what one might cost or how to obtain and install one. Also, many weren't sure what the benefit of this service was, or for what occasions they would use it. Most damning, the instructions for sending a video email or card weren't at all clear to prospective users. Indeed, most weren't even aware that they were first required to download a piece of software before using the service.

Through user experience testing for this client, we also learned that the largely text-based homepage did not excite people about the possible outcome of using the site. That is, users did not, by and large, share the developer's enthusiasm for being able to send user-friendly video emails and cards with videos.

Based on consumer input obtained through our testing, the company took the following steps to make their homepage work for them:

- They displayed the image of a web cam and a direct path users could follow to purchase one at a discount without leaving the site (which was especially important for those that didn't own such equipment but wanted to use the service).

- They created a visual flow chart that employed graphics to show how the site could be used to send a video card or email.

- Finally, they placed photos on the homepage that illustrated the emotional benefits that could result from using the service—namely, the satisfaction of sharing videos of family reunions, the birth of children, college graduations, and so on with friends and family.

Similarly, we worked with a healthcare site that was introducing a radically new healthcare solution for consumers. On many levels, this solution parted ways from traditional managed care. Initially, user experience testing suggested that consumers simply didn't understand what the site was about. The final solution to this problem was to redesign the homepage so that it began with a brief explanation of how and why consumers would benefit from using this service versus managed care.

The main lesson we learned through these examples is that the key to effectively introduce a product or service that no one has ever heard of or used is to take responsibility for educating people about the service. In this "take no prisoners" approach, users must be made aware of both what they stand to gain by using a given web service or purchasing a product online, *and* what they stand to lose by failing to do so. We offer the following simple guidelines on how to effectively bring this about:

- Don't try to tell people everything they need to know about the service—certainly not on the homepage. Give them just enough to let them know what's in it for them and what they might miss out on by not acting on the opportunity.

**Figure 3.1
(Next two images)**

The homepages for
the relatively unknown
eVineyard.com and
4Tests.com enthusiasti-
cally greet the customer
with the benefits of
the site.

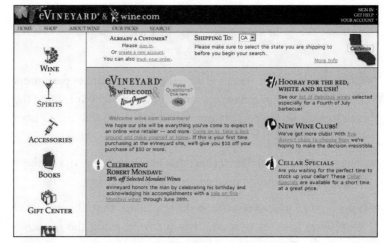

www.eVineyard.com

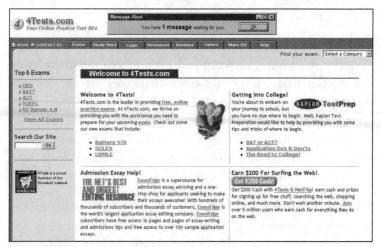

www.4Tests.com

- Provide a direct link to get more information—for those who want to "know it all."

- Provide a link to a demo that walks the user through a real life transaction.

- Use graphics and photos wherever possible, either to describe the process in *simple* terms or to illustrate what people stand to gain by using the service or product (for example, happy grand-parents and excellent healthcare at a reduced price).

Strut Your Credentials, Particularly Where They Matter

In some cases (for instance, the purchase of commodity items such as books or branded shampoos), many consumers will be unfamiliar with a particular dot-com. For this reason, it is critical for users to have a sense that the prices and rates are fair and the site is legitimate. The web can be a scary place for the faint-of-heart, and users need to know they are not being taken to the cleaners by one of the many fly-by-night operations that prey on Internet newbies and the generally unwary.

When the web sites in question pertain to industries such as healthcare, education, or financial services, the importance of credentials increases exponentially. In fact, strong credentials are often the make-or-break point for consumers considering whether to use such weighty services or purchase products from these sites. It is critical to getting users to put their faith and their dollars in you. This holds true whether you're speaking of consumers making "high ticket" purchases (such as cars, furniture, and antiques) or of the many businesses for whom the "cost of doing business" entails the purchase of costly goods and services from other businesses.

Consider the following examples. When Fleet, a major bank in New England, was about to launch web banking, testing showed that consumers clearly wanted the site to look just like the bank branch. They rejected a new logo in favor of the one already employed on signage, letterhead, and so on. Moreover, most of those tested wanted their account information to look just like their statements and expected the site to be a visually obvious extension of the bank: In every sense, its online shadow and not, as one consumer put it, "something a twelve-year-old in Wisconsin had created in his basement." The bank took these recommendations seriously, and consequently, at launch, the site was a mirror image of the bank and was as easy to use as the bank's ATM. Thereafter, usage far exceeded projections.

In another case, the first version of a homepage for a site that sold children's educational books and software made no mention of who or what was behind the site. Users thought anybody could be

**Figure 3.2
(Next two images)**

As with its famous
bricks and mortar
counterpart, the home-
page of McDonald's
greets visitors with the
familiar yellow arches
and striking red
background—in other
words, exactly what
they expect to see.
Likewise, Pier 1's site
mirrors the look and
feel of their stores.

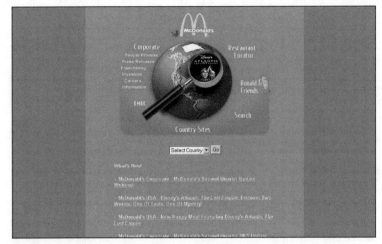

www.mcdonalds.com

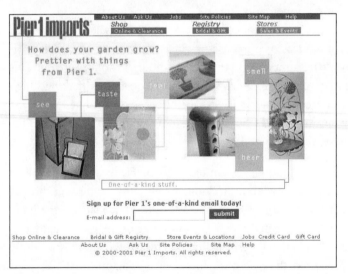

www.pier1.com

behind it, and consequently they simply viewed the site as a specialized e-commerce site. This was a missed opportunity insofar as
the company in question (unlike competitors) carefully selected
and sold products based on strong ratings given them by both top-
notch educators and parents. For the second version of the homepage, the proud trumpeting of these credentials front-and-center
on the homepage was extremely comforting and appealing to parents, who thought these credentials added much value to the site.

Finally, when we tested a prototype of a site for trading metal, we found that the first thing target users wanted to know was "who was behind the site." When they learned that the site was developed by significant people in the industry, their interest in using the site increased substantially. As a result, the company placed "About Us" as the first item on the homepage.

As these examples make plain, in cases where users need to really trust a site in order to enter the "front door," companies need to make the most of their credentials by making them prominent features of their homepages.

Don't Have Credentials? Beg and Borrow (But Don't Steal) 'Em!

So far, we have established that credentials are important. But the question of how companies set about actually establishing their credentials online is an entirely different matter. How is this to be done?

In many cases, the best way to obtain credibility when it is needed is to "borrow it" by featuring well-known brands or brand affiliations on a homepage. Borrowing is an effective technique because it enhances the user experience by generating a sense that, although the site and its parent company may not themselves be known to consumers, they are "known" through association with more familiar and trusted companies. This is made still more effective when a given company's affiliations (such as the parent company, key clients, or partnerships) are also prominently displayed on the homepage.

Of course, the significance and need for credentials will vary from web site to web site, and established companies will generally have less need to borrow. Nevertheless, even established companies might want to emphasize their bricks-and-mortar presence on the homepage. Doing so "cements" (so to speak) their enduring character in the minds of consumers and suggests that they have established customer service policies and will honor their commitments. If a company's offline presence is prestigious (for example,

**Figure 3.3
(Next two images)**

eBay is one of many sites that features prominent brand names and logos on its home page. DVDFile effectively leverages several recognized brands on its homepage as well.

www.ebay.com

www.dvdfile.com

if the company maintains stores in London, Paris, and Tokyo), or if it has a track record of longevity (for instance, if the company makes much fanfare of the fact that it has been in business since 1890), those important aspects should be cited on the homepage.

In contrast, when you're developing sites for start-ups that are not extensions of well-known brands, establishing credibility is tougher. The need for homepages that borrow from more familiar brands is thus made even more acute. In user experience testing, we have seen firsthand the significance of borrowing better-known names and branding for start-ups. For example, a retail chain with a wonderful reputation worldwide was opening stores throughout the U.S. and launching a new site. They learned how important it was to feature both the brand names and logos prominently on their site to successfully win the confidence and interest of site visitors.

In another case, creators of a music site that would enable the user to download music to his computer discovered how crucial it was for their site to feature well-known artists from a broad spectrum of genres on the homepage. This convinced visitors that it was worthwhile to check out the site in question *and* take the time to download the requisite software.

Use Your Real Estate Wisely

The question of establishing credentials touches on the broader issue of how to make effective use of real estate on the homepage. Using borrowed credentials is one example of how to assist in making the unknown into the known.

Still, many companies fail in other ways to make the most of space on the homepage. Some sites commit the sin of extreme minimalism, which frustrates users who want to get right to a particular location but are forced to spend valuable seconds hunting. Or, alternatively, they swing to the opposite pole, making the homepage so busy, so inundated with detail, that the consumer is fairly bewildered about where to begin.

In our experience studying the reactions of users, most web site visitors would prefer to see a happy balance between these extremes—a balance that announces the following information:

- What the site is all about, for example, a place for buyers and sellers of Product X to meet.

- The key features and functions available to users on the homepage, so users know what they can do and learn there.

- Any special areas (perhaps time-sensitive), such as a holiday package or a featured story on alternative medicine.

Although homepage minimalism usually leaves visitors confused, we have observed that if a site becomes too busy, several potentially devastating consequences arise:

- Visitors "block out" those sections of the page that they decide are less important or "advertising."

- Users simply don't scroll below the fold; they don't explore beyond what fits on their screen when the site first appears.

- In the worst cases, users become so overwhelmed that they either retreat to the left navigation bar to be taken off the page, or they exit the site altogether.

In each case, they miss out on key content and functionality because the page was not streamlined and prioritized. The problem of crowding and homepage "overkill" can seriously impede the effective viewing of a web site.

Why? Users will mentally "block out" advertising and any other sections that seem extraneous or hard to decipher. Similarly, they may never get far enough down the homepage to view areas of the site that may be of interest to them. Yet, left to their own devices, most will not scroll below the fold.

In user experience testing for a major retailer, we examined reactions to three variations on a homepage. The one to which consumers responded best was the version that was simplest, which clearly displayed the different products and services in the left navigation bar, introduced the different departments on the top navigation bar, and announced the "special" products, services, and for-sale items in the center frame.

Users consistently ask for homepages that are simple, clean, organized, and prioritized by content. As a rule of thumb, users tell us that the "stuff" above the top navigation bar is typically advertising and is therefore ignored, that the "stuff" below the fold is perceived as not all that important, and that the content in the right column is often perceived as less important.

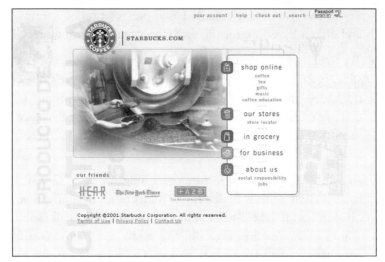

www.starbucks.com

Figure 3.4
(Next two images)
The Starbucks and Gap homepages are both clean and well-organized; they are prioritized by content and fit into the area above the fold.

www.gap.com

Knowing these perceptions, you can strategically use the homepage to direct users to where you want them to go. We suggest that you use the following order of importance in developing an effective use of homepage space:

● First announce who you are and what you offer.

● Prioritize the presentation of features, listing the most popular first.

- Try to use a brief and visually based presentation of a feature and offer a hyperlink for the user who wants to learn more.

- Try to limit the homepage to one online page. If this is not possible, place items that are least important to your site's objectives last—and don't be surprised if they're missed. Also, if you do have to place items below the fold, make sure that the placement of the "page break" doesn't obscure the fact that there is indeed "stuff" below the fold.

- Avoid the temptation to feature everything you offer. One way to avoid doing this is to determine (in focus groups) how users "bucket" and "label" what you have to offer. This will enable you to group features logically and create names that clearly announce to the user what to expect. Grouping features helps reduce clutter.

We believe that following these suggestions will help you make effective use of space on the homepage. Of course, such is not the goal of design per se. What consumers really want are homepages that can be used intuitively—meaning that they can understand what you offer without having to second-guess your labeling, figure out the navigation path, or seek additional help. Establishing credibility and the wise use of real estate are two steps in this process. A third involves ensuring that the overall design of the page is in service of a given company's "concept."

Make Sure Your Design Is in Service to Your Concept

We can't emphasize enough the importance of staying closely tethered to purposes for which the site was conceived in the first place. In writing this, we are keenly aware of how many misguided attempts to be different—to "break through the clutter" or adopt the latest technology—have resulted in web site designers failing to remember how important it is for their site to be in service to the following:

- The audience

- The goals the site is trying to achieve

- The brand

- The industry

If the site is intended to sell Armani, it had better look "Armani." If it is an educational site, it must convey an image of intelligence and knowledge—intangible elements that are not simply built into perceptions of a store. If the site is an extension of an offline brand, it must successfully convey the image of that brand. And if it is a financial services site, it shouldn't look like a disco (too funky or far out in its design and color scheme) to foster the seriousness of a place people trust with their money.

Also, some designs "fight" communication of what a site is all about. We've seen several sites use a magazine format on the homepage, which obscures the fact that the site is primarily an e-commerce site that also has editorial content to support the selling effort. When a user sees a "magazine," she thinks "this is a place to read articles about cosmetics, not necessarily to buy them."

Your Homepage Should Serve Your Strategic Goals

It is of critical importance to the success of a site to make sure the homepage clearly directs people to the strategic activities the site was designed to promote. Thus, if the goal of a site is to offload customer service from the call center, it is critical that the homepage points people clearly in the direction of online customer service—and makes it as appealing and apparent as possible. To this end, the homepage must announce what a given site was designed to accomplish in the first place, whether that's to sell, to inform or educate, to extend your brand, or to provide an additional customer service channel.

As simple as these goals may sound in principle, we've seen many sites fail to accomplish them. They neglect to make it clear to users what functionality and content they are offering.

For example, one major brand constructed their site expressly for the purpose of creating an additional channel to sell products. At the outset, they used a small shopping cart icon on their homepage to direct shoppers, even though the majority of the page contained corporate and industry news. Not surprisingly, few users understood that they could shop, let alone where they should go on the site to do so.

Similarly, a major computer company wanted their site to provide online customer service, to assist in handling high call volume for obtaining and installing printer drivers and patches. Yet the homepage offered no direct route to obtain these, and customers were forced to drill down through their product line, numbers, and models to find the needed driver or patch. Many of these customers were first time users who didn't feel confident about what a driver or patch was, so it wasn't long before they were headed for the 800 #.

We offer, as a final example, the case of a successful TV news channel that wanted to extend its programming and audience by creating a web site. While users enjoyed the site and felt that the show largely established the site's credibility, visitors didn't immediately see how the site related to the show. In research, we discovered that prospective visitors to the site anticipated much more from this site than a recapitulation of the day's headlines. Where was a calendar that showed upcoming programs and features? Where was a summary of the shows they'd missed? Why didn't the homepage direct them to more information about a particular company or topic covered on a show? After all, wasn't the Internet supposed to be *the* place to get as much information as possible on a given topic? Essentially, the site was losing out on key opportunities to extend the brand by providing practical information online that supplemented the television channel.

Each of these examples points to the relevance of using the homepage in near single-minded fashion; whatever other functions it serves, the page *must* successfully direct users to the more strategic pages on the site. Visitors to the homepage will thus view it as a "sign post," guiding them to where they *really* want to go.

www.oprah.com

www.marthastewart.com

**Figure 3.5
(Next two images)**

The homepages for television personalities Oprah Winfrey and Martha Stewart are online supplements to popular offline brands.

Figure 3.6

GQ.com both complements the newsstand version and offers consumers a way to subscribe online.

www.gq.com

Designers must learn to conceive of the page in this manner as well, imagining themselves as first-time visitors and walking an electronic mile in the user's shoes. If you are a designer, the questions to pose to yourself are clear:

- Is it obvious what you want the user to do?

- Is it obvious where the user is to go?

If not, have your team brainstorm what the homepage would need to do to fairly scream the relevant categories (for instance, "SHOP," "COMPARE PRICES," "GET HELP," and so on) from the homepage. Indeed, if these and other links don't all but leap off the homepage to grab the consumer's attention, you can well expect these pages to go unviewed altogether, regardless of the toil that surely went into their construction.

The More the Merrier
Figure Out Who Your Customers Are and Welcome Them

Most sites serve multiple audiences with diverse agendas and a variety of reasons for visiting the site. To name but a few, different types of audiences include first time users and frequent visitors; subscribers and non-subscribers; commercial and residential customers; students and educators; patients and doctors. Such overlapping purposes can make the task of informing each of these audiences that they have "come to the right place" difficult. Once it has been decided which target audiences a site is intended for, an immediate question arises as to the way in which this multiplicity is effectively managed on the homepage.

To illustrate our point, consider the following case. A major retailer for whom we conducted research wanted to use their site to better serve its commercial customers—that is, people who buy in volume or buy special products that meet the needs of businesses as opposed to individual consumers. By contrast, their homepage featured lots of consumer-oriented products and specials and a variety of customer service offerings tailored to the needs of "regular folks."

As you might guess, when commercial customers were shown the homepage, they immediately assumed that the site offered nothing for them, and felt that they were better off going to the store or using the catalog. The "Commercial Customers" button on the top navigation bar simply wasn't enough to entice them. Had they selected that button, they would have found a page completely tailored for them. However, few commercial customers got that far, and our research surmised that the homepage was in trouble—at least from a business-to-business perspective.

Testing revealed that what was most compelling to commercial customers (such as volume discounts, tax exempt status, and special products tailored to their industries) was all but absent from the homepage. We therefore recommended that the homepage be redesigned so that a major piece of real estate—the page center—would be devoted to reflecting the needs of commercial customers.

**Figure 3.7
(Next two images)**

The MasterCard site reaches out to both consumers and commercial customers (through a special area of the site).

www.mastercard.com

www.mastercard.com/business

This section communicated the benefits of registering as a commercial customer and, in so doing, created a compelling path to that area of the site that was more expressly designed for their needs.

Sites that serve multiple audiences with diverse needs must use their homepages wisely to generate an impression with members of each of its audiences that there is a special place for *them* on the site. This is especially important for the homepage because it is here that visitors will find "front doors" to other areas and pages of the site.

The following are a few tips on how to achieve this goal:

- Be sure to call each target group by a name they call themselves (for example, "commercial customers" or "B2B"). This definition may be influenced by company size (for example, companies of fewer than 100 employees); if so, this needs to be made clear.

- Give each audience equal "weight," so that each feels significant, and so the site is designed for that group in particular.

- Avoid content or advertising that might appeal to some among one audience, but which you suspect could offend or perplex others; for instance, stock price info on a health insurance site or candy advertising on a diaper site).

- Again, use visuals to your best advantage wherever they are relevant to direct your audience. For instance, you might use a photograph of kids and parents employed as a guide that leads each group to its own section of the site.

- Cite benefits of interest to each target audience so they know both how and why they would want to click further.

Tell the Truth Up-Front
Bad News Is Worse in the Check-Out Aisle!

Finally, it is important to emphasize that, ultimately, no one site can hope to be all things to all people, no matter how many audiences developers believe can be realistically served. Companies that fear informing their visitors of the site's limitations fail to realize that abrupt discovery of the "truth" is infinitely more annoying once a user has invested ten (or more) minutes of time. Here are a few examples of "truths" that we feel should be self-evident on the homepage:

- Nations or states to which one *cannot* ship your product (such as wine).

- Products you offer that are not available online.

- Products and services that are not available.

- Areas of the nation/world that aren't yet covered by the service in question.

Being honest communicates integrity. Moreover, it's a simple matter to provide a mechanism that will inform prospective customers when the desired products and services *will* become available. As opposed to duplicity, this strategy will quite possibly foster future relationships with customers—preferable, by any standard, to severing a fragile trust with half-truths and apparent dead-ends.

A Few Hard Questions

To summarize, when you or a team of developers is constructing a site's homepage, ask yourself whether ambiguity surrounds the following "hard questions." If so, you might consider clarifying the page:

- What is the site all about?

- For whom is the site intended?

- Why should people stick around, anyway?

- What do people need to know about the company to place their trust in its web site?

- What should people know about a site so they are not misled and do not waste their time?

CHAPTER FOUR

Understanding How Users "Bucket" Your Space

Better Use Their Language, Because They Are Not There to Join Your Company

We all love a homepage that zings, not only with graphics but also with words. Language used in buckets—a word we use for the major categories of information on the homepage—can be upbeat and energetic, but users have to know what you are talking about and whether or not you are talking to them. When web site visitors perceive that you are offering them content and functionality they clearly want and need, they make the leap in logic that this is what your company is all about.

And This Site Would Be About...?

All too often, users take a look at the homepage of a web site and quickly come to the frustrating conclusion that, although there seems to be a lot there with respect to content and functionality, the one thing they need simply isn't there! Worse still, they see nothing at all that is relevant or useful to them.

Unfortunately, it is often the case that what users really want is, in fact, right under their noses—front and center on the homepage or in another prominent place. Be that as it may, they still can't find what they are looking for. There may be a number of reasons for this. Perhaps it is because the desired feature has a name that means nothing to them, which might as well be in another language. More likely, site features are frequently categorized in ways that appear logical to the parent company, but which are anything but intuitive to the uninitiated. More often than not, sites that are developed to mirror the organizational structure of the parent company also confound employees.

It seems that before he can use a site effectively, the user must first identify *himself* as a particular kind of customer with particular needs. Then he can cross the threshold into a successful, fulfilling user experience.

What this means is that if the categories of information, or "buckets," on your homepage don't make immediate sense to users, visitors probably won't stick around long enough to explore the rest of the site. Inevitably, the end result is disappointment and frustration for the user, and a needlessly missed opportunity for the sponsor. This chapter covers strategies for avoiding pitfalls that can so cruelly thwart a company's good intentions and the best-laid plans of designers.

I Love Your Org Chart...
Too Bad I'm Not Looking for a Job

It seems like a simple rule of thumb that a web site should be a reflection of the company behind it. Assuming this, the user should be able to go to your site and see exactly who you are and what you are about. Well, at least in theory.

The problem inherent with this seemingly innocent idea is that it becomes far too easy for developers to justify building sites that are the online mirror image of the companies they serve. Accordingly, such sites end up being organized by department (Sales, Marketing, Research and Development, Customer Service) or by company (in the case of many large umbrella corporations) or, equally problematic, by the target segments the company has defined for its products and services. Government sites are also guilty of this.

This is to be expected when, for better or for worse, the organizational structure of a company all but defines the world in which employees work. But the same inference cannot, of course, be extended to customers. Shouldn't sites that are intended for the public at least make sense to *known* customers, to say nothing of random visitors?

To illustrate our point with an analogy, these departments may be thought of as organs that function together to ensure the smooth and continued circulation of the life-blood that enables the continued existence of the company. The "blood" may be thought of as that valuable stream of products and services made available on a web site. Lack of harmony between the person and these organs,

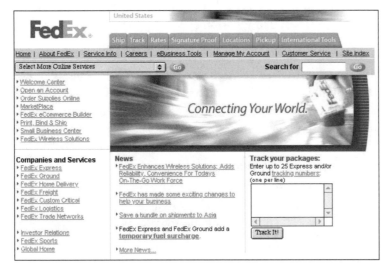

Figure 4.1

The FedEx homepage includes "Companies and Services" that may not be intuitive or familiar to the user.

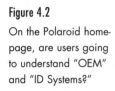

Figure 4.2

On the Polaroid home-page, are users going to understand "OEM" and "ID Systems?"

and among the organs themselves, inhibits the flow of blood, withering the company's potential for success.

So, for instance, the sales department is responsible for getting products into the hands of customers and, for the web site, this generally means that online product sales will be accessed through a button called "Sales." Although this seems intuitive, the flow of products and services (the much-needed blood) is complicated by the fact that an unruly or unpredictable customer might want to see product descriptions. And you might almost hear some site developers protest, "How dare they spoil a perfectly good system with unreasonable demands!"

Such situations can be remarkably complex. While Sales handles order fulfillment, actual marketing materials are developed and distributed through the Marketing department. Therefore, if a user wants to see a product description, he or she needs to click on the "Marketing" button, which leads to a selection of appropriate materials, all under sub-categories that reflect the separate groups within the Marketing department that handle these materials. The company can only hope that users will understand the labeling of these groups well enough to obtain the product information they need.

Insight

Based on their day-to-day interactions, users most likely have a much different view of your organization than you do. If they want product information, for example, that's what they want. They don't care what part of your organization is responsible for product information. The same goes for customer service, product updates, company information, and so on.

And to access information on services? This, too, can be a mysterious process for consumers. After-sales services may be the responsibility of the Sales department. Or, that might fall under Customer Service. Current customers wanting to learn more about future product enhancements, or the locations of regional offices, might find this under "About Us." Or has it also been placed under Marketing? Research and Development maybe? Again we say, until online usability is made truly intuitive for the target customer, companies can only trust that the native intelligence of consumers will guide them through a minefield of possibilities.

In this book, we insist that the relationship between the web site and the user need not be so fraught with the potential for failure. Now if the roles and responsibilities in the Sales department, for example, were consistent from one company to the next, then

setting up the categories on the homepage according to the organizational structure might almost work. But sadly, organizations don't form utopian networks of seamless usability in this way, and are unlikely to do so in the future. To put it bluntly, web site visitors don't really care about how a company is set up—unless, of course, they are seeking employment with the company in question. Only then would they want to know what departments to target (and even in this unlikely scenario we are not convinced). Would they find what they're looking for under "Career Opportunities?" or would the department they need have been renamed "Human Capital Administration?"

What Fascinating Categories You Have! Each One a Mystery Unto Itself

Time and again, we have seen companies use categories on their homepages that were, for all practical purposes, meaningless to their users, employing words or phrases that spoke to only a tiny sub-set of the intended audience or, worse still, that were totally misunderstood by everyone.

Every industry has its own language, a language that keeps non-practitioners feeling like outsiders. High technology is a most egregious offender, with its culture of techno-elitists endlessly spinning acronyms and jargon that seem intended for the sole purpose of separating "us" from "them" (terms that are recognized only by the most tech-savvy among us, like "server" and "DSL"). To cite another example, people in the automotive industry use words for manufacturing and marketing processes that seem like a virtual foreign language to anyone outside the field. Industries like fashion and healthcare also have unique sets of concepts and vocabularies that are not easily grasped by outsiders, and on finance-related sites, we often come across jargon words like "transaction."

But even setting aside the question of entire industries, most companies, too, have their own "dialects." While many of these are rooted in the broader lexicons of specific industries, novel terms and "buzzwords" also spring to life with an often alarming frequency. These words are often related to company-specific

products and processes. Again, high technology companies top the list of offenders because of their tendency to overlook the deeply esoteric character of the numeric code used to refer, for example, to a specific line of laptops or printers. These terms may skip easily from their own tongues and the keyboards of their PCs alike, but to all but the most dedicated among their customer base, they remain a total foreign language. Instead of a number, colorless and sterile (such as Series BJC-85W), wouldn't a simple term like portable color printer be much more helpful to those who are relatively uninformed by the frequently arcane jargon of computing? We believe so.

Insight

Although some of your site's visitors will have a high level of sophistication and familiarity with your products and services, some will have significantly less background information. Don't risk alienating users through the use of acronyms and insider terminology.

The web site of a major health insurance company used terminology that especially threatened to turn users away. Apparently, making an effort to cover a multitude of sins, they first referred to themselves simply as "providers" (a commonly used healthcare term). To some site visitors, the term was associated with insurance companies. Others, however, assumed that the term referred exclusively to those that "provided" healthcare services, for example, physicians. This resulted in widely mixed expectations of the site's capabilities.

This company also gave current customers a way to quickly find out what drugs were covered and under what circumstances. Great idea. But they referred to this function as "Drug Formulary." Although this probably made the corporate attorneys happy, it left site users completely in the dark. Early usability testing uncovered the impact of simple, user-friendly language—Find a Doctor versus Provider Search.

I Know the Web Is a Creative Place, But You're Losing Me

In an over-zealous attempt to lure users to their sites, developers frequently load up their homepages with boxes and buttons that hawk an array of trendy-sounding terms that mean next to nothing to site newcomers. Most common among these are youth-culture words, such as "cool," which presumably denote the presence of "cool stuff" on the site. This can confuse the user who, in this case, is simply looking to find the latest product information. If the site uses teen or twenty-something slang-du-jour, there is a real danger that it will be outdated before it hits the web, or that it will be viewed as confusing by those who are not in that demographic and, more humbling, will make them look dumb by those who are.

Insight
"Hip" and "cool" language passes in and out of fashion. Furthermore, when in written form, it can appear more forced than trendy.

From Russia with Love and the Limited "Role" of Russian Dolls and Rollovers

In their efforts to make homepages more "user friendly," designers have resorted to a number of organizing tactics, of which two in particular stand out: the so-called "Russian doll" and the "rollover." Both are useful to a limited degree, but a designer's over-reliance on either can lead to user frustration and a willingness to abandon the site altogether.

As the name suggests, Russian dolls sites (named for those brightly colored wooden dolls that, when opened, reveal more dolls nested inside) involve the initial use of a broad category, behind which are any number of sub-categories that grow increasingly narrowly defined as the user continues to click into them. In contrast to true Russian dolls, which can be artful and mysterious, these electronic counterparts frequently prove frustrating for consumers because they oblige users to continue clicking through page after interminable page in an attempt to find the content or function they need.

Even where designers opt not to use Russian dolls, we have seen an interesting evolution with rollovers. In the early years of e-commerce, a user rarely thought to explore the homepage with her mouse and was surprised when rollovers first appeared. In such tentative experimentation, the user often assumed that rollovers signaled the presence of new pages, and when she would click on them, she was frequently confused when they simply disappeared. Despite these early problems, recent years have seen users becoming increasingly accustomed to rollovers to the point that they now expect and look for them, especially if buckets on the homepage aren't clearly labeled.

A significant difficulty with some rollovers is that they are overly long or are placed in such a way that they obscure other options that appear on the screen—for instance, other links in the left navigation bar. Obviously, a problem such as this has the potential to unhinge the very user-friendliness that the rollover is designed to create. At other times, we have observed that the terminology used to designate rollovers overlaps with terms associated with the links themselves. In one such confusing scenario, a rollover designed for a site's "Contact Us" link was called "How to Contact Us."

Insight

Use rollovers judiciously. Avoid wordiness as well as redundancy.

Although such instances certainly betray a lack of imagination when it comes to the use of nomenclature, a more serious problem is that they all but invite users to mistake their respective meanings. We feel that instead of muddying the waters in this way, rollovers should enhance links by briefly describing the options offered. Generally, they are to be thought of as a strategy used to avoid overloading the homepage with so many options that navigation and clear understanding of bucketing are impeded. Of course, the urge to display all relevant information on the homepage is a noble gesture, but if users have to dig too deeply too soon to get at the information they want, they tend to give up. Overkill on the homepage reflects nothing so much as a failure to prioritize. The guiding principle should always be this: "What are the functions or content that your users want the most?" In the case cited above, for instance, the "Contact Us" link could include language regarding the ability to email or get 800 numbers.

Figure 4.3

This clothing site offers users a clear, detailed list of what is contained within the selected category.

SHOP BY OCCASION	SHOP BY ITEM	WARDROBE ADVISOR
	Sweaters	
	Fashion T-shirts	
	Blouses & Shirts	
	Pants & Shorts	
	Skirts	
	Suits & Separates	
	Dresses	
	Outerwear	
	Accessories	
	Shoes, Bags, Belts	
	Legwear	
	Fragrance	
	Gifts	
	Petites	
	Sale	

I Don't Want to Put Myself in That Category Either, and Don't Call *Me* a Baby-Boomer!

In an attempt to make their sites usable to the key target audiences, companies frequently take the opposite tack: Instead of worrying about which buckets to include and how to label them, they confine their homepage to a limited set of basic "doorways," each labeled with a name chosen for appeal to a specific audience. The user clicks on his doorway of choice (assuming, of course, that one of these doorways is germane to his needs), and he is then shown the appropriate features and functions. Some users appreciate this approach because it can make a large, unwieldy site more manageable. However, web site "minimalism" can also be problematic for a variety of reasons.

The labels themselves present the first conundrum, insofar as doorways can be too restrictive. A healthcare site, for instance, might use two labels, "Members" and "Providers." Although this might grab the attention of the majority, there will always be those who don't quite fit either label. In this example, if the site visitor is endeavoring to choose an insurance company but is not an existing member, which e-door should he darken?

Insight

Avoid being myopic when you are choosing identifying labels that you will provide your users. Most likely, they don't refer to themselves in the same way you refer to them. Job titles, demographics (male, female, teen), and intention (shop, purchase) can all serve to alienate users who don't quite see themselves the way you do, or who don't want to label themselves at all.

Business-to-business sites have been known to choose common job titles to label their doorways, such as "Purchasing Manager" and "Department Head." This forces the user to take a step back and think about which of these hats he or she wears; and he understandably expresses concern that he will choose the wrong doorway and, consequently, limit the choices to which he is exposed.

A common refrain might run as follows: "I am looking for office supplies. Am I going to see only bulk purchasing options if I go in as a Purchasing Manager but not as a Department Head? And where will the prices be lower?"

At the other extreme, bending over backwards to cater to the pedestrian shopper, many retail sites oblige users to label themselves (or others) with terms like "Preteen," "Teen," or "Adult." Unfortunately, terms like these inevitably carry with them unintended meanings. Are we to suppose, therefore, that the selections featured in the "Adult" category will be less "trendy" or "hip" than those consigned to the "Teen" bucket? How such questions are answered will have dramatic consequences for who sees content on a given web site.

Still other e-commerce sites may take a more functional approach, employing such terms as "Browse," "Customer Service," and "Purchase." Are we to imagine that shoppers will have no choice other than to buy what they look at? This would, of course, be nonsensical—and yet such is the very logic of a web doorway that invites you to simply buy, without (seemingly) giving you the exercise of free will in the matter of e-shopping.

What's worse, we've seen sites with very large, complex product inventories create sets of target names like "Baby Boomer," "Home-Lander," or "Code-Breaker" to pigeon-hole people according to a small number of types, in order to facilitate the sale of particular products and services they believe will be most appealing or relevant to each of these groups. Sites that sell gifts or furniture will often collapse people into classes that define particular tastes or styles: youthful, traditional, chic, or what have you. Although that is occasionally helpful, we have observed that most consumers react with some annoyance at being stereotyped in this way. They fear, with reason, that their choices are being arbitrarily limited by anonymous companies whose boards of directors take it upon themselves to decide who they are and what they want to buy.

The guiding principle here is that users don't like labeling themselves. To be sure, it takes but a few moments to figure out how they are expected to categorize themselves, but these are still moments they would rather use getting what they want from the site.

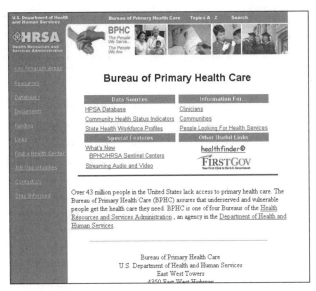

www.bphc.hrsa.dhhs.gov/

Figure 4.4

The Bureau of Primary Health Care, of the US Department of HHS, offers users a range of options as they enter the site. For example, a user can identify himself as a "Clinician" or "People Looking for Health Services." Users can also go directly to data sources, search, and look for topics alphabetically, as well as choose from among other options.

When shoppers aren't sure how to label themselves, or even if they want to, the experience of conducting online commerce has the potential to turn sour. And such labeling practices cause still greater anxiety for less-experienced users.

For these reasons, the option to enter directly into particular areas of the site should also be available, even when a company is bent on labeling. In this way, those who already know where they are headed will have the option of heading directly to the page that interests them. As for others, those who want to browse to their heart's content and then make up their own minds as to what is relevant or useful, will be able to do so. Another solution might be to allow people to answer a series of questions about their particular needs, which subsequently become the basis for categorization and bucketing (in this way, a family PC owner becomes more relevant). Each of these proposed solutions has the virtue of placing control of the site exploration firmly in the hands of the user.

Insight

If there is a rule of thumb regarding the use of self-identification, it harkens back to the concept of control. Make self-identification an option, among other clearly-labeled options, for those who want to navigate your site outside of your pathways.

Site maps can also be useful here, although we find that users are often loathe to take the additional step of clicking on a site map when they are intent upon getting to their desired destinations as quickly as possible.

A photography supply company tried limiting its homepage to a small number of doorways, the labels for which included "Home Photographers," "Professional," and "Prosumer." The site designers assumed that this would make it easier for users to get to the products and services that were most relevant to them. After all, why would someone taking pictures of a new baby want to see high-end digital cameras costing hundreds of dollars? Well, as it turned out, that is precisely what occurred.

Some of those visiting the site were actually professional photographers who were taking photos at home, who had assumed they should choose the Home Photographer doorway. Inversely, others among the Home Photographers were indeed amateurs. Yet because they were parents and doting grandparents, many of these wanted only the biggest and best equipment to capture those precious moments with Junior. Their disappointment at being presented with what they perceived to be lower-end merchandise was palpable. That these were inexpensive posed no difficulties; but that they were non-digital and even disposable cameras was wholly unsatisfying.

And as for "Prosumers?" Nobody even knew what that meant.

Confronting the Unfamiliar: Start by Looking Outside Your Organization

It is perhaps part of human nature to cling to the familiar. As in other walks of life, we in the business world act on assumptions about how our customers think and behave: the decision processes they pursue, and the ways they perceive our products and services. We stay focused on what we think and experience—as insiders—rather than looking *outside* our organizations. Yet, developers are building a site for outsiders.

Although these assumptions are based on past experience, they are nevertheless inadequate barometers of the world beyond insular business cultures. Our intuition may well be correct when it comes to looking inward to the practices of our own company; such assessments can hardly be extended to reflect the wants and needs of Internet users in general, especially those prospective customers we are interested in luring to our site.

Moreover, the use of the web is changing rapidly throughout the world. Even if we could adequately judge the beliefs and behaviors of users according to our own, the rapidly evolving nature of web commerce and Internet usage generally cannot be well understood today without constant vigilance and reassessment tomorrow.

So, a key concern for web site developers will be how to overcome such deeply entrenched bias. Exactly how are they to set about anticipating user needs that fall beyond the purview of their corporate culture and which are, in any case, evolving very rapidly?

One means of getting at this information is to examine the homepage for how it mirrors the way customers make decisions or use information—assuming they will begin with Point A and go on to Point B, and so forth. In user experience research on non-commerce sites, for instance, we have found it useful to peruse a list of topics, select those that stimulate the most interest, and then ask specific questions about the items that are found within those topics. Similarly, on e-commerce sites, we first gauge reaction to product lists, then to categories, and finish by examining products within that category one by one.

It is important to approach such research methodically, because occasionally users will want to start somewhere in the middle of the process; for example, they'll want to look at the latest content regardless of category. More problematic still, they may envisage a category as "latest updates," whereas the term used on the site is "recently archived." Although this makes user testing difficult at times, such reactions also provide important clues to the nature of the user experience.

So a general insight of research is that, although one's own assumptions and expectations will inevitably be difficult to overcome, by paying close attention to what users are thinking, the terms they are using, and the roles they are playing, by starting from ground zero and learning about their thought and categorization processes, their experience will become less mysterious to designers. By learning about what intended users *most* want to come to your site for, designers will find more options open to them with respect to what they feature on the homepage.

One large technology company was so intent on satisfying the needs of each and every person that came to its site that their left navigation bar featured an interminably long list of categories. Many of these were subsets of others, just in case the content of one bucket was not clear.

Rather than clarifying the options, users were overwhelmed by what they viewed as a list that was too long by half. They began to question whether the company behind the site had really thought through what they wanted to offer on the site. On further investigation, they also noticed overlapping between categories, which made them question how organized the company itself was.

Figure 4.5

The Smithsonian is made up of different museums, like Natural History and Air and Space. The Smithsonian Store could have built a site with a separate area for each of these museums, making the experience much less time-consuming for the user. Instead, the homepage is organized by how the user might approach shopping, for example, price, occasion, gender, and age, followed by a range of options.

www.smithsonianstore.com

○ ○ **Insight**
○ When organizing your content and functionality into buckets, the best place to start is at ground zero. Make no assumptions. Find out from prospective site visitors what their expectations are.

By taking a step back, the company learned that users had a small handful of priority functions and content, which they referred to using terms like "Marketing Materials." They then revamped the left navigation bar to include only those basic categories.

The buckets on your homepage need to map with the way users think. If they don't perceive a connection, they will assume you don't offer what they need.

Just Because Every Department *Wants* a Button on the Homepage Doesn't Mean They Need One

It is all too common to take a democratic approach when developing the web site, embracing the assumption that each department should have a button of its own on the left navigation bar. The familiar scenario plays out something like this: Each department chooses a web site committee, which then meets periodically with the goal of brainstorming about the *essence* of their department. That is, they discuss the various personal abilities at work on the team, the departmental missions, and maybe even *some* content and functionality that the team might perceive to be useful.

The result of all this "idea creation?" More often than not, it results in an overall look and feel that is inconsistent from one area of the site to the next, and offers functions that fail to complement one another or work together (for example, identical products and services might be named differently across categories). In our view, a site that is sufficiently uncoordinated makes visitors wonder about whether that is a reflection of the company that stands behind it.

Although team brainstorming is often a means of avoiding in-fighting within a company, this approach often fuels the development of web site categories that resemble an organizational chart. Furthermore, by approaching research in this way, departments often protect their own turf by offering some, but not all, of the information or functionality that might contribute to the overall mission of the site.

Insight

What is the mission of your site? Figure it out. Define it. Make sure everybody involved in the site knows. Redefine as necessary. And let it guide both development and ongoing maintenance of the site.

We believe that it is more important, wherever possible, to avoid this problem at the outset by asking these important questions:

- What is the overall mission of the site?

- Just what is it that we, the company, want to achieve here?

- Are we trying to promote the company? Support customer service? Sell products?

To reiterate: What *is* the mission of the site? Of course, customer representatives should also be part of this process.

And Don't Forget to Ask: "Are We Offering What Target Users Want and Expect?"

Is the tail wagging the dog? In the process of making decisions about what to offer on your web site, you may discover that the web is but the tip of the iceberg in terms of looking at how you serve your customers or prospects.

The mission of the web site is essentially a marriage of what customers and prospective customers want and need—their expectations and priorities—and what the organization is ready to provide. Somewhere along the way (before, during, or after the process of learning what customers and prospects expect from a web site), some productive navel gazing is in order.

Easier said than done, however. In fact, companies often discover that what they expected to offer is not what customers want, or what customers *do* want is not what they have been prepared to offer.

Beyond the minutiae of "bucketing" and nomenclature, however, this issue needs to be addressed on a broader scale to reflect ways in which the web is changing how customers and prospects interact with companies. Some parallel functionality is expected (for example, the ability to purchase online as well as offline). This may mean shaking up distributor and reseller arrangements, or making departments like distribution and marketing work more closely to provide a streamlined sales experience for customers. It might also

mean that the toll-free customer service number is still required, if not taxed further, until all of the customer service functionality in the site is in working order and customers have been trained to use it.

Technology meets organizational politics. This means not only looking at some re-labeling to clarify what you actually intend to offer, but also taking a look at your intentions for the site, and what this is going to mean for your organization.

Research Tip

Begin the dialogue by asking prospective users to describe their off-line behavior. For example, how do they gather information, and what are their decision-making processes like? What are the gaps that your web site might fill? This is the starting place for your web site mission.

The View from 30,000 Feet

Homepages don't have to be boring. Language used in buckets can be upbeat and energetic, but it has to be understandable and relevant. When web site visitors perceive that you are offering them content and functionality that they clearly want and need, they make the leap in logic that this is what your company is all about.

A Few Hard Questions

- What are the main reasons users want to come to my site? Are they reflected front-and-center on the homepage?

- What words do the intended audience use to refer to this content and functionality?

- Does the labeling of buckets not only make intuitive sense to users, but are their expectations met completely in terms of what is actually behind these labels?

- Do rollovers expand users' understanding of the labels in a meaningful way?

- Are there some departments in my organization that will have a lesser contribution to the web site than others, in keeping with the goal of serving the needs of users?

CHAPTER FIVE

It's Okay to Be Different: Just Make Sure People Know What You Offer

As web sites evolved from being little more than online corporate brochures to being important venues of commerce, they also became showcases for innovative design, color, moving images, and sound. On those sites where they have been used judiciously, these elements have added much value. Nevertheless, it often seems that web sites have been created as entries in a design contest, replete with bells and whistles that confuse, frustrate, and ultimately alienate the user.

The desired "glitz" can quickly cloud the purpose of your site and send users scurrying away in pursuit of a more embracing and manageable experience. In this chapter, we will tell you how to avoid going overboard.

Loved the Show, But Save It for Broadway
May I Please See My Checking Account Balance Now?

We've all been to sites like this: You enter an innocent-looking URL and expect to encounter a run-of-the-mill homepage that (at a minimum) identifies the sought-after company and perhaps displays a logo and pleasant photo along with a list of options. Somewhere in that list, you hope to find the information or function you need. And as you continue to navigate the various pages, you reflect that this hardly seems overly ambitious or too much to ask.

Instead, you click, and for your trouble, you wait in vain for this utopian scenario to unfold. Perhaps more than one photo is displayed on the homepage, and that accounts for the interminable download? But to your dismay, the screen turns inky black and a disconcerting jingle commences. Before your eyes, a distant tiny image—barely visible—appears onscreen. To your increasing dismay, it grows ever larger, weaving and oscillating across the screen until, as the tempo of the music intensifies, the still obscure image fragments and multiplies, at last bringing into focus what appears to be a number of animated dancing bears. As if auditioning for "A Chorus Line," they join paws and shamble through a Busby Berkely in time to the music.

Bewildered, you continue to hope for images of a less exuberant Board of Directors, fervently hoping that you are not already watching them! "Please," you mutter with mounting agitation, "please turn that music OFF!"

Of course, this is an exaggeration. But we have seen some instances that weren't so very far removed from this scenario. We've seen clothing sites, for example, that forced users to sit through tedious fashion shows before providing any useful options for navigation. In another case, a travel site opened with one exotic panorama after another and was accompanied by equally lurid music, but it conveyed virtually no actionable information to the site visitor. It was as if the site's only purpose was to encourage daydreaming about tropical vacations or, indeed, a vacation anywhere *but* the workplace! In another case, the web site of an auto company for a time confronted the viewer with aggressive rock music keeping the beat for a guy flying across the waves on a surfboard. Before moving on to the real content, the user had little choice but to watch a brief demonstration on the fine art of riding some "tasty waves, dude!"

Adding insult to injury, it goes almost without saying that this assault on the senses that is staged by some site developers or designers is only possible at all to the extent that users are able—and willing—to load the Flash plug-in (or whatever other technology is forced upon them by virtue of a complicated web site). And if the technology brings the user's computer to a screeching halt, the injury becomes even more severe.

Therefore, although elaborate and flashy introductions can certainly set the mood for a site, overly ambitious preludes such as the ones cited above also tend to put the user in an uncharitable frame of mind, increasing the likelihood that he'll make a quick exit. This tendency is compounded exponentially with repeat performances, because visitors are often obliged to endure the spectacle each and every time they visit the site. If they're regular visitors or, worse yet, customers, what purpose is served by bludgeoning them in such a way? In theory, after all, they're already in the fold.

Does that mean that animation, and even some whimsical diversion, are inevitably counterproductive to the success of a site? Absolutely not. But if users are distracted (for even the briefest of moments) from realizing their objectives, such grandstanding increases the risk of diverting them right out of the site. If users are left no choice in the matter of whether they witness the prelude—especially after being exposed to it a first time—the risk of losing them grows exponentially.

We have observed that where the homepage is preceded by a splash page that gives site visitors the option of escaping, this risk is dramatically reduced. Where possible, the splash page should be kept short, so that even those visitors using older, slower modems are not forced to sit through an excessively long download. Additionally, users should be able to choose whether to skip the splash page altogether, even on the first visit. On subsequent visits, designers might consider skipping it for them by using a cookie.

**Figure 5.1
(Next two images)**

Here are examples of the use of "entertainment" at the entryway of the site.

www.subaru.com

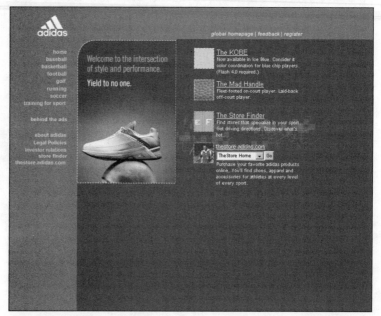

www.adidas.com

Research Tip

A good rule of thumb is to give users a choice of whether or not they want to view long introductions to web sites. Make the "show" optional. Or, even if the first show is inevitable, at least do users the honor of setting up a cookie that allows them to avoid such introductions on subsequent visits. This principle should also be adhered to for animations within the site.

Knock It Off, Picasso! Art is for the Walls

There is nothing intrinsically wrong with wanting your homepage to be a work of art in the conventional sense. In fact, it *should* be tasteful, elegant, and interesting to look at. Nevertheless, striving after that goal must not supercede a site's primary purposes. A homepage, therefore, must be clear about two things: what the site has to offer the user and the identity and nature of the parent company. If these things are true, users are never left to their own interpretations or to engage in guess-work. After all, one distinguishing feature of any work of art is that interpretation is generally left up to the viewer. When speaking of web sites, however, this aesthetic virtue may be a decidedly economic vice.

To the extent that the analogy we offer between web sites and the world of art is apropos, homepages that are self-consciously artistic generally fit into one of two categories: *minimalist* or *chaotic*.

We apply the term minimalist with some care, given it's wider field of application in the arts. Users like homepages that are minimalist insofar as they are attracted to simple, straightforward designs. Elements that generally stand out include a balance of visual elements and white space, clearly labeled buckets and functionality, graphics that don't dominate the page and cause long download times, and attractive colors that aren't dizzying in their variety or intensity. This level of minimalism frequently appeals to a wide spectrum of users. Minimalism *does* have its limits, however, and we often see homepages that overzealously transcend these straightforward principles.

An office supply company experimented with a homepage that featured a single bright color—lime green—with an abstract image in a slightly milder shade and, at the bottom of the page, their logo. Whatever the page's aesthetic graphic appeal, with respect to user experience, it at least bears mention that this was a design one might have expected to see on the walls of an art gallery or design firm rather than on the homepage of an e-commerce site.

More specifically, the sponsor of the site was an office supply company. Their customer base, while perhaps appreciative of art and design, were hardly visiting the site to peruse collections of Flemish Masters or French Impressionists. Rather, their objectives in visiting the site were to access product lists and attain customer service. Users were predominantly office managers and purchasing agents for whom time was precious, and who seldom had the luxury of an extra hour in which to explore the site at leisure. Most were so busy, in fact, that they even complained about the extra click it required to take them from the homepage to the next page, which displayed the major areas of the site—but which forced them to sacrifice a valuable thirty seconds, or more, of their day.

In addition to minimalism, a second quasi-artistic approach to page design also results in user confusion. It is what we call the "chaotic" approach. We frequently see homepages with interesting design elements, abstract graphics, or interesting photos, the intended purpose of which is to intrigue first-time visitors. For example, the site for a particular cosmetic company incorporated abstract drawings of women and cologne bottles that users mistakenly assumed must also be clickable. Instead, users had to survey the page for various tiny text links before viewing available products. In another case, a bottled beverage site tried to appeal to a younger audience by including graphics of hip-looking teens interacting. Again, users assumed these images would be clickable, though they weren't necessarily sure what might lie behind them; but again, the navigation links were much less obvious.

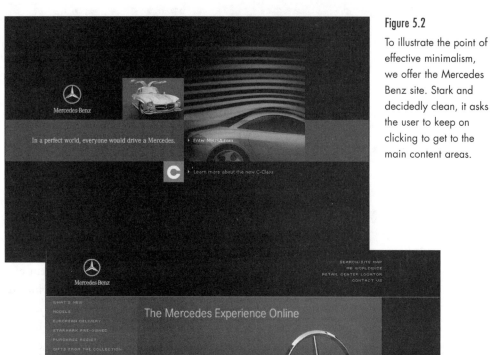

Figure 5.2

To illustrate the point of effective minimalism, we offer the Mercedes Benz site. Stark and decidedly clean, it asks the user to keep on clicking to get to the main content areas.

www.mercedesbenz.com

Similarly, even when abstract images are indeed clickable, some might be so abstract that the user doesn't really know what the images refer to. Again, the user is forced to think and re-think what to do instead of being able to intuitively move on to the next step.

As a result of both these approaches, the initial confusion experienced by users on the homepage is exacerbated as they move more deeply into the site. Art for art's sake can also result in a homepage that makes the user feel like he's found himself in the middle of Times Square on a Saturday night—the senses assaulted by neon lights and billboards, each of which is intriguing in its own way but none of which screams "start here!"

A developer or designer might have much to offer in a site, and the words and symbols chosen to denote certain kinds of content and functionality might be right on target: dazzling colors and images splashed across the homepage. The goal of this extravaganza is to stimulate the user to explore the site by providing a feast for the senses. But this amount of stimulation can quickly turn to excess, and then exhaustion, followed shortly by the need to find a clean, calm place to rest.

Figure 5.3

Clean and simple in its design, HP's homepage gets users directly to the key areas of the site. It is unique in its category for speaking clearly to the intended audience.

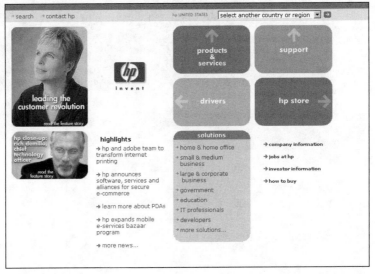

www.hp.com

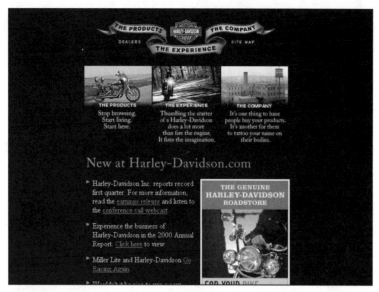

www.harley-davidson.com

**Figure 5.4
(Next two images)**

Both Harley-Davidson and mimeo.com offer uncluttered, well-designed homepages which, in their simplicity, reinforce brand image and speak to their target audiences.

www.mimeo.com

Designers Work in Mysterious Ways
Iconography Is Only Compelling in Church

Users love icons. In fact, as we will discuss in other chapters, they often like icons more than they like words. And icons can certainly support brand image, especially for companies that make use of images (such as a cartoon character) that have long been associated with the brand. But if a web site's icons are not immediately recognizable, so that the user can successfully associate them with expected content and functionality, they will invariably fail to fulfill their purpose.

An extreme example was that of a site that was devoted exclusively to music, whose homepage featured the image of a keyboard with undulating shadows dancing across it for a striking visual effect. In a deeply unfortunate oversight, the designer didn't notice the vague resemblance these shadows bore to the swastika symbol (as more than one site visitor commented during testing).

Of course, not all problematic icons present difficulties because they provoke controversy. A more widespread, if banal, problem is that some icons are visually interesting or appealing, but are nevertheless totally confusing; they come across as abstract, colorful "whatevers" that, unless defined by a caption or rollover, simply sit on the page and look pretty. We worked on an entertainment site that featured a prominently placed icon in the form of a luminous red heart. Users were certainly attracted to it, but they had difficulty pinning down its exact meaning. Some thought it might be a way to get to the most popular artists; others thought it would allow them to create a list of their own favorite artists. Still others guessed that the site was performing a valuable public service by allowing users to sign up to be organ donors. All these were interesting possibilities. Unfortunately, no one guessed that clicking on the heart would allow them to sign up a friend and receive a premium in return.

Icons can also fail if, despite all their apparent clarity, they are misleading. A shopping cart, for example, is the universal icon for that area of an e-commerce site where the user collects all the items he wants to purchase. Seemingly little interpretation is needed there.

Yet, we have come across sites in which clicking on the shopping cart leads the user to a shopping area and more lists of products rather than to the checkout. Another site included a shopping cart which linked to a list of bricks-and-mortar stores where products could only be purchased offline.

However much these examples suggest the contrary, we again emphasize that web users *like* icons. The web is, of course, a primarily visual medium and, as we will discuss in subsequent chapters, users generally prefer visual representation to text. Nevertheless, icons need to be grounded in offline experience in order to be intuitive to users. In other words, they need to be simple, easy-to-understand representations of concepts users are accustomed to in "real life." Few users want to be forced to sit and think before clicking. All of which is to say that although it's not particularly sexy, there is a reason why the humble shopping cart continues to work so well.

Research Tip

During testing, when you're observing users navigating your site, pay particular attention to their use of icons. You can ask users the following questions: What does this icon mean to you? What do you think is behind it? What will happen if you click on it?

www.bn.com

Figure 5.5

At the Barnes & Noble site, the ubiquitous shopping cart and several other key icons are intelligently paired with text that helps define them.

Bells and Whistles Can Sink Your Anchors

A subtext of this chapter is that users expect to find certain elements on all homepages, regardless of industry affiliation or purpose. These elements, called the "anchors" of the site, must also be in sync with the priorities users have when they come to a site. These anchors are defined here:

- *Customer Service*. FAQs, e-mail addresses, an e-mail link, online support, and instructions for product returns if it's an e-commerce site.

- *About Us*. The mission of your organization or company, the location of the main office, names and biographies of executives and board of directors, and affiliations.

- *Search*. Users are invariably impatient, and some want to start by searching rather than using any of your navigation options. Search needs to be a prominently displayed open text box.

- *Home Button*. Even if a logo is clickable, users still expect to see a small button, often in the top navigation bar, that indicates how to get "home."

- *Contact Us*. Users want a quick way to get a question answered or even comment on a site. Contact Us may overlap with Customer Service, but it still needs to be a discrete option.

Beyond these basic elements, sites also incorporate site anchors that link to a site's functionality, or to aspects of a site's mission—News, Products and Services, Shopping, Account Information, Calculators or other tools, even that pesky Shopping Cart! These also need to be front and center on the homepage and be clearly labeled.

Now, if bells and whistles do, in fact, serve to highlight these site anchors, especially those that are unique to your site, so much the better. It's when the anchors are obscured that you run the risk of losing site visitors.

Let's say a developer has in mind a variety of interesting anchors, above and beyond "the basics" mentioned previously, and he isn't

sure which ones to feature on a site. Should they be of equal prominence at all costs, even if that means trying to shoe-horn a dozen
or more icons onto the homepage? The labeling might make
perfect sense, but a large number of icons will still leave the user
overwhelmed and confused, even where they are not obscured by
flashy design. The standard of measure is simple: If users can't immediately see what they are looking for—with or without the flash
and color—they won't remain at a site. They'll walk away
believing that your homepage was needlessly cluttered, or painfully boring, or (at best) beautifully confusing. No matter how you
look at it, you've lost them. In the category of online entertainment, the general consensus among consumers is this: "I should get
what I want quickly, easily, and preferably for free." Paradoxically,
many music sites find themselves striving to distinguish themselves
from the herd for a single jaded online audience that has "heard it
all before." Although the most obvious way to achieve this goal is
to insist that your site is "all things to all people," by trying to do
everything for everyone, developers more often than not end up
doing nothing for anybody. And ultimately they alienate their original, core audience.

In this case, our client was a music web site that did, in fact, have
a point of distinction. They offered users an array of original content that was unavailable on other music sites. In addition, their
ability to offer substantive musical content across a wide variety
of musical genres was impressive. The major difficulty was that,
due to ineffective homepage communication, few users had any
idea that these features were part of the site.

We conducted testing that included both focus groups and user experience interviews, and we found that their site's success all but de-
pended on the communication possibilities of its homepage. Site
anchors are an integral aspect of initial homepage communications.

Our recommendation to this company was that they use the home
page to play two roles on the site: those of "messenger service" and
"traffic director." That is to say, we advised them to use the homepage to inform visitors about key features of the site and how these
could be accessed. Although this may seem obvious, we often find
that these principles are lost on web designers and producers who

are already overwhelmed in their attempts to simultaneously communicate their site's business model, mission statement, and philosophy on the homepage. What they too often lose sight of is that, to the average user coming to a music site, the company's mission statement is irrelevant should they be impeded from finding the songs they want.

The question of how much is too much is not always an easy one to answer. For any given web site, there are generally three or four basic reasons why people visit—notwithstanding whatever other great content or functionality they might also encounter there. These nonessential elements might entice visitors to stay longer, and might even give them reasons to return. But the most relevant three or four reasons should be situated front and center on a homepage—clearly labeled, easily accessible, and working the way users need them to work.

To obscure these with bells and whistles is to invite speculation as to whether they even exist. Moreover, users may also become suspicious of smoke-and-mirrors approaches to marketing, wondering if the developer has something to hide.

Research Tip

You may get visitors to sit through the floor or the light show—and maybe even return for an encore. But if they can't find anything useful at your site, chances are they won't be back. Remember that too much stylization can obscure your purpose.

Go Iconoclastic! But Navigate at Your Own Risk

As we have discussed, web site navigation begins with the icons that users see on the homepage. When the imagery or labeling is not clear, users become confused. In addition, navigation that is initiated from other elements of the homepage, notably the left and the top navigation bar, may also suffer the effects of poorly thought out design. In particular, overstylization of the homepage can also extend to these areas, with the corresponding problems.

Let's begin by taking a step back. Think of what you do when you get up every morning. Most likely, you have a routine that begins with fumbling to turn off the alarm clock, and is followed by groping for a cup of coffee and maybe a quick glance at the newspaper. And how about at work? You might begin the day with stopping for another cup of coffee, turning on your computer, and checking for voicemail. Human beings develop lasting habits easily. Not only do they resist veering away from established routines, but they also become easily frustrated when such comfortable routines are interfered with. (When was the last time your coffee maker— let alone your PC—mysteriously ceased to function without your being frantic to repair it on the spot?)

Web site users have also learned certain habits, many of which are related to the homepage. Navigation links in the top navigation bar, for example, tend to be more global (such as the "About Us" link), whereas the left navigation links tend to be more specific (such as those that identify specific content areas or functionality and are used to begin searching). Some users immediately peruse the left navigation bar, whereas others begin in the center of the page.

Although design elements like color and iconography certainly impact how users approach a homepage, so do the user's own habits. Users establish a frame of reference and a sense of comfort when all the elements they expect to see are neatly in place. It's when these elements are missing, or are obscured by design, that comfort level is placed at risk.

Insight

Prioritize, prioritize, prioritize! But don't do it unassisted. Ask prospective users to tell you why they would come to a site like yours, what content and functionality they need, and what they would call it. Once you get some answers, you will also know what to highlight. "Right-size" the site to fit the needs of your target users.

Make Sure the Site Is in Sync with the Brand

If a developer represents an established brand, the web site design elements need to take brand imagery into account. This might mean incorporating into site design the overall "personality" of a brand, and not merely the logo or current advertising. The web can also expand this exposure, by taking the site visitors one or two steps beyond how they currently perceive a given brand.

We worked with the site of a large insurance company that uses a popular comic strip character in its advertising. The homepage of the web site featured this character prominently, along with consumer-oriented features such as calculators. All of these elements served to make the site more approachable and friendly, as well as taking it a step beyond the traditional image of an insurance company.

However, those familiar with this company were generally also familiar with the company's use of this comic strip character; it was the additional consumer-oriented content and features *in tandem with* the character, that were embedded in the user's consciousness. The page also referenced serious content like account and product information. The result of this careful juxtapositioning of the comical and no-nonsense was that during research, users reported that they felt welcomed by the homepage, but also that they could continue to place their trust in a company that was solid and conservative.

On the other hand, we have also worked with sites whose sponsors were so eager to push aside their established brand imagery that, beyond the company name, they totally rejected any reference to recognizable imagery or personality, wanting instead to create a site that appealed to a younger, more "web-savvy audience" that they feared rejected their current image.

Instead of extending the image, a focus on design—disconnected from the current brand imagery—rendered a site unrecognizable to current customers, while missing the mark with the target viewership.

Likewise, sites from sponsors that do not have a current brand image are equally liable to misstep. As discussed previously in this chapter, long production numbers do not create a brand. No matter how creative or intriguing, designs do not succeed if they are not strategically organized around a straightforward brand image. What does the brand stand for? How is the brand positioned vis-à-vis the competition? These questions need to be answered before, not after, the homepage is designed, and it is not the responsibility of the homepage design team to establish the brand.

Insight

Build brand imagery into the development process. Start with an understanding of the brand, as well as the imagery, personality, products, and services associated with it. If the brand is not established, explore a viable brand. Then ask users to help you determine if the brand is indeed reflected in the site.

The View from 30,000 Feet

If there were mantras for web development, among the list would be simplicity and control. Certainly the word "control" seems to pop up with increasing frequency during site development. Although we have been discussing the principle simplicity throughout this chapter, it cannot be considered independently of user control, with which simplicity goes hand-in-hand—in fact, they enable one another.

As we often say, users want to be in control of the web experience. Over-design, coupled with an excess of bells and whistles, increases the risk that the role and branding of a site be misperceived. When users feel overwhelmed by the design or inundated by bells and whistles, the efficiency and convenience they want most from the web flies out the window.

A Sachs Insight

Test your design with users. How do they react to it? What images of your brand does testing provoke? How are they interpreting your labeling? Such considerations are the ultimate test of whether or not your design is on target.

A Few Hard Questions

- Are the basic links, like "About U" and "Home," obvious to the user?

- Are the three or four or five things users would be most likely to come here for front and center?

- Can any initial bells and whistles be avoided after the first visit?

- Is the intent of the icons and labeling totally clear by design?

- Is your brand identity reflected?

CHAPTER SIX

People Don't Read: Don't Make Them!

We have noticed a growing segment of web users that we have affectionately dubbed "click first, think later." If successful navigation requires reading instructions first or filling in an inordinate number of fields, this portion of your audience is lost before it even begins! This is because they typically rely on visual cues—for example, a button that has the instructions on it or one whose meaning is implied by its very design.

Some users out there *will* patiently read instructions and Help screens, but they are few and far between. This being the case, in this chapter we focus on how to keep those sometimes zealous and impatient tendencies of readers and non-readers in mind when designing a customer experience.

If They Want to Read a Novel, They'll Buy One

Unlike print media, people expect the web to be interactive, and they are generally confused or annoyed by web sites that simply replicate the experience of reading print in electronic format. Bluntly, when most of us want to read a newspaper or a novel, we pick one up at a bookstore. On the web, users are typically looking for a qualitatively different experience—one in which they can pick and choose from various options easily and directly, without having to wade through mountains of tangential information.

We've observed that, particularly with respect to younger users, this tends to be the case. When interviewing college applicants, for instance, we found that any text not obviously a headline was simply ignored. They are so used to browsing among a myriad of high-level choices that any text requiring scrolling to advance to the next selection is regarded distastefully. In another instance, the presence of complex cooking recipes on a site had the unintended consequence of making participants long for a Print button. Far from wanting to scroll through the necessary ingredients and procedures, they just wanted to see the whole thing at a glance! We thus learned in user experience testing that scanning recipes for ingredients to purchase was one thing, and following online instructions in minute detail was quite another.

The moral to this and many other stories is, of course, that if a site designer wants users to hang in there until they find the selections that are right for them, the designer must first figure out exactly what information is needed or desired by their target viewers, and then offer it. Especially when considering whether or not to include long or detailed text on a site (such as recipes, travel information, and health or financial data, to name but a few), designers need to offer clear instructions for printing (most obviously a "Print" button) that makes the user feel secure in the knowledge that even if he has no desire to gaze at a screen for hours at a stretch, he can still print the desired text.

The goal of text links—like the lead story on the front page of a newspaper—is to tell users exactly enough to entice them, without requiring them to make a choice in the dark or scroll interminably to get to other choices. Figure 6.1 shows a good example.

Figure 6.1

Take a look at the homepage of *People*. Whether you are a reader or you need visual cues, the home-page draws you in.

http://people.aol.com

People.com marries eye-catching photos, headlines, and just enough information to let the reader decide if an article or feature is interesting enough to want to read more.

Of course, some want to scan a recipe or product description on-line but know they will want to read about it or file it for when they are in the kitchen making the cake or in the showroom buying the car. Those are good uses of the Print feature, as is the case of a long article that a technical or business reader may want for the long commuter train ride home at the end of the day.

Epicurious.com gives the reader immediate access to a printable version. That makes it clear what you're going to get when you go to the printer.

Homedepot.com, while intending to offer the reader the means of printing the information she needs, makes it far more difficult to predict the printed outcome!

Figure 6.2

Don't like reading from the screen? Epicurious makes it easy to print it out (and avoid unwanted spills on your keyboard or spatters on your screen).

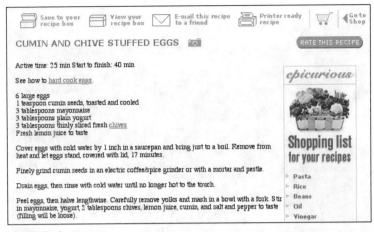

http://epicurious.com

Figure 6.3

Will the user know exactly what will be printed? Will he notice where the print function is located?

www.homedepot.com

Insight

What works in print does not translate to the web. People want and expect to save time by only viewing details they are truly interested in. Therefore, you need to remember the following tips:

- People don't like to scroll as a means of advancing from one choice to another.

- Users are willing to embark on a second (or even a third) click if they are fairly certain they are on the path they want.

- Make sure you offer a clear "Print" button that lets users know the content will print in an easy-to-read form.

Let Your Pictures Do the Talking

One of the most effective ways to announce content on the web is through images. For example, if a designer wants to communicate that multiple paths on a site all lead to distinct commerce areas, he might display an image of a well-dressed woman, man, and child. By doing so, the designer tells the user what he is selling and how to get at the merchandise—all without saying a word. Notice how the Saks Fifth Avenue homepage uses virtually no text, yet effectively communicates what they have to offer to whom and how the user can get it. They also strongly reinforce their brand image without any use of Flash or animation.

One note of caution to be observed by designers, however, is that people can be amazingly literal in their interpretation of the images and text on the web. If a user is viewing a photograph of gloves, for instance, it might well not occur to her that the same site sells scarves. If a designer employs an image that is at all figurative, viewers will almost inevitably vary in the meaning they ascribe to that image. For the success of an e-commerce web site, in particular, this can be dangerous. Take, for instance, the example of a healthcare client of ours that used the image of a woman jogging to illustrate health tips. Virtually everyone who viewed the site thought that the content was meant exclusively for women.

www.saksfifthavenue.com

Figure 6.4

Is there any doubt in your mind whom this site is for and what the Saks Fifth Avenue brand is all about?

Another client's web site featured the image of a PC set up with a printer and speakers. Their goal was to show what the PC they were selling was capable of supporting. Unfortunately, most site visitors assumed that the model described below that image came with a printer and speakers. It was an ominous misconception when they took into account the price tag that accompanied the system. It really wouldn't matter if the fine print said "for illustration only" or that "the set available does not include peripherals." People don't read on the web.

Pictures Don't Have to Say a Thousand Words, But They Need to Say Something That Makes Sense

If you use visuals simply as "wallpaper" to set a tone or mood, you will find that many people click on them thinking that they mean something other than what you had intended.

This is particularly true of splash pages that are designed to set a mood, be it luxury or relaxation. You may use images of elegant parties to convey that you sell elegant party food. People will think you are a restaurant or a caterer. If you do set a mood, make sure that you use their time to communicate what you offer and what you want them to do—be it to browse or shop or call you for more information.

Take a moment to compare the sites of two telecommunications companies: Sprint and MCI Worldcom. Note that Sprint lists on the homepage all the features they offer to each of the markets they serve. Not visually stunning, but (in a rather uncluttered way) it provides one-click access for each category that isn't easy to condense or explain. By contrast, MCI Worldcom uses a large, abstract "unclickable" image to set the mood for the company. Good branding, perhaps, yet the page offers the viewer very little information about what the site will offer the prospect or the customer. It might be better to offer more intuitive images as well as some text.

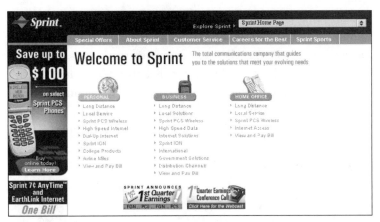

Figure 6.5

Sprint provides users with an overview of features so they can click and move forward in the site.

www.sprint.com

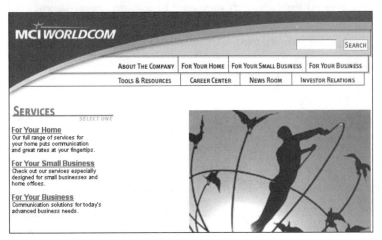

Figure 6.6

MCI Worldcom presents users with an interesting image that necessitates extra clicking to move forward.

www.mciworldcom.com

An Image Can Be Worth a Thousand Words... But Not If It Whispers

A common problem that confounds many a user is a visual that quickly changes images, expecting the user to guess (as in a video game) when to click on the moving image to get to the page about the image of interest. Many a user doesn't want to click if it will take him down an unintended path if he's late; others simply miss the idea that the image is clickable. In instances like this, we recommend slowing down the images so that users who want to navigate via image have time to do so. And, importantly, offer other clear ways to get to the content behind the visual.

Looking at the Oxygen site, a site devoted to women, you see a prominent visual that changes to illustrate the top three articles. As the images change, the pointer moves to the related article. However, the article's headline is not clickable. So, if a user doesn't "get it" as to how to click on an image or how the image relates to the article, she may miss the desired path. The solution: Slow the images, make the headlines clickable, and if possible, make a stronger visual connection between the image and the article so it is very clear that the pointer is pointing to an article.

Figure 6.7
(Next three images)

The Oxygen site uses interesting imagery, but users may not immediately understand how to select an article.

www.oxygen.com

Images Often Work Harder Than Words

As any of us who have succumbed to the eyeshadow that Gwyneth Paltrow was wearing in *Vogue*, or the restaurant featured in *Gourmet Magazine* can attest, images are seductive. Most of us are more likely to be enticed by an image—one that is at once meaningful and moving—than by reading a sentence or two. Moreover, it should go without saying that certain categories more than others actually *require* visual images in addition to text. For example, few of us would be willing to purchase, or bid on, an art object without first taking a look at it. Other categories where the choices are either generic or well-known are less dependent on visuals.

So our advice to designers is this:

- Use images sparingly. For most users, they take forever to load.

- Use images only to announce content or direction.

- Consider the implied meaning of every image and make sure it is very difficult to misconstrue.

- Use images in categories that are aspirational—to sell product more effectively.

- Make your images clickable. Wallpaper is for your kitchen, not your web site!

Insight
The lack of images on your site is no worse than using images that don't make sense or that otherwise confuse or annoy your users.

People Are Just as Literal with Words

For those of you who have searched for the "Any" key when asked to "hit any button" or have typed out the word "anywhere" when asked to "click anywhere to begin," you already know what we mean by literal.

Figure 6.8 (Next two images)

Gap.com confounds the shopper by inviting them to "PURCHASE THIS ITEM" before they have selected color, size, or fit. This button leads to a second page that offers the choice to "ADD TO CART"—a case of putting horse before the cart!

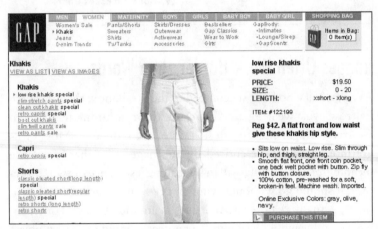

www.gap.com

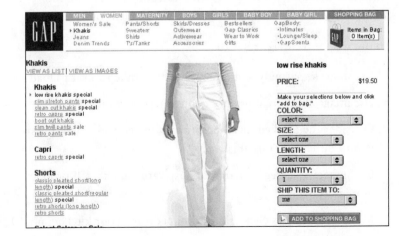

This extends to using words for instructions that "get ahead of themselves." For example, if you use the word "Send" to mark the set of steps leading up to "sending a document," or if you create a button called "Buy" to show users the set of steps leading up to making a purchase, know that many people will be unwilling to make that kind of commitment. This supports the idea that people are incredibly literal in their interpretation of web-based language and symbolism. If they see a button labeled "Buy," they will think you are inviting them to make a purchase, when all they really want to do is comparison shop. Little surprise that they simply ignore this button and abandon the site in favor of another right away.

First Things First
Begin with Important Features

The best way to enable people to make informed choices without forcing them to read a thesis–length text is to present all the high-level choices first and allow users to make their own decisions about drilling down further on an anchor tag, or "More" button, if that is what they want to do. Note that most users read into the order in which content is arranged on a page to signify its relative importance. Many might think, "If it is really good, why do I have to scroll two pages or use four mouse clicks to find it?"

The American Cancer Society uses mostly text—no icons, no scrolling—just clearly written links with explanatory text where needed to announce whom the site is for and how to get immediately to the reader's area of interest.

Two tough questions confound many a company: What are those first, most important choices likely to be? What kinds of information are users going to make a priority in exploring a web site? Focus groups are a great tool for answering this question. For example, if the most important things about women's sweaters (apart from size) are fiber, content, and color, this information needs to be prominently featured. We've found that many shoppers see a red turtleneck thumbnail sketch and assume that the sweater

Figure 6.9

The American Cancer Society site is a good example of how to effectively use text to communicate site features and help the user to get moving.

www.cancer.org

comes only in red. It's a missed opportunity—in New York anyway—if they don't know the sweater also comes in black!

We are not saying that you need to test every modification of your site in a focus group, such as each season when your clothing line changes. In the previous example, focus group respondents suggested ways in which the availability of alternate colors could be made clear, through "swatches" that accompany the thumbnail, or text that briefly offers this option. This learning guided the presentation of new products as they were introduced each season.

Similarly, five years of experience researching web sites have taught us that web pages are more effective with users when they are kept short and to the point. Nevertheless, we still see product pages or search results that read like encyclopedias: itemized lists, pictures, headers, and full descriptions. A lesson we have learned is that most people want just enough information to avoid having to click in error and be forced to backtrack. Give them any more than that and site designers flirt with a high "piss off" factor—and run a real risk of having much of their content skipped. Therefore, it is important that you learn how to summarize very effectively so the average visitor can acquire a good sense of what a choice is and why he should want it in a sentence or two. The shorter, the better.

Tell People—Briefly—What You Want Them to Do

We spend countless hours in our lab, watching people try to figure out if and when an online image can be enlarged, or what to do with a pop-up window after reading it. If users are to be comfortable on a site, they must be given a clue about these things. If you are the designer, we advise you to do the following:

- Tell them where and how to "click to make it bigger."

- Let them know where to "click to close the window."

These are only a couple examples of what users commonly say about images. Depending on your users and the purpose of your image, you will need to offer additional explanations as well. Only your own testing can effectively illuminate the issues that are unique to your site.

If few or no instructions are supplied—or worse yet, if newly devised icons are simply assumed to make sense—people will follow paths in error and will ultimately (probably sooner rather than later) become frustrated. That's guaranteed.

We worked on a fashion site whose designers invented new icons that ostensibly enabled people to enlarge images, rotate them, or zoom in closer. They also used male and female icons to indicate gender. Unfortunately, most users either did not notice these icons or failed to recognize them for what they were. When replaced with buttons clearly marked "Women," "Men," and "Zoom," among others, people were liberated to navigate with ease.

Figure 6.10

A VeriSign pop-up makes it clear how to close the window, saving the user frustration.

Figure 6.11

Eddie Bauer specifically tells the user how to enlarge that baby seat.

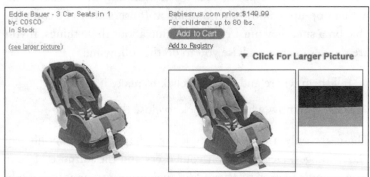

Save People from the Garden Path

Many sites use relatively small print to forewarn users of the key steps they will need to take before exploring a site in more depth. For instance, small print might warn of the need to register before making a trade, of the need to wait for a confirmation number, of the ever-present danger that one's purchase of movie tickets might not reach completion, of the requirement that a site be informed as to which among its competitors the users do NOT want to see, or what a person is bidding on a piece of property. Because people do not read—even when the stakes are somewhat high—it is critically important that you protect them from themselves. This means that you should make it crystal clear what steps they need to embark on, a feat which can be accomplished in several ways:

- Make each part of the process a "step," and prevent users from proceeding to Step 2 before acknowledging that they have completed Step 1.

- Highlight anything they need to know in bold—or perhaps make it a pop-up window that they can close or at least never be forced to look at again.

- Make the rules of your site short and very clear, and don't be afraid to display them in various contexts on the site. In other words, don't rely on people going somewhere else to read the fine print (that tickets are non-refundable or that travel times cannot be changed, for example).

Wells Fargo does a good job of showing potential loan applicants the four easy steps to applying for a loan. Steps 1 through 3 help a borrower determine what he might be qualified for. Those that have already researched their creditworthiness can proceed straight to Step 4 to apply online. This approach helps either type of user zero in on where to start and helps reduce anxiety over borrowing money—an area that makes the average consumer nervous. It also helps Wells Fargo pre-qualify potential customers.

Insight

Presenting information in steps helps set the user's expectations about what is ahead, while also providing context.

www.wellsfargo.com

Figure 6.12

Wells Fargo outlines the steps that loan applicants need to follow, so that they know what's ahead of them and they have a frame of reference once they are involved in the process.

If Your Mom Can't Read It, the Print's Too Small!

The ravages of time have undoubtedly had their effect on our vision, as they have on so many other things. This caveat notwithstanding, it still seems as if much text on the web is unnecessarily small, fine, and unintelligible. Occasionally, the difficulty is that the font is diminutive. At other times, it seems as though the text is shown in an unduly pale color with no appropriate background contrast (our favorite is fire-engine red), or inversely, that the lettering is made to glow so radiantly that it obscures the message or at least makes it unpleasant to look at. Unlike a trip to the optometrist's, however, browsing a web site is not an endurance test that users have little choice but to sit through. They are under no obligation to accept the imposition of such unpleasant conditions, however inadvertent, and they may choose not to.

Follow these tips on how to use text on your site so that the average Joe or Mary can read it comfortably:

- Make sure that body type and font are large enough and clear enough to be read. It seems a simple principle, but we frequently see type that is too small to be comfortably read onscreen. While many people will print out an article from the web if it is interesting enough, they are more likely to skip it if the text size is excessively tiny. The equivalent of 10-point type is the smallest size that is readable onscreen by most users, and 12-point type is preferable.

- Make sure text that denotes navigational buttons or menus (such as the selections on the left navigation bar) stands out from other text on the page. Some simple ways of doing this are to make important text larger, bolder, or in color. However, not everyone is endowed with the physical capacity to perceive those colors deemed distinctive on a site, so wherever color is employed to convey information, remember that it should be accompanied by other visual cues (graphics, labels, and gray scales, for instance).

- Make sure that the contrast between type and the background is high. Three typical problems are associated with this:

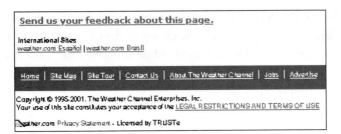

Figure 6.13

The type in this example could be a challenge to those among us who are less visually gifted.

1. *Inverse text*. When the text is lighter than what is behind it, it is generally difficult to read.

2. *Clashing colors*. When the colors of text and background cause visual dissonance, as with orange type on a lime green background, it's hard on the eyes.

3. *Low contrast*. Similar shades of a color, or similar levels of gray in different colors, blend into the background and make it difficult to make out the letters.

- Stick to colors that do not "glow." Obtaining an easy-to-read shade of red can be particularly challenging.

- Make your design work well for a variety of font sizes. Instead of hard-coding a size for text, let your users use their browser font settings to determine what works for them individually.

- Finally, discipline your copywriters (with a whip, if necessary!) so that even the lengthiest text accompanying a navigation button is short enough to be readable (particularly if it is embedded *in* a button).

Insight

Text is inevitable. But judiciously edit—*and test*—to make sure you are using the best wording possible, that it's clean and clear. Then present it in a way that your user can comfortably read it.

The View from 30,000 Feet

People's expectations of the web are far different than their expectations of "print" media, and for most users, reading is simply an undesirable activity. Perceptually, it is faster to click three times to drill down to the precise information you want than to scroll down a single page to move from one choice to the next. However, there are no clear-cut rules. The needs of your users, your users' backgrounds, and the goals of your site, all must be taken into account. Text certainly has a role.

Research Tip

Who are you writing for in your site? What terms do they use? What needs to be explained, and what doesn't? How are users interpreting your descriptions and your labels? You should explore all this during user experience testing. Ask users to provide their interpretations, upon first exposure, as well as during the process of navigating and using the features of your site. Can they read your text (is it easy on the eyes)? Are they missing important text? Also ask them when it is enough, too much, and not enough.

A Few Hard Questions

- What is the "common denominator" in terms of the backgrounds of your users? Are they novices or are they insiders? Do you know what information you must offer to enable them to makes choices?

- Are your navigable choices brief?

- Do you use images to announce content or simply to provide context?

- Do your images clearly state their purpose—and are they clickable?

- Does your site display text when the meaning could more clearly be conveyed with an image?

- Does the user have to scroll only to read the body text, or does he have to scroll to navigate?

- Is the information people *must* know clearly stated, in context, so that users do not run into trouble?

- Is your text easily readable?

- Have you told people how to enlarge your images and close your windows?

CHAPTER SEVEN

Just Because the Competition Does It That Way, Doesn't Mean It's Right

We wish we earned a dollar for every time a developer says, "I designed it that way because that's the model everyone uses in the greeting card (or email or travel) category." Even the thought that there *is* such a uniform, static model, used by all and sundry, at this still early point in the web's development is unfortunate and even comical. Statements such as this assume that a modicum of research has been done to ascertain the truth of such models. In fact, there is little reason to believe that one's competitors have even tested their sites with target consumers in order to confirm that their language and logic has a customer seal of approval. Where web site development is concerned, if there is one rule of thumb that continues to endure, it is that there is no consensus among designers.

The bottom line is that many sites are so badly designed—and are often so counterintuitive—that copying them is not a good idea. The fact is, even if a designer does follow the lead of others on the off chance that what they are doing is spot on, it is far from certain that the competition's approach will translate well to one's own site, brand, or category. The best way to build a model for how to interface with customers relates to the discovery of a target customer's language and logic. Step by step, how do users select and fill out greeting cards, create email, or book travel? Understanding the way they behave and speak—and identifying opportunities to overcome problems they have had navigating and understanding other sites—can be the first step towards creating a winning model.

Jump Off the Bandwagon!

Many companies exhibit an overwhelming desire to pack up their current sites and replace them with new ones that more closely emulate what their competitors are doing. If frames are "in," their reasoning is, "let's do frames." If left nav bars are "out," they think, "let's get rid of ours." Change to a magazine format? Add a context-sensitive secondary top nav bar? This wish-list of innovations goes on and on.

Our belief is that before instituting any major change, designers should understand very clearly what is *not* working on a site, what *may* be working on other sites, and (most importantly) what their target customers seek. At all costs, they shouldn't "fix what isn't broke"—particularly if customers visit a site in order to make transactions. On the other hand, if a designer *does* decide to dramatically change a site or introduce new elements, he should make sure that current users can still track their orders, and that they're not confronted with a painful learning curve.

This is admittedly a difficult balance. Originality and creative expression must not interfere with the user's ability to navigate the site. As always, this is an opportunity for testing.

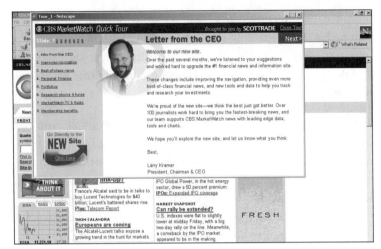

Figure 7.1

Next tour leaving in 20 seconds...

http://cbs.marketwatch.com

And, if you do decide to change your site to enhance the customer experience, do it for a good reason. We've seen many sites that introduce a site's "face lift" or overhaul with a tutorial on how to use it. That logic is counterintuitive, because if the new site is so easy to use, it should not need a tutorial. The new look and functionality should speak for themselves.

Model Online Processes After Offline People
Design with Logic That Is Easy to Follow

We often find sites where the sequence of events people are asked to follow does not coincide with the way people do things in an offline world.

For example, a client informed us that he had people fill out an electronic greeting card by first addressing the envelope and then filling out the card. "That is how the industry leader does it," he insisted. "Okay," we responded. "But how do *you* fill out a greeting card?" He replied, "First, I select the card that is most appropriate for the person or occasion. Then, I open it, write a salutation and message, close it, insert it in the envelope, address the envelope, and mail it in time for whatever occasion the card celebrates." Based on research with real users, we agreed that this made sense—it followed the order in which most people actually fill out paper greeting cards—and we asked him to consider designing his online greeting card with that in mind. In all cases, it is important that the online process mirror the offline logic of users and not put the cart before the horse (or the address before the message).

This principle holds true across industries. For example, you can tell your travel agent that you love early morning flights—except on Sunday—or that you only like to fly on 727s, or that you prefer to fly United except to London where you'd rather take Virgin. Know that an online travel site will work for you only if you have the option of entering these bits of information beforehand so that they will be taken into account when search results are tabulated. Otherwise, search results might initially be hopeful, yet on closer inspection they'll show that you're flying on a United 767 to London. Then the site cannot be said to have been very helpful. Another example might be purchasing a ticket to a hockey game: You'll take mezzanine seats, but this will only be satisfying if your view isn't obstructed by a massive concrete column. When the tickets finally arrive, you have the mezzanine seats you wanted, but at precisely the wrong angle.... You're facing the pillar! These problems crop up because, as a user, you don't have the benefit of a logical process that allows you to make informed choices about the outcome of your online expedition until it is potentially too late.

For example, the order and logic of the purchase process must make sense online as well as off. How many of us have put something in our electronic shopping carts only to be sent back to the homepage, or have unsuccessfully attempted a return to the shopping cart to view and reevaluate an item that has already been selected? Or, more annoying still, how many of us have placed something in our shopping cart without knowing the price, despite our best efforts to find it? These things just don't happen at the supermarket. If we put apple juice in our shopping cart and subsequently decide to return it because we'd rather have grape juice, we are still in the juice aisle.

You get the point!

As we will cover in depth in Chapter 19, "Business-to-Business: Challenges and Opportunitis," this premise is particularly salient for business-to-business sites. If a buyer needs to obtain two levels of authorization in order to purchase a major piece of equipment, their site needs to accommodate that process. If most companies that will purchase a company's products use purchase orders, their web sites need to make this option available. Finally, if buyers need to know the dimensions of an item, its weight, or its compatibility with other items, B-to-B sites must provide that information—if they want to continue to make sales, that is.

Insight

Remember, for a web site to be successful, the sequencing of online choices must reflect the ways users behave in the offline world! Therefore, it pays to figure out *in advance* what this behavior is so that users don't become easily frustrated and leave your site.

Don't Reinvent the Wheel Online, Either!

We encounter numerous design firms and in-house development teams that claim to have engineered the coolest new way to search, browse, or advance to the next screen. And, in fact, many of these challenges have indeed been successfully tackled by others facing the same kinds of questions as those we raise in this book. Therefore, an important aspect of building better web sites should be to learn from the successes (and failures) of your predecessors.

For instance, insights that have been learned the hard way include understanding that consumers expect their search results to be clearly visible and distinguished onscreen from other elements of text; that they will be able to click on an informative (but brief) header to get more detail; that when advancing (or backing up) a page, they will see the total number of pages that are available; and that they will be able to move at will from page to page and from the top to the bottom of any given screen and back again. Although these points now seem intuitive to designers and users alike, they are just a few of the lessons that had to be learned through success and failure, trial-and-error. For this reason, it would be foolhardy to disregard these and other principles too hastily, even if you're attempting to design a better user experience.

We typically find that designers are on dangerous ground when they decide to play too freely with accepted web conventions. Our research with customers convincingly shows that developers shouldn't assume too much about their site visitors—especially not that users will want what they offer so badly that the users will be willing to abandon conventions that are second nature to them.

This is not to say that a designer can't design a really cool advanced search capability that is geared to optimize search within a category, or that she shouldn't develop great new ways for users to browse or inspect merchandise. It means simply that designers should think hard before introducing new conventions that ask the user to deviate from, or even relearn, what they had thought to be instinctive knowledge of the web.

Insight

New ideas can be really cool and *still* not be cool enough to replace the old conventions! Consider how much new information the user will be required to absorb before adopting new navigational tools and icons.

Call Us Crazy, But We Think the Left Nav Bar Should Be Left Where It Is

Without doubt, Amazon.com has done a wonderful job of facilitating browsing, primarily through effective use of the top navigation bar. However, with few exceptions, we find that most users instinctively look to the left to find their high-level options. This means, among other things, that if they select a category in error or are finished checking something else out, their natural inclination is to look again to the left to see what their options are and to plan their exit.

For this reason, designers who remove the left navigation bar (on any of their web pages) do so at their own risk, for they are more likely to encounter disoriented and (frequently) disgruntled visitors than they are success. (Left navigation, by our definition, refers to the global navigation links, arranged in a set of rectangular-shaped links arranged in a vertical bar that resides on the left side of the homepage and basically follows the user throughout the site.) The thing to consider when designing a site that has no left nav is whether or not people can quickly learn how to use the alternative option, and whether it enables them to move intuitively from one key area of the site to another. If so, that's great; but if not, designers might want to think about sticking to the tried and true, and not throwing the baby (that is, the value of left nav bars, repeatedly proven in our customer experience lab) out with the bathwater.

www.ibm.com

Figure 7.2

If you are interested in "Clearance Corner," you will lose the "Home/Home Office" component of the left nav bar, making it hard to remember your place. (See next image.)

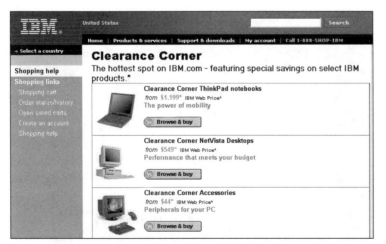

www.ibm.com

Figure 7.3

From this point forward, you no longer have a link back to your "Home/Home Office" section, or to its set of links.

Whatever designers decide with respect to the left nav bar, however, it is important to remember that consistency is key. Thus, metaphors and links that *are* employed in places other than this bar should appear on every page. We have learned from customers that there is nothing more disorienting than to grasp the meaning of a new metaphor, icon, or image, only to see it disappear as one drills further into a site. It's like arriving home only to discover that your furniture has been rearranged by persons unknown!

People Just Want to Go Home! Don't Count on Your Logo to Get Them There

Many web designers will tell you that it is standard protocol to use the company logo as a link that returns customers to a site's home-page. Yet many, many people we've interviewed aren't even aware that this protocol exists. Rather, they have come to rely on a simple "Home" button situated close to the top of pages throughout a site, which very clearly conveys its purpose: to take the user home.

Two Kids, a Dog, and a Split Level

As we discussed in Chapter 4, "Understanding How Users 'Bucket' Your Space," many sites have attempted to create pathways that are based on a user's profile. These generally assume that

Figure 7.4

The home button, while important, doesn't have to be too obvious. Take me home, Betsey!

www.betseyjohnson.com

if you are married and have kids in school, you'll inevitably be interested in this piece of furniture or that stereo or this vacation in particular, or that if you are single and urban, you will certainly appreciate these sneakers and that CD. Or, if you run a small business, you will want this computer line in your office.

To reiterate, we have found that, most often, web users don't like to be pegged in such ways. Therefore, designers should consider incorporating lists of potential criteria from which individual users can select, so they can decide *for themselves* what their taste in music is likely to be. Research shows that where they do so, it almost always adds value to the shopping experience. On the other hand, if a designer insists on fitting users into buckets that are not of their own choosing (but rather based on shared age, income, and/or life-stage), we have found that users frequently resist what they correctly interpret as an effort to pigeon-hole them. In our view, the web is about control: a user's capacity to exercise control to obtain what she wants and to screen out what she doesn't want. We've heard many users tell us that being indiscriminately lumped into a group assumes too much about what such categories indicate concerning the likes and dislikes of users. Most importantly, user segmentation along these lines may cause users to miss out on products that might be of interest but which are excluded from consideration merely because they lie outside a set of arbitrary parameters defined by the designer. In short, the user loses control over his or her own experience.

In sum, it is wise to resist any temptation to "lump" people together based on broad dimensions such as those previously outlined—which may or may not help users get where they want to go on your site. We believe that it is best to include users in this process by asking them a series of relevant questions that get them to hone in on the information or merchandise they want. When they take an active role in the process of labeling, users see what criteria led to their stereotyping, and they are more likely to buy into the information or products selected for (and *by*) them. Personalization works when users feel that the choices presented to them are ones they themselves have had a hand in choosing. Not only does this refine the individualization process, but it also provides a degree of control and adds value to web experience. If this

Figure 7.5

Ann Taylor organized its clothes for the summer season usefully, according to three types of occasions, to help shoppers choose appropriate clothes. A user can also "shop by item" if she wants.

www.anntaylor.com

Figure 7.6

Ann Taylor helps its users buy gifts for themselves or for others by asking three questions and supplying answers in drop-down menus.

www.anntaylor.com

stands in contrast to what the majority of web site developers are up to, then so be it! Just because they're doing it, that doesn't make it right!

The View from 30,000 Feet

Customers have a language and logic all their own that web site developers ignore at their peril. We have discovered in research that, most often, the logic of web use proceeds from the logic of the offline world, which finds people writing cards before signing envelopes and having highly individualized input into the selection process of plane fares, sports tickets, and many other products and services. In fact, in our experience, nothing sticks in the user's craw so much as being forced to do things he doesn't want to do: He doesn't want to shoehorn himself into prefabricated categories on the basis of age, income, and other factors, or learn new content and navigational strategies just to get what he wants out of the web experience. In other words, what users really want is the power to choose for themselves!

To build better web sites, therefore, we recommend prudent use of proven models with user experience research. (A case in point being the left nav bar; we reiterate, "if it isn't broke, don't fix it!") This dual strategy permits designers to incorporate powerful knowledge about what does and doesn't work into the grassroots of the development process.

A Few Hard Questions

- Does your site rely on trendy models borrowed from other sources? If so, do you have any clear idea of whether they are grounded in consumer research?

- Does the design of your web site reflect the offline experience of users?

- Have you learned which aspects of design actually work, so that there is no need to "reinvent the wheel?"

- Have you been tampering with the left nav bar? If so, you might want to consider consulting your target users. Many of them might have a different view!

- In contrast, do you depend on your logo getting people back to the homepage? If so, again, you might consider consulting with users, who may not always make that connection.

- Finally, does your site limit the user's options for self-definition by forcing her into prefabricated categories that predict her likes and dislikes on the basis of variables such as age and level of income?

PART III

Making Sure They "Stick" Around

Your Day-to-Day Challenge to Enhance User Experience

8 A Frustrated User Is No User at All: Don't Let
   Him Leave Your Site!   123

9 Adventures in Downloading
   "But Do I Have To?!"   137

10 When I Need Your Assistance, Believe Me, I'll Ask!
   *Getting Information, Directions, Help, or
   Anything Else*   151

11 Hieroglyphics Are Only Interesting When You
   Are Visiting the Pyramids
   Icons and Language   175

A Frustrated User Is No User at All: Don't Let Him Leave Your Site!

It has been our experience that few users have a saint's patience in their encounters with unruly web sites and, unfortunately, the window of opportunity for making a favorable impression on them is narrow. Particularly if a web site introduces new technology, unfamiliar processes, or a new way of navigating, users frequently "hit the wall." That is, even if users really desire what your site has to offer, at some moment in time frustration prevails, and then users give in to their sense of confusion and non-comprehension, concede defeat, and abandon their efforts. When this happens, odds are they will not return and, more dangerously for the success of the site, they will persuade others (perhaps many others) to do the same.

For the web site developer/designer, the trick is to anticipate this impasse and, wherever possible, preclude it. With the foresight afforded by user experience testing, web site development teams are empowered to create solutions they can be confident will retain the interest of users, even before the site is launched. Such a pre-emptive "strike" is not only desirable but in fact critical for a new generation of designers to build successful, intuitive sites. Knowledge of when people will take a wrong path or have trouble entering a field is no luxury in a hotly competitive marketplace, and insight into the handling of a host of "error conditions" will contribute to a more productive user experience and more profitable e-commerce one.

Hitting the Wall
Strategies for Recovery

In earlier chapters, we emphasized the general importance of user experience testing in building better web sites. But such research becomes all the more imperative with respect to sites that incorporate ground-breaking technology, new interface design, or innovative concepts. Testing will both identify ways in which users tend to run aground on a given site and reveal—in the user's own words—those aspects of navigation and content to which developers *must* pay attention if they hope to lure disgruntled (former) users back, let alone attract new ones.

A client had developed a way for web users to create and send video greeting cards, and they engaged our services to conduct user experience testing on their site. Though virtually all users expressed at least a moderate degree of interest in what the site had to offer, research among both novice and advanced web users revealed significant difficulties with respect to the following issues:

- Understanding that before using the site, they had to download software

- Installing the software (once successfully downloaded)

- Sending the video cards they had created

At each stage in the process, it was clear that if this had been a "real world" experience of the site and not laboratory research, most of the users in our study would have left the site in sheer frustration, their patience exhausted. To many, it seemed that no avenue they pursued or icon they clicked brought them any closer to the Holy Grail of sending a video card, and all promises of exciting functionality notwithstanding, many were increasingly distressed by successive failures to realize the goals of the site.

Upon demonstrating the site designer's intended content and ways of navigating the site, we successfully entered into a dialogue with respondents, who were able to make important recommendations about how to clarify aspects of content and site navigation. This new information, when passed on to the development team, allowed for an expeditious redesign of the site in accordance with the user's point of view.

This example highlights a common problem in site design: A trio of developers working separately had built three discrete portions of the site, which, taken individually, were considered by them to be relatively easy to use. What no one took into account was how to smooth the transitions from one part to another so that, for example, in the midst of a download, the user would *also* be informed how to locate and install the file. If they had taken that into account, the development team might have realized that it made more sense to auto install files so their users would not be obliged to become technicians before using the site.

Insight

If your site involves complex or new technology, know that many users will experience difficulties even if you test the site *ad nauseum*. During testing, it is crucial to ask people how *they* would explain an instruction, so that you can build their perspective into the site's design. Also, ask them where in the process they would find such explanations helpful. After all, help is only helpful in context.

Death by Frustration
Who Will Save the Day?

Whether it is a purchase path that is serpentine, a product that seems unavailable, a search result that always come back "0," or simply an ambiguous set of instructions, users are comforted by the certain knowledge that they will always be a phone call away from a real human being whose job it is to listen to and assist them. Nevertheless, many sites make it impossible to find an 800 number, a call-back feature, or even—for those into "snail" mail—a postal address to which they can send feedback or return a gift. Failure to offer visitors these avenues of offline communication is simply bad business because it carries with it certain potentially damning implications. Many of the people we've interviewed leave such sites believing one of two things:

- The company running the site doesn't want the customer to interact with them—particularly offline.

- The site (and hence the company) isn't professional enough to provide state-of-the-art customer service.

For instance, we tested numerous sites where PCs are sold, and many users told us they generally wanted to avoid entering sensitive information online (for instance, a credit card number). Still, they would be perfectly happy to venture as far as the shopping cart if only they could be *sure* they would be able to speak with a customer service representative at that point. If what a site offers might require discussion (perhaps because it is "big ticket" or a complex purchase), web site designers should be certain that an 800 number, a call-back button (our research has shown that many home users who do not have a second phone line resent being called while they are themselves denied the option), an address, and all other pertinent contact information is readily available. It should be easy to find and access on a site, both from the homepage and from any other key pages and areas where users are likely to have need of it.

Essentially, these measures are important because they address the issue of control: Who in the consumer/producer relationship is empowered to dictate when and how contact is made? Of course, live chat is still the best of all online options, provided that the customer service assistant is sufficiently knowledgeable and can see what the user is seeing (in real time, because users find few things more tedious than being forced to verbally rehash their online navigation, hours after the fact).

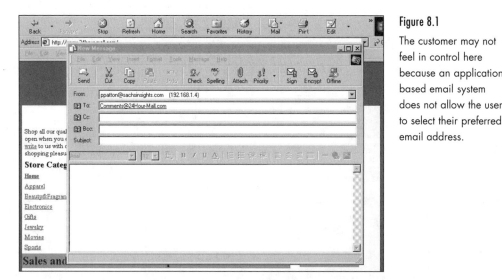

Figure 8.1

The customer may not feel in control here because an application based email system does not allow the user to select their preferred email address.

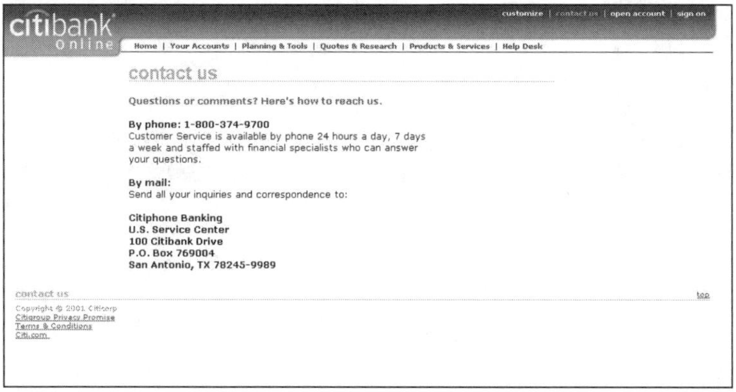

Figure 8.2

Aren't we on the Internet here? There should be an email option for contact in addition to phone and snail mail.

https://web.da-us.citibank.com

Figure 8.3

Now the user does feel in control because he decides which email address to use.

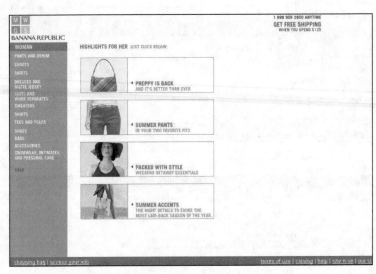

Send us your questions or comments

Please fill out the form below. Click the "Continue" button when done.

Your Name: _____

Your E-mail Address: _____
(Please enter the e-mail address associated with your Amazon.com account.)

Subject: [Select a Subject ▼]

17-digit Order Number: _____
(optional) (example: 102-0340758-0764393)

Comments:

www.amazon.com

Figure 8.4

A "floating" 800 number means users are never stranded. Furthermore, if a page becomes problematic, the user can call for help without having to leave it.

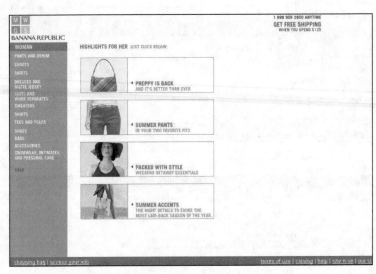

www.bananarepublic.com

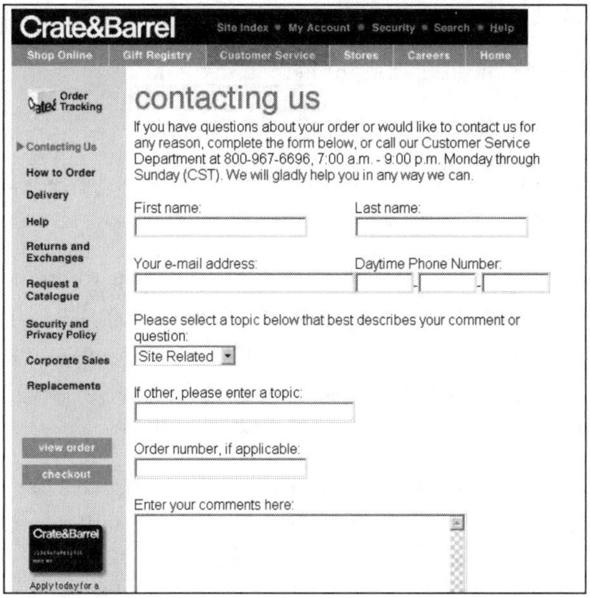

www.crateandbarrel.com

Figure 8.5

Right up front, users are given the option of calling so they don't feel forced into using email.

The Customer Is Always Right

Rules of Thumb for Managing Error Conditions

Many of us know what it is like to spend countless hours filling in data fields only to have them hurled back at us for one of the following vague reasons:

- "Your Password Doesn't Have Enough Digits."

  Well, for goodness sake, *tell me* how many digits to enter!

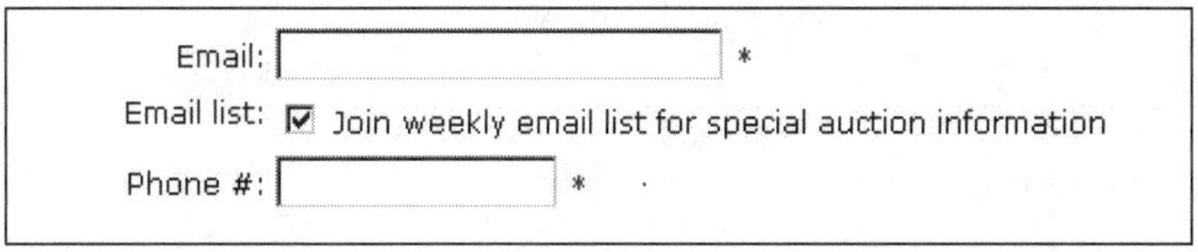

www.auction-warehouse.com

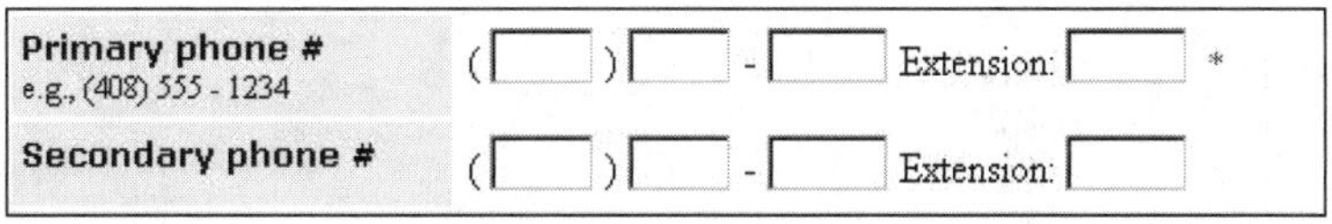

www.ebay.com

Figure 8.6

You should get it right in the first place. Be very specific when asking users to enter information. It eliminates the need for error messages.

- "Your Credit Card Number Is Incomplete."

  Really? I'm holding it right here in my hand!

- "Please Reenter Your Order."

  At least tell me what I did wrong, so I don't waste *another* five minutes!

Our most elementary rule of thumb is that the customer is always right. The use of words like "Error," "Incomplete," "You Forgot to…," and other semi-accusatory language is hardly going to win converts to a site, let alone make it any easier for the user to complete the field and get on with the task at hand.

Based on the user experience testing we've seen, we offer the following tips on how to resolve error conditions without making it unduly unpleasant or impossible for the user:

- Make usage instructions concrete and clear. For example, tell the user how many digits you need, and make it clear which fields are optional.

- Keep instructions short and sweet (or at least to the point).

Figure 8.7

Here is another example of getting it right. This address is from a search result; you may not be able to link to it directly. It is page one of eBay's U.S. registration page. Notice that it prompts the user to include "@serviceprovider.com."

www.ebay.com

- Avoid industry speak in your labels and instructions; aim your language to the "average" user.

- Because people don't always read, be sure to embed instructions in navigational buttons.

- Make sure to bold anything users *must* read in order to not screw up. However, at the same time, keep text streamlined. A large block of text, even with important information in bold, is still a turnoff.

- When a user makes an error, return him to the *exact* place he needs to be in order to correct the problem and provide brief instructions on how to do so.

- If Search nets no results, offer tips on how to increase the user's odds of finding what she's looking for.

- Even in those cases when the user *has* made a mistake, we recommend that—by way of your web site—you bite the bullet and take the blame. For instance, employ language like "We're/I'm Sorry, We/I Didn't Understand What You Entered. Please Try to XYZ."

- Place "help" buttons next to difficult steps and offer context-sensitive help. This may involve defining terms, explaining why you need the information, or instructing the user on how to enter information (for example, dd/mm/yy).

Users Aren't Programmers: Don't Assume They Know What You're Talking About

Because most web site development teams are far better versed in using the web than most users are, they often make a number of assumptions about what "average" people are willing and able to do online. This failure to anticipate the abilities of users affects a range of online conventions, and extends from terminology and jargon to the navigational protocols whose meaning may be second-nature to designers, but which is utterly mysterious to many users.

To help you build better web sites, we have identified a number of fairly common protocols that participants in our user experience testing frequently don't understand.

1. How and When to Back Up

Generally speaking, we are in favor of internal navigation that spells out when users should move back or forward within a site, because we have found that people are often confused about how and when they should venture to do either. This situation is frequently exacerbated by the apparent failure of technology to cooperate. Sometimes the browser's "Back button" works, and sometimes it doesn't (for instance, when the user tries to back up too far or backs past the credit card entry). We have found that simply informing people they can "go back to search results" or "go ahead to check out" is the most effective way to build a comfortable dialogue with the customer and eliminate his confusion.

We also advocate creating step-by-step instructions (especially for more complex sites) that methodically take users through such processes as "Advanced Search," "Purchase," or "Registration." The knowledge that the user has arrived at "Step 2 of 5" and that

Figure 8.8

The link back to the previous page tells you exactly where you will "land" when you click it. Personalization like that used in this bridal registry is a plus whenever possible.

www.weddingchannel.com

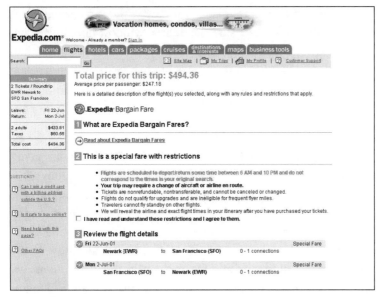

www.expedia.com

Figure 8.9

This page, from Expedia.com, indicates the purchase path in a series of clearly labeled steps.

he can always go back to "Step 2" enhances confidence in navigation. It also mitigates the creeping fear that he doesn't know how long he is in for or what he has to do in order to retreat from an uncertain navigational choice.

2. How to Manipulate Windows

How we wish we had a dollar for every user who, having once opened a window, thereafter lost sight of it forever! Even where such catastrophe is avoided, the comparatively straightforward opening and closing of windows can sometimes be a tricky endeavor. Believe it or not, many users sit for minutes gawking at a screen, fervently hoping that the window they are looking at will somehow close itself.

Although designers might be tempted to laugh in disbelief, we advise that you respect the user by always helping him out:

- Provide an instruction within the window that explicitly offers to close the window in question.

- Display windows in a size that doesn't swallow the entire screen.

- If the user attempts to open a window without realizing that it is already open, make sure the desired window does indeed become visible. (It has been our experience that more often than not, the window fails to appear in such cases—often causing unnecessary confusion.)

3. How to Enlarge or Shrink an Image

If you think everyone who uses the web knows what "thumbnail" or "minimize" means, we suggest you speak with a random selection of friends and family members. In fact, many people view the word "thumbnail" and imagine just that—and are perplexed as to how this might relate to the web or computers. Short of being directly informed of the possibility, others have no idea how to use the assortment of tiny Xs and Os on the page to enlarge an image. Our point is that people tend to interpret language and iconography on the web very literally. Therefore, we highly recommend that you use unambiguous language that spells out precisely how to go about accomplishing the task. For example, to be brief and to the point, you could include the phrases "to make bigger/ smaller" or "to see a larger image/picture" in connection with an obvious button. The ideal web path is, in this way, similar to a conversation where both parties feel at ease and are not unduly challenged by words and instructions that they don't immediately understand.

4. How and Why to Add a Plug-In/Upgrade Your Browser

The world at large is not conversant about the pleasures of Java or Flash, and users don't always know or care what "encryption" means. If you must have people upgrade their browsers or install plug-ins, make it as painless as possible. Where possible, allow users to accomplish their upgrades within your site and then be led back to their point of departure. Most importantly, you must explain clearly and briefly "what's in it for them" so they will be willing to play along with this unexpected digression.

Absolute Power Is a Good Thing
Don't Mess with the User's Control

Unlike the many forms of media over which individual members of the public exercise little or no direct control, the web offers the user an unlimited amount of input into his or her own online experience: The user can click on the buttons he wants to click on, avoid the advertising that bothers or bores him, or forgo registration with your site if he decides that it is "not for him."

For their part, users (naturally enough) cherish this level of control and are loathe to relinquish it. Therefore, we believe it is best not to try. The following are some common mistakes web teams make in this regard, and how we think these should be addressed:

- Don't oblige people to register in order to get a sense of what your site is all about. Many users assume they'll have no choice but to register on a site before using it, and often take for granted that they will have to pay a fee as well. In our experience, both can lead to ambivalence and tension. Instead, make it clear to users what benefits they will receive in advance of registration, so they know what to expect. Furthermore, it is helpful to allow users to register while they are completing an order, by simply asking them to complete an extra field or two and explaining that this will allow them to access the site later using a login and password.

- Although demos are wonderful things, most users prefer to control the pace at which they browse a site. It is frustrating to be forced to sit through a demo they didn't request—comparable to someone yanking the remote control out of your hands and channel surfing at will.

- Refrain from asking intrusive questions—particularly when the site fails to explain why the user is being asked in the first place. On the other hand, if the user knows that entering her mother's maiden name will increase security or that entering her favorite kinds of music will personalize her choices, this might make her more (not less) open to exploring the site further.

- If your site offers the ability to use email to alert people to promotions, or if you sell names, make it clear to users that they can opt in or out of these features. Although it might be a timesaver to check these options automatically, it conveys the impression that users are being conned into accepting an unwanted intrusion into their lives. And this, in turn, is guaranteed to raise the suspicion of any jaded Generation-X web afficionado.

The View from 30,000 Feet

The ambition of any good web designer is to create a dialogue with site visitors that feels comfortable and intuitive. It is your job as a designer to figure out where users might travel on the site and anticipate their needs. As in many areas of life, if people feel understood and have their desires realized, they will be satisfied—particularly if they feel in control of their destiny.

A Few Hard Questions

- Does your site have transitions between steps that are intuitive and lead a user to know what to expect next?

- Are the language and navigation free of ambiguous industry-speak and jargon?

- Is the user in control of site navigation?

- Have you built into your site responses to error conditions that are friendly and instructive?

CHAPTER NINE

Adventures in Downloading

...But Do I Have To?!"

Plug-Ins!!! Plug-Ins???

Web sites often feature some form of download, and major functionality on a site generally involves downloading software. Shockwave or Flash may even be required to view the homepage or, at the very least, to experience the special effects. Using downloads to their best advantage means presenting them in a way that meshes with the comfort zone of the user. Alternatively, it may mean not using them at all. These are the issues that we will address in this chapter.

So You're Ready to See My Site? Not So Fast, Mr. User

Consider the following scenario: In your browser, you enter the URL for a web site that interests you. For instance, it might be the name of a company whose product line you find intriguing. The homepage pops up on your screen. Maybe it has a few icons on it, maybe not. In either case, prominently positioned in the center of the page are words to the effect that, if you want to see this site, you need to have Flash installed: "Click here to download." Perhaps this option is accompanied by a warning that many of the features of the site will not be available to you if you opt out. You might also be asked to indicate whether you have a 56K modem, or T1, or DSL.

To many of us, this request would seem relatively straightforward. You are being asked to proceed with the installation of Flash, Shockwave, or whatever software is called for. For most, this poses no immediate problem because plug-ins are currently so readily available, and most users own computers that meet the basic speed and color requirements needed to take advantage of them. So, why not enhance the sexiness of your site with some additional "Flash?"

This is an important question to ask. But let's start by thinking about the best ways to ensure that users' appreciation of plug-ins matches that of web site designers.

Download a Plug-In? The Only Thing I'm Downloading Is Confusion! What Does This Stuff *Do*, Anyway?

Quite apart from being uncertain about the nature of Flash or Shockwave, the average user may not even know what a download is. This is understandable because, in all fairness, even those who are relatively experienced with the online world sometimes confuse "download" with "upload." Imagine, then, the dismay of the inexperienced user, who has had a nasty experience downloading something (maybe an attachment in junk email) that not only took what seemed like forever but was overly complicated or even indecipherable. In any of these cases, the result is confusion, frayed nerves, and the perception of time wasted in trying to make something work. Occasionally, they will succeed only to discover that they have inadvertently propagated a nasty virus and, as a result, have decided that all downloads are just plain "bad."

In all likelihood, those reading this book will not have such a low level of familiarity with basic web-related tasks like downloading. However, such people *do* exist, and we believe them to be a litmus test for the success of a designer's site—because if they can understand what a designer is trying to accomplish at a site, then anybody can!

Experienced users, on the other hand, will have other kinds of concerns and will generally want an answer to the question of how long the download is likely to take *before* they begin the process, even if it means abandoning the site and returning to it at a later time. Most likely, if the download takes more than a few minutes, they will abandon your site altogether.

If you are offering new users the opportunity to download a plug-in that will enhance their use of the site, you also need to provide them with a means of getting a quick definition of what a download is. This seems like an obvious point, but it's one that cannot be overstated: Users will want to know what a plug-in does. For both new and more experienced users, the time involved will also need to be clearly stated, as will the nature of what is being downloaded. More download-savvy users may understand how to download a document or a photo attachment through their email, but a plug-in is most likely another story. Also, some users understand Flash but don't know what Shockwave or Real Audio is. And chances are that other plug-ins are on the horizon that users may also want to take advantage of, and those plug-ins are likely to be even more unfamiliar.

Insight

Users may need to know two important pieces of information: What is a plug-in (or a download), or whatever it is you are asking me to download? For that matter, what is a download? They need an exact definition of what it means to download, as well as a description of the plug-in they are about to receive.

The question of "how" requires some elaboration, so we will address it in more depth later. Questions that crop up in relation to the broadest question of how a download is to occur include: "Does this involve going to another web site?" and "What happens then?" These users need a brief step-by-step explanation of the process and a citation of aspects that have been automated. Designers need to keep in mind that if they don't make the process sound painless enough, users will most likely find excuses to postpone the download or avoid it altogether.

Insight

Exactly what is going to be involved in this download process? Some users will have an idea; others won't. The process needs to be briefly outlined for those who need it. And most will want some approximation of the time required.

In our experience, many of these questions can be answered through the addition of a simple link that takes the user to an overview page on which all the basics are laid out. As a corollary, we have observed that this is generally a good place to include a note about the site's security because, although the site for the download will almost certainly address this concern, some users are going to want to know this information well before they get to that stage.

Another Burning Question: "Why Should I?!"

Whether the issue is time, fear, or plain ignorance, there can be no dispute about the fact that a download requires the user to take an extra step he probably wasn't expecting. This can be unsettling, and even more experienced users (who generally understand what's involved in a download) may not be sure if they want to take the time to do it. These concerns beg a question that users often articulate when being placed in this situation: "Why do I *need* to take the time out to download something just to look at a web site?" To address this, two other questions must first be answered:

- Is the download actually required to view the site?

- If so, is there a tangible benefit to the user?

Let's start with the issue of whether downloads are required. We have, in fact, worked with various entertainment sites that require a download such as Shockwave. In some cases, sponsors of the site were providing content like movie previews, and they felt that users would not have a powerful experience without plug-ins. Other times, they believed their target audience would already have the plug-ins installed or would be willing to do so to experience the site. We believe this to be a risky strategy, and that the need to provide "wow and zow" needs to be weighed against the potential of having some percentage of users feel as if they were turned away at the gate.

Plug-ins also have a higher chance of causing serious crashes for users. It may not be your fault that your movie causes someone's computer to crash, but it will be you they blame when the system locks up and they lose their other work. How much do you want to gamble your brand on the quality of someone else's code?

Insight

As much as you want to show off your high-tech Flash, and even if you can't get around being flashy, the truth is that not all users will have access to plug-ins like Flash. Some users will have to go the low-tech route or avoid your site altogether.

Generally, we recommend that plug-ins be optional and that the user be clearly informed on the homepage that special effects within the site are better experienced with them than without them. Where appropriate within a site, the user also needs to be informed that he has clicked on an option that either cannot be experienced at all or will not be experienced to its full effect without the plug-in.

We worked on a site in the financial services sector that used this approach. On the homepage, users were informed that special effects in the site required the download of a plug-in. They were also asked to indicate whether they were accessing the site with a high-speed line or a standard modem. The majority of users were able to easily answer the question regarding the access method and understood that they could opt out of the plug-in if they so desired. Therefore, they felt they still had a measure of control over the web experience: Not only did the site show respect for their time, but it did not inspire fear in the hearts of those who were not "download-savvy."

That addresses the requirement issue. Now, to the benefit.

Let's assume a designer has taken the time to define "download," explain types of downloads, address whether or not they are required, and estimate the time needed to carry out the process. So far, so good. But do site visitors understand why they might want to actually take the time for the download? If it is not required, this may be a moot point—though we find that users are often left with the nagging suspicion they may be missing something if they don't take the time for the additional plug-in.

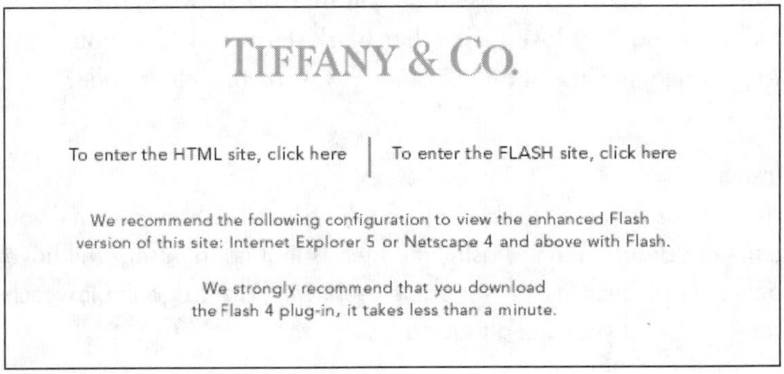

Figure 9.1

The Tiffany site gives users the option of viewing the enhanced version of the site, which requires the Flash 4 plug-in. Additionally, the user is reassured that this will not be a long process.

TIFFANY & CO.

To enter the HTML site, click here | To enter the FLASH site, click here

We recommend the following configuration to view the enhanced Flash version of this site: Internet Explorer 5 or Netscape 4 and above with Flash.

We strongly recommend that you download the Flash 4 plug-in, it takes less than a minute.

www.tiffany.com

Generally, the plug-in allows the site to provide special effects like sound and music, which can of course be beneficial. However, plug-ins can also be used to enable additional interactive features like self-tests and other interactive tools. If a user wants to experience this level of functionality and the plug-in is required, she is indeed at risk of missing out on something potentially useful if she doesn't take the time for the download. This is a benefit that needs to be carefully spelled out, and not hidden under general terminology like "additional functionality." Names of interactive tools, or what they do, should be included.

The guiding principle here should be to inform the user—before the fact—as to what he might be getting into through the use of download and why he might want to download.

Insight

The user's need to control the web experience should also guide the use and presentation of plug-ins. Users need definitions, a brief how-to, and a specific benefit if they are going to take this step. And if the plug-in is merely there to enhance the "bells and whistles," it needs to be optional.

Help, I'm Lost! And Where's That Download?

Inexperienced web users, or at least those with minimal experience downloading, have a basic fear of clicking on that "Download Now" button. They fear that they will be taken to some other web site where they will be exposed to arcane directions and mysterious questions about their PC configuration that they won't be able to answer. As anyone who has faced this situation knows, it's likely they are correct.

In addition, if they *do* click the "Download Now" button on the site of the plug-in, they will be asked to register their use of the download, which often leads to slippery questions about cost. Exacerbating this, they will subsequently be asked *where* they want the download to occur—which is, in our view, a *definite* show-stopper. Most users have no idea where it should be downloaded, beyond having some vague sense that they want the maximum benefit for the least amount of hassle.

Insight

What do you mean, "what location?" Even if they're able to start the download, many users won't know where it should be "deposited." With vague fears about Internet security, coupled with basic confusion, users may avoid the process at this point.

Now let's say that these issues have been successfully navigated and the user actually has the thing downloaded. Beyond a cursory "thank you" and a confirmation of completion, users report that they don't know where to go next. Do they hit the Back key in the browser until they get back to the original site? Great. The page they end up at is the same one they visited before they clicked "Download Now" to get the plug-in. In this needless and confusing cycle, we have witnessed users trying again and again to download the plug-in, fearing they may have missed a step and not wanting to pass up the opportunity to download the same information all over again.

All they want, at this point, is to make the thing work. And it might—assuming that they know where the downloaded plug-in ended up. Some users simply close the browser and start over, anticipating that *this* time the site will know where to look. Others click around and around, experimenting with different possibilities. Did the plug-in need to be installed first? If they receive a message to that effect, then where is it? And what do they click on to install it?

Again, the result is frustrated users, who may at this point find an alternate site that doesn't require all these extra steps.

So ask yourself that question one more time: Does it really make sense to require this plug-in?

Insight

It is not only the actual process of downloading that causes users to be fearful, it is also knowing where the download occurs. Whenever users have to leave their current web site to move to another one, they have concerns about how to get back to the original site, as well as how to resume whatever process was interrupted in the original site. This same concern has caused users to avoid banners.

Déjà Vu All Over Again
The Same Concerns to the Power of 10

Up to now, we have addressed the issues associated with downloading basic web site plug-ins, like Real Audio, Shockwave, or Flash. Some sites, to be used effectively, require the use of downloadable software, either from that site or from another still more complicated site. Although this software may provide a range of benefits—and users absolutely must understand and embrace these benefits before they move forward—the potential concerns are magnified.

Will the software be virus-free? Will it somehow conflict with software I currently have installed? Will it be so difficult to use that I will go through this potentially annoying process for nothing? Again, these are questions that need to be answered, perhaps through a list of FAQs the user can peruse before she is asked to "Download Now."

On the other hand, are your users really going to take the time to go through a list of FAQs before taking the next step? They're likely to do so only if the application is mission-critical. Even savvy users have limited time and patience.

We worked with a web site on which this concern was met in a proactive manner, though not without a few painful iterations. The site itself provided users with a range of document production services, copying and binding, with a range of colors and cover options. Basically, it enabled the user to send a document off for production as easily as he could send it to his own desktop printer.

To accomplish this, however, the user first needed to download a piece of software from the sponsor's web site, a request that would normally strike fear into the hearts of experienced and inexperienced web and software users alike. Briefly, they were presented with a short explanation of the benefits of the site: how they could have quality, hassle-free, guaranteed photocopying and binding at a reasonable price from any location. Then it was explained how the process worked, in terms of the simplicity with which documents could be sent.

Once sold on the benefits, users were informed that a simple download of software would be required, together with the reassurance that this would involve little more than clicking a button to initiate the process and then responding to a few questions along the way. This discussion was accompanied by information on download times and security and a list of simple steps required to carry out the process. When the user felt she was ready, she was asked to close all other applications and then click a button to get started.

The site was true to its word: The download process began, and the user was informed as to what was happening and when it was complete. Afterward, she was furnished with additional information to help answer any questions she might have, such as whether the installation software should be placed on the hard drive or on the desktop.

Figure 9.2

The CNN site does a great job of communicating plug-in information to its users. It explains what is being downloaded, why, and even shows what taking this step is going to do for the user.

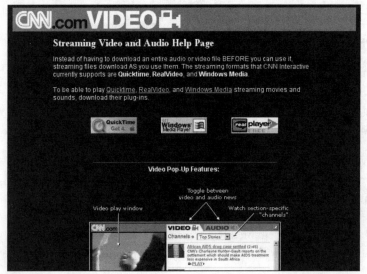

www.cnn.com

Following completion of this process, users were informed that they could begin using the site. Aside from a few initial glitches, which were identified during the initial testing process, the site was found to be running smoothly. This is one of the best illustrations we have seen of how users want downloads to work, because it illustrates just how much more secure users feel downloading software when the site does all the work for them.

Insight

Don't even consider making the download process simple. Users want you to do it for them. Here's a solution: Earlier on in this chapter, we mentioned the importance of letting the user know that downloading is a "painless" process. By "painless," we mean more than just easy. To most users, a truly painless process means "do it for me and tell me when you're finished. And by the way, make it work for me, too."

A Download Kind of Crowd?
Finding a Starting Point

In the discussion of various user concerns potentially associated with downloading, we at times alluded to an additional question, which we often encourage our clients to ask: Is the download even necessary?

We all want our sites to be presented in the best possible light and for the user to have an optimal experience. Quite frankly, as developers and marketers, we also live in a world where we are surrounded by the latest technologies, and designers frequently succumb to the temptation to include new downloads whether they are really needed or not. In contrast, many users are neither experienced nor sophisticated in their web practices. For instance, not everyone has a computer at home, and even those who do may prefer to access web sites at work (and vice versa). So it stands to reason that many will not appreciate the inclusion of complicated, if flashy, downloads with the same zeal developers might.

◯ ◯ **Insight**
Increasingly, sites are automatically checking for plug-ins when a user first enters the homepage. This is all done behind the scenes. If the download is not available on the user's computer, the user is given the opportunity to take the next step—either accessing the site without certain special features or first downloading the plug-in.

For the sake of argument, let's say a designer's web site has a business-to-business focus. However, Internet usage is increasingly being monitored in the workplace, and users may not be able to download plug-ins due to firewall restrictions. Is that going to mean the site will run aground even before it has set sail? A consumer-oriented site might likewise face restrictions. Consumers don't always have high-speed lines at home. Consequently, if a site is optimized for such a level of access, the download that happens quickly on a DSL line may be quite a different experience than it is for a home user with a slower computer and a 28.8 modem line. If they stumble upon a site while they are at the library, a friend's house, or an Internet café, chances are even more remote that they will be able to download additional plug-ins. And, as we have already stated, some consumers simply resist the idea of downloads. Every time a major virus is circulated, their reluctance to view downloads as anything other than potentially dangerous invaders is increased.

◯ ◯ **Insight**
Don't forget who your user is. Are you targeting people who have the latest plug-ins (not to mention software) in place and who are comfortable adding more? Or is it a crowd that is less tech-savvy? Make sure you have gauged their comfort level before you decide what to require of them.

So again we ask this: Does a site *really* need plug-ins? That is a question only the designer is entitled to ask, but which only the user can answer.

Branding a Download and Downloading a Brand
Be Consistent!

Established brands are associated with various images, and as we have discussed, users carry these images in their minds when they visit different web sites, and they compartmentalize them into discrete categories. So, for example, they tend to be disconcerted if they are bombarded with rock music and video clips while visiting the site of a bank or an insurance company. Still, some animation, if it's judiciously used, is useful precisely because it can help to *update* a more staid corporate image. Moreover, sophisticated functionality, such as that which accompanies many interactive tools, would certainly be in keeping with the expectations for sites from companies in industries like finance.

Conversely, when visitors come to the site of a music studio or a "hip" consumer brand, they expect special effects that are in keeping with their image of the brand. For this reason, even when a given company's brand imagery is not yet established offline, special effects and functionality can go a long way toward establishing a desired brand image.

Research Tip

Ask the potential users of your site about their orientation to downloads. What is their current level of understanding? What are their fears? What would make them want to do a download in relation to your site? What would make them *not* want to? Does the download process work for them? Take them through it, and they'll tell you where the landmines are located.

The View from 30,000 Feet

Users have varying levels of resistance to downloads. Their guiding principle, however, is that they want to both control the web experience and have their time and energy respected.

As implied, downloads fall into two major categories: necessary and unnecessary. The rules are relatively simple:

- Additional "bells and whistles," such as animation and sound, can certainly add to the web experience. As we discussed, downloads required to enable special effects *need* to be optional.

- Downloads may be consistent with the basic functionality of the site, such as a music site that requires users to download a plug-in like Real Audio or a film industry site that requires Shockwave or Flash. If so, the user needs to be guided through this process so that it is as transparent as possible. Still, users who cannot or will not download need to be able to at least access basic information.

- Downloads may also be required for certain functionality, such as interactive tools. Again, these downloads need to be optional, such that the user is presented with a choice both at the beginning of the site (with a clear explanation of why the download may be valuable) and at the moment he chooses a specific function that requires the download.

A Few Hard Questions

- Is the plug-in absolutely necessary for fully experiencing the site? Are you prepared to lose a chunk of your audience because of these technology requirements?

- If not, is it clear that the download is optional? What are the benefits of doing it and the penalties for not?

- And if it's required, is it totally painless to the user? Are you prepared to do a lot of extra work testing, explaining, and supporting the download process?

- What about my brand? Is the download in keeping with my brand image, and if not, does it expand the image in a way that is both logical and beneficial?

CHAPTER 10

When I Need Your Assistance, Believe Me, I'll Ask!

Getting Information, Directions, Help, or Anything Else

"How much?" and "when?" are questions that repeatedly emerge in regard to both helping the user and providing her with the right content. As intuitively obvious as factors such as navigation and functionality need to be, users frequently still need additional guidance in getting to the next step, and frustration results when not enough (or too much) information is provided.

In this chapter, we discuss the ways in which users react to information such as directions and help, and how to avoid presenting this information in such a way that it misses its mark.

Thanks for the Great Directions, But I Already Know How to Do That

An axiom of web site development is that icons alone are not sufficient, in and of themselves, to completely guide the user. No matter how well they seem to illustrate a function, additional explanation is generally necessary. At the macro level, the need for supplementary information or directions becomes even more pronounced, because once users become involved in a process, the potential for confusion is multiplied by the number of steps they need to go through.

A paradox is that in attempting to help users avoid frustrations before they encounter them, web site developers often swing to the opposite extreme and, bending over backwards, provide an annoying excess of directions. When this happens, users enter a site and, before they have a chance to explore different options for themselves, they are presented with a long and tedious explanation of how to accomplish certain tasks. We have seen sites that present extensive pages of information about a function, point-by-point, that require the user to do much scrolling and a lot of reading (for many users, possibly the two most detested aspects of web experience), before she can even get started. "What am I supposed to do?" the user asks herself in bewilderment. "Memorize it?" Or should she print out a copy and tape it on the wall next to the computer so she can follow the instructions and finish the task?

Here's an example of what we mean. The web site for a hotel chain featured the option to change from standard to express booking. This allowed regular customers to use personal information already stored through a "frequent guest" number, and consequently avoid having to input the same information (like their address and preferences) every time they visited the site. The potential commercial benefits of express booking were obvious: It would save time and reward frequent customers.

Nevertheless, what worked in theory failed miserably in practice. As it appeared on the web site, the frequent guest number was neither user friendly nor a timesaver. To the contrary, users found it to be a punishingly tedious way to eat up time they might spend in other, more productive ways. Why? Because the icon in question presented the user with a long page of text to be read, beginning with an explanation of what "express booking" meant, in spite of the fact that this function was only available to those with a customer and PIN number. The non-sequitur here, of course, is that if potential customers were familiar enough with the hotel chain to have chosen this option (which was also used offline), they would also, in all likelihood, be familiar with how express booking worked. So despite the fact that many users almost certainly did not need this information, they were still obliged to scroll through it. There wasn't much about this that was "express"—rather the opposite.

Again, the main lesson here is that, to reiterate what we have said in previous chapters, users have very specific reasons for coming to web sites. Especially with respect to those that are transaction-oriented, they expect to accomplish tasks in a straightforward manner and with a modicum of convenience. No matter how comprehensive or well-written, lengthy definitions, explanations, and how-to's only serve to impede progress and obscure the goal. In any event, chances are that the user will read the first paragraph or so, assume she knows it all already, and skip the rest. Make sure the one sentence you want her to read is at the top and jumps out at her.

That is, unless she has asked for help.

⊘ ⊘ **Insight**
⊘ Users are focused on achieving their specific tasks and are not interested in anything outside of the process of reaching their goals. Anything that threatens to derail them from that process will be ignored.

Next Steps
Can I Please Have a Hint?

Let's start with a quiz. What's the opposite of explaining too much? Not explaining enough? Well, yes... sort of. Why only sort of? Because not only do users benefit from information in the right doses, but they also benefit from information provided at the right time. After all, timing is everything. The result of aggregating explanations and how-to's in one place, if not on one page, is that sooner or later the user is going to get to a point in the process where he *does* need some additional information.

There's a lesson here that software developers learned a long time ago. Users want help just at the moment they need it. They don't want long lists of steps at the outset. Neither do they want that same litany of directions when they are halfway into a process. What they want is help with a *specific* step or question at the moment it occurs. And that's *all* they want—not more, and certainly not less.

Let's revisit the example cited previously concerning the hotel chain's web site. Admittedly, some regular customers of the chain in question might not be familiar with express booking or might have a few questions about it (for example, how to use a credit card number). Other users, who are even less savvy about using web sites to make hotel reservations, might need additional instructions, if for no other reason than to double-check their actions before going to the next step. Still others might simply need some reassurance that what they are doing is correct.

What each of these users has in common is that, at some point along the path, they need an opportunity to get clarification. *Where* on a site and *when* in the process they get it doesn't really matter; what matters is that the users need information, and they need it right there and then.

Insight

Even though all users travel along the same path, a step may be clearer to one user than to the next. To keep everyone oriented as they traverse the site, users need the opportunity for clarification as questions come up along the way.

This is a challenge for web site developers. Building better web sites starts with remembering the premise that each user is unique and has a distinctive approach to gathering information and completing transactions. Therefore, while each user is potentially willing to conform to the process spelled out for him by the site, most are still going to have their own set of concerns and questions. Long-winded explanations at the head of the homepage cannot hope to meet their needs 100% of the time, but ignoring these needs is not an option either.

We suggest the following as a productive middle ground between these extremes: Each time the user is at the point of completing a step, he should be provided unproblematic access to information that describes what he is about to do or receive, what is involved in the next step, and what is provided in the next layer of content. Moreover, he will probably also need to have the option of being shown precisely where he is in the process at that time. We will return to this issue later in the chapter.

Returning to our hotel web site example, we discovered in research that what the site really needed to make visitors appreciate the experience without becoming annoyed was links to information, which made it possible to meet the needs of *all* users (including the less savvy among them).

Insight

Frustrated User: "How the hell am I supposed to do this?"
Savvy User: "What are you telling me all this for? I know what I'm doing."
Frank Sinatra: "I did it my way."

Users need the option of obtaining as little, or as much, explanation as they need, when they need it. Generalities have little value because individuals process information differently. Remember: Timing is everything!

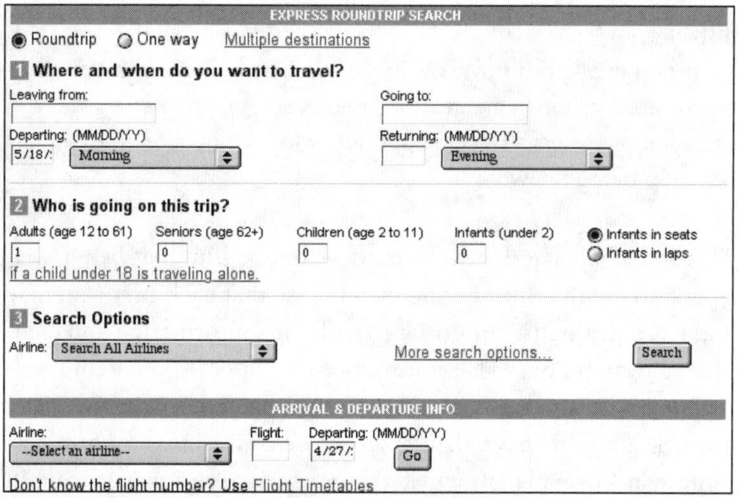

Figure 10.1

Notice that on the Expedia site, the user is given the opportunity for additional directions (for example, "if a child under 18 is traveling alone"). If it doesn't apply, the user simply ignores it.

www.expedia.com

By the Way, What's in It for Me?

As a corollary to the issue of providing too much how-to and explanation before the user embarks upon a function, we note that the emphasis on the how-to can be overstated to the point that the user no longer understands the nature of the benefit he is supposed to be receiving. Developers shouldn't lose site of the fact that web site users are only "in it" for themselves. As we have discussed in other chapters, they seldom visit a site in the absence of an expectation that they're going to be rewarded for the experience, even if this reward consists of only the most fleeting idea of what the site is actually offering them.

This self-absorption also has an effect upon whether users embark upon a specific path within a web site. Above all, they desire an answer to the question "What's in it for me?" At first blush, the benefit to be obtained by navigating in a specific direction on a site may seem obvious. Thus, if a user clicks on "Customer Service," she is probably going to get some kind of assistance. Likewise, if she opts to view some type of content, such as a stock quote, the benefit is also relatively intuitive.

Or is it?

Insight

Whenever possible, users should be reminded that they are making the best use of their time; in other words, remind them of the benefits of the site. This is especially true when users are being invited to embark upon a new path within the site.

If a site features online customer service reps who can offer immediate, real-time assistance, this capacity should be highlighted—if not on the homepage, on the first page of the customer service area. Otherwise, users may venture no further into the site. If stock quotes are in real-time, this benefit should also be highlighted. Similarly, the benefits of undergoing a more time-consuming process (like purchasing a product) should also be emphasized, especially if developers offer features that go beyond what is normally associated with purchasing online. A good maxim for web developers to follow, therefore, is that they shouldn't assume users will take the time to figure things out on their own—no matter how intuitive everything seems to site designers in the development process.

A luxury goods web site we worked with exemplifies what can happen when you emphasize how to at the expense of potential benefits. The product purchase path was adequately explained throughout the site. However, the company also offered free shipping, which was only presented to users at the *end* of the purchase path, that is, *after* they had completed their shopping and were ready to check out (assuming they even made it that far).

This problem was especially unfortunate in light of the fact that, when it was brought to their attention, users were highly impressed that the site offered free shipping—so much so, in fact, that this benefit alone would have influenced their decision to venture further into the site had they known about it. After all, it wasn't something that other sites (even those offering similar products) were offering.

Insight

Do you have a benefit that might really hook your users? Make sure it's highlighted, maybe even more than once.

Figure 10.2

In the Drugstore.com site, the user's attention is clearly directed to the fact that the site offers free shipping.

www.drugstore.com

Brand comes into play here. In the web site of an established brand, like a major retail chain or organization, the benefits are often relatively clear to users. They generally know what to expect from that brand, or at least what the brand is all about. When this is not the case, and the brand is not so well known (as is often the case in a "pure play" web site), clear presentation of the benefits is crucial to establishing a sense of brand identity. The lesson here is that no amount of explanation, no matter how carefully it's presented, will be helpful to the viability of a web site if users don't initially *perceive* a benefit to moving forward. Understanding what benefits users want, and which ones your company can actually offer, is critical to whether users take that most important of next steps. Such perceptions are frequently founded on brand recognition, but not always.

A bartering web site for the steel industry had all the right capabilities, including industry-relevant terminology, adequate security, user-friendly transactions, and well-written explanations. Everything seemed to be in place. So, why, the designers wondered, was it not a "no brainer" for companies buying and selling steel to register for and use the site?

Research with potential users answered that question, and theirs was a painfully straightforward answer at that. Despite being of professional quality in the ways mentioned above, the site never provided visitors with a good enough reason why they should register. Like many industries, the steel industry is based on personal relationships, and transactions are conducted over the telephone and through fax machines. The industry had not yet made the transition to the web; in fact, many companies in the industry were not using the web much at all. Therefore, the site was lauding the virtues of conducting these transactions (even anonymous ones) by way of a medium that people in the industry did not yet trust, and in many cases even know. Generously put, the site was ahead of its time.

Insight

If you are offering capabilities that your target audience has not yet experienced and may not feel ready for, communicating a compelling benefit is critical to getting them to take that next step.

What the site needed was a radical departure from the status quo. To make this transition, prospects needed a compelling benefit, which the site certainly offered. The problem was that it was not clear when it was most needed: before visitors even thought about exploring the site. In other words, without a clear and compelling benefit, beginning on the homepage, there was no perceived compelling message to keep exploring.

The site did provide a demo, but not front-and-center on the homepage. Again, without a benefit in mind, users did not necessarily see a reason to use the demo. Instead, both the functional links and the demo funneled the user into a very nitty-gritty process of how the site worked, without first "hitting the user over the head" with the reasons why he should be there.

And what did users want?

They wanted to know who the sponsor of the site was. After all, they were being asked to trust their businesses with what was essentially a complete stranger. As it happened, this was a major benefit of the site insofar as it had been developed by a seasoned management team with extensive experience in the steel industry. In earlier versions of the site, users were forced to hunt for this information.

Given that personal relationships are the cornerstone of this industry, users also wanted to be sure that these would be protected, and they needed reassurance of this before they would be willing to move forward. The site did indeed explain that personal relationships were inviolable, but this explanation fell largely on deaf ears (or blind eyes) because it was positioned a few layers into the site. This design choice was made on the erroneous assumption that users would first embark upon using the site and wait to be reassured at the point where they were viewing buy/sell offerings.

Insight

Do your users have natural barriers toward certain functionality, such as security? Sure, you should address this concern at the appropriate time. But don't forget that they might not even take the first step until they feel like all their questions have been answered.

There was yet another dimension to prospective users' concerns about the benefit of using the site. As discussed, the steel industry has processes that are very entrenched—processes that were, for the most part, working well. What could a web site possibly offer beyond what they were currently doing? In research, we discovered that the site had the potential to greatly simplify the day-to-day business dealings by cutting out the administrative phone/fax relay game, but that most test-users weren't willing to spend enough time at the site to determine this on their own.

The site also provided an excellent means of making new business contacts and offered an outlet for selling scraps that might otherwise be useless. However, these benefits had not been announced or promoted on the site. User experience testing highlighted these concerns as well as providing a forum for exploring ways in which the site might be modified to better showcase its benefits.

Insight

The web remains a new medium for both users and industries. If a site is asking users to both adopt a new technology and modify their business processes to make use of this technology, this is a double whammy. Relevant benefits, based on the needs of the prospective user, need to be presented where they will do the most good. This may require that a relatively large amount of this "selling in" be presented up-front in the site.

I'm Not Going into That Room Until You Turn a Light On

We've discussed what can happen when users are exposed to lengthy explanations of how to use sites. Often, they are spoon-fed much more information than they need, although they frequently don't understand why they would want to take that next step, let alone how they stand to benefit from doing so. Paradoxically, an emphasis on benefits, when not coupled with the ability to get questions answered (the "fine print"), can also be a deterrent to users.

A site for a major music club, for example, highlighted the offer to "get 12 CDs free" on the homepage and touted membership in a

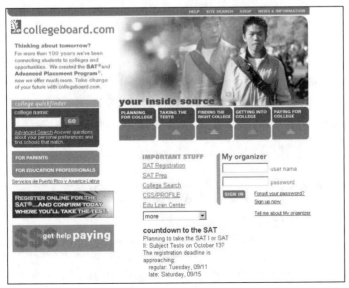

Figure 10.3

The homepage of the College Board site says it all: Who is behind the site, and why you want to be there.

www.collegeboard.com

music club. Site visitors who were not currently familiar with this music club immediately wanted to see an explanation of membership, along with the requirements (especially requirements that might involve future purchases). They also wanted this information available directly from the homepage, in a form such as an FAQ list.

It is not that the site didn't offer this information: It did. However, the requirements were located deeper into the site than the homepage let on, and users were forced to *begin* (to their dismay) with a registration process when all they really wanted was an understanding of the requirements. Subsequently, they then wanted to peruse the list of CDs to decide if the list was sufficient for them to actually want 12 of them for free. Once these information needs were met, they would consider registration. Before they had the facts, however, the whole process seemed presumptuous, if not outright deceptive.

Current members of this music club were also confused by the site. Most members were receiving mailings from the club, making whichever selections they wanted, and then mailing back a standardized order form. The web site offered numerous benefits beyond what could be offered through these mailings, but that was unclear from the homepage. Current members were willing to peruse the site in order to gain an understanding of how the web site might be a better option than mailings, yet for most this information did not appear to be available.

Clearly, getting the right mix of benefits and detail can be complicated, and it is not something you will necessarily accomplish on your first attempt to design a site. However, we have discovered that as users grow more experienced with a site, and provide feedback, this balance emerges in sharper relief.

It's 10:00 P.M.: Do You Know Where Your Users Are (and Vice Versa)?

Users need to know where they are in the site, both in general and specific terms. They need to know precisely where they are situated *within* whatever process they have undertaken (such as information gathering or transactions).

When talking to users, we sometimes feel like many of them wake up in the middle of the night from dreams in which they are lost in a labyrinthian web site—sinking deeper and deeper, and committing more and more of their time and personal information to the site. Often, they become panicked over how much further they have to go or whether they are even on the right path. We also wonder if developers don't have the same dream, only they wake up with a sense of calm and well-being because they imagined having explored the depths of a perfect web site—one that, in reality, was a dark and mysterious place.

Somewhere along the way, the paths of designers and users have to cross, and the former need to tell the latter exactly where they are and how much further they have to go to get to whatever they want or wherever they are headed. This leads to an obvious question: Should the steps of a process be shown to the user up front, or should the steps be presented as they go along? Well, why make it an either/or situation? The answer is "yes" to both.

Users are, of course, first and foremost human beings. They have their own ways of processing information and their own comfort levels with using the web. Some users, generally the more experienced ones, can peruse a list of steps and be comfortable with it if it "maps" with what they are accustomed to, either offline or within comparable sites. Then, they are comfortable moving forward, with no questions asked. Others, especially those with less experience, may need to be reminded where they are in the process.

Some sites accomplish this orientation through the left navigation bar. The role of the left navigation bar will be discussed more when we cover web site navigation issues. However, for now it is important to keep in mind that users look to the left navigation bar not only as a way of getting around the site, but also as a means of orientation.

Here is an example of how the left navigation bar serves to help orient the user: When the user is searching for product information, the options in the left navigation bar may expand. On the homepage, the user clicks on "Products" in the left navigation bar, and he is presented with a page, one layer down, and a list of product categories. Then, in the left navigation bar, a subheading appears under "Products" (perhaps in a different color), indicating that the user is on the "Product Categories" page. The user then clicks on a category, and on the next page, the actual name of that product category appears in the left navigation bar under "Product Categories," again highlighted in a different color.

Figure 10.4

The IBM homepage shows clear product categories in the left navigation bar.

www.ibm.com

Figure 10.5

When the user clicks on "Home/Home Office," the product categories within Home/Home Office are displayed in the left navigation bar.

www.ibm.com

Insight

Don't underestimate the value of the left navigation bar. It is used as a quick reference "site map" to what the site offers, as a reference to current location within the site, and as a fast path navigator.

With this model, the user soon realizes that by looking at the left navigation bar it is possible to keep track of his current location.

Other sites place "breadcrumbs" at the top of the page in the form of a series of sequential links that outline the current location and pathway in the site. Something more may be needed here, however, because many users often feel the need to know what lies ahead as well. A site that helps parents save for a child's college education addresses this issue in one interesting way. During the registration process, the user is presented with a brief description of all the steps in the process to the immediate right side of the screen, where the current step is highlighted. This provides the user both an overview of each step and an orientation to what she will be doing as she moves forward. For users who are less familiar with entering registration information on a web site, this orientation also provides an additional sense of security.

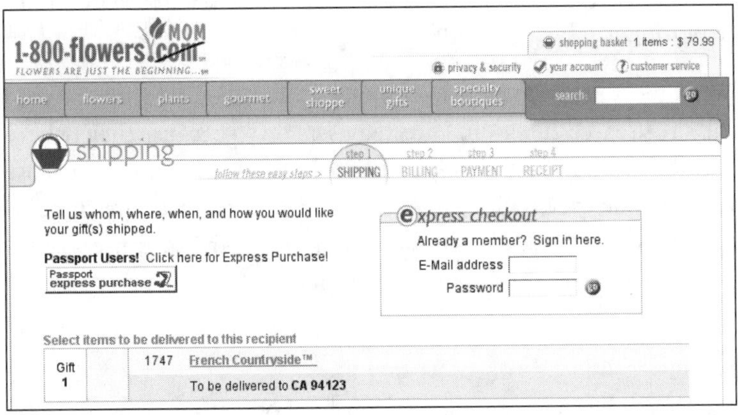

www.1-800-flowers.com

Figure 10.6

When purchasing from the 1-800-flowers site, the user is instructed to "follow these easy steps." As he progresses through the path, the appropriate step (Shipping, Billing, Payment, or Receipt) is highlighted.

Research Tip

Designers need to learn how people gather information and accomplish tasks in the offline world. Where in their processes do they run into problems? When do they need help, additional definitions, or background information? Gaining an understanding of offline processes is a starting point toward developing priorities for how to organize this content on a web site.

Searching and Advanced Searching
I Know There's a Quicker Way to Get There, But I Want the Scenic Route

We often find that some users want to go directly to their desired information as quickly and painlessly as possible. Others are less focused and want to take some time along the way to explore routes that may or may not be related, and perhaps even venture off in another direction altogether. As we have seen, users cannot be easily stereotyped. How they attain their goals frequently depends on such factors as their familiarity with the general concerns of the site and the amount of time they are prepared to commit to exploring it.

What most users *do* have in common is that they gravitate toward the site's search function. Directed users do so because they believe it to be the quickest route, and less-directed users do so because they assume they will be able to meander. Therefore, sites need to accommodate both experienced and non-experienced users without forcing either into a specific method.

Insight

The search function is a critical element of a web site. It needs to be designed to accommodate both directed searching and meandering, if not a combination of the two.

The search issue is in many ways the exact opposite of what we have been talking about in this chapter, yet it is merely the flip-side of the same issue: that users want help and directions, but at a time of their own choosing. Sometimes, they do not want these at all. Searching a web site can be an exciting, educational process, where one secret after another is yielded as each stone is unturned. For users who have the time and the inclination to approach a site this way, they should be permitted to enjoy themselves while they smell the roses. If, on the other hand, they want help in the form of an advanced search, just make sure it is an obvious choice.

The operative term here is *choice*. If the user wants additional assistance, he will ask for it.

I Don't Have Time for "War and Peace"
Notes on the Content Pages

Presenting content is always a complicated issue. First, users tell us that they don't like to do a lot of reading online. If an article goes on and on, they would rather print it out and read it on the bus ride home. Yet, they need to see enough about what's in an article to know if it's interesting enough to print out, because they are also going to complain if, a whole ream of paper later, it was not the article they wanted. But then again, if they have to go down four layers of short pages to finally get at the information they are looking for, they complain that they would rather do some scrolling (but again, not too much) before they get at the one factoid they are looking for.

Basically, each individual user has a slightly different approach, depending on the time of day, her mood at that moment, her sense of urgency, and the specific topic. The only way to win is to anticipate every approach as much as possible, through a combination of hypertext links, icons, and the left navigation bar.

Users are usually first exposed to articles and other documents, such as those that come from newspapers, by a summary. In a few words, the basic gist of the article or document is presented so people can decide if this is indeed what they are looking for. This seems simple enough, but even at this stage of the game, users report problems.

Insight

Users don't necessarily love to read on the web, and they are usually in a hurry. They want to skim through summaries and then decide if they want to burrow down further into longer articles. The more easily they can step through the layers, the better.

We worked on a technology site that was comprised primarily of "white" papers, that is, long articles on technology-related topics. When the user selected a specific topic, such as personal computers, she was presented with a list of documents, each described in a brief summary. This seemed simple enough. The user could then read through the list and see an expanded version of a white paper by simply clicking on it. Very simple. However, the summaries were apparently written by the author of the white papers, and were frequently one sentence in length. They reiterated the title without illuminating what was in it. Other summaries were more-or-less sales pitches, informing the user why she should read this or that white paper, without actually telling her what was in it. Other "summaries" went on so long (two or more lengthy paragraphs) that the user didn't really need to read the article because she had already been provided with the condensed version.

What users want in a summary can be summarized with the basic Journalism 101 elements about a news article: who, what, why, where, when, and how. Users need to know enough about what is in the article to know if they want to read further. They don't need every detail of the article in short-form, nor do they need a sales pitch on why they should read it. If it is a news article, the date and time of the article needs to be front and center, as does the source. Documents with more editorial content or facts need to be summarized so the user can get a feel for what she will be reading, the focus, the kinds of facts being presented, and the source.

Now, what the user is exposed to after she actually selects a document to continue reading is not necessarily governed by hard and fast rules. A news site may include short articles of one or two pages, perhaps supplemented by additional links. These links might allow the user to gain further detail, view additional graphics, or see related articles.

A site with heavy informational content, like a historical reference or educational site, might include hypertext within a paragraph that provides a way for the user to get more in-depth information on a certain topic. Embedded in paragraphs might also be graphic images, with icons that allow the user to expand the image for closer examination. These links are all specific to the actual content the user is reading.

Most likely, users are going to be glancing over at the left navigation bar as their directional point of reference, as well as using it as a menu of features. The major content categories and functions are established on the homepage, as we discussed earlier. Users take a mental snapshot of these buckets, once they have processed them (and assuming they are labeled in an intuitively logical manner), and then they expect the site to conform to these buckets. This is a subconscious expectation.

As they get further into the site, it is the general convention in web sites that the left navigation will contain these buckets. Additional reference information that the user might need while within the site (including a Glossary, perhaps a Tutorial, and a Help feature) might also be listed. These features go above and beyond any hyperlinks that might be included within the actual function or text.

Insight

Even though it takes up real estate on the page, the left navigation bar should remain on the page even as users move into heavy content pages. Users want to be able to move around, and they want to get to supplementary content like a glossary or a tutorial.

With the left navigation bar serving essentially as the pivot point on a standard web page, let's talk about the other elements on a content page.

But what about more general questions or concerns that might arise as the user is accessing this content—questions or concerns that may not be so specific to what the user is reading? This is where the left navigation bar serves a purpose as a menu for additional information. For example, perhaps the text is describing a period of history, like the American Civil War. While reading it, a question pops into the user's mind about the location of a certain battlefield, which does not happen to be explained. The left navigation bar could contain a Glossary for the user to click on that would allow her to look up the name of the battlefield. Or maybe it would contain a Tutorial with topics like how to do research on the site, as well as more specific informational topics.

In a commerce site, the same principles hold true. Product pages are a prime example of how users' varying needs for depth, or lack thereof, need to be accommodated. Some users come to product pages with the goal of perusing a brief description of a product, its basic functionality, what it's used for, a brief benefit, and maybe a small photo. Others want measurements. Product pages also play a special role as the user is traversing the purchasing path. Therefore, product information will be discussed in more depth in Chapter 18, "The Challenges of Transferring an Established Brand to the Web," which is devoted to e-commerce.

The target users for a specific web site often have their own expectations for how articles and other documents need to be presented. These expectations are the result of factors that include their mindset; for example, a scientist's expectation of how articles are presented will differ greatly from the the expectation of the average news hound. Ultimately, the decision about how to present this information needs to be based on understanding this mindset.

Figure 10.7

A web site about the Underground Railroad, sponsored by UC-Davis, is an excellent example of the use of hyperlinks. The user can click on a link to get more information on the sponsors and, further into the site, more detailed historical information.

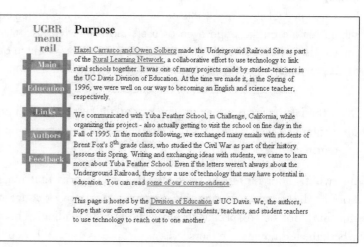

www.ucdavis.edu

Insight

The desire for control over the web experience also guides how users interact with content. They want to explore at their own pace and be able to move in directions that interest them and avoid materials that do not. Content needs to be presented in such a way that allows for individual exploration.

Thanks! Just When I'm Starting to Have Fun, You Tell Me It's Illegal

Sometimes there are restrictions on what certain users can see or do on your web site. No, we are not talking about pornographic sites. Instead, we mean sites that, due to legal restrictions for example, cannot treat all users equally. Here is an example:

A wine site offers a vast array of interesting wines from both large and small wineries, most of which are located in California. In an early version of the site, users could shop at will, perusing the brands, getting an idea of what the wine might taste like (dry, sweet, and so on), and filling their shopping carts. From there, they went through a standard e-commerce checkout procedure, entering their credit card information, shipping address, and… whoops!

When users got to the shipping address part of the process, they were in for a potentially nasty surprise. Why? Because as it turned out, not all states, or even counties, in the US actually allowed wine to be accepted through the mail. And that's not all. Some brands, due to distributor agreements, could not be shipped to certain states.

Insight

Although users like to be surprised on the web, they don't like to have their time wasted. This is especially true when they are completing transactions.

As a result, users spent quality time on the site, got their taste buds worked into a frenzy, and then discovered that they would still be obliged to settle for whatever they could find at the corner store. Needless to say, they weren't exactly feeling benevolent toward this web site.

Once this issue became apparent in user experience testing, the developers of the site added a step to the beginning of the purchase process. Before an item could even be placed in the shopping cart, the user was asked where the wine would ultimately be shipped, all through the use of a simple question and a drop-down menu with state abbreviations. If the user entered one of the states that restricted wine shipments in some way, he was then routed to a page that explained why there was a restriction and, when possible, he was provided alternatives (for example, guidance on any brands that were unrestricted).

The web site of a computer hardware manufacturer had a "Buy Now" option. Users clicked on it, and from there, they went through a basic purchasing process choosing products, then choosing options, and finally indicating readiness to actually make the purchase. At that point, the user was informed that certain products could indeed be ordered online. However, other products, including personal computers, could be purchased from a dealer. And even then, instead of laying out the facts, the designer offered users a screen in which they could indicate their ZIP code because the site had a handy store locator. Basically, users were left to surmise that the product could not be purchased online.

Users can play by the rules, but not if the rules are not stated up front. When the rules are clear, users can then decide on their own whether they want to move forward.

Insight

What's worse than too much information? In our view, not enough. In the minds of users, apparent subterfuge would be at the top of the list, especially if their time is wasted in the process of getting to the truth.

Is It an Ad or Is It Information?
If It's Not Useful, It's Pollution

Banner ads on web sites have certainly gone through an evolution. In the early days of commercial web sites, it probably seemed like banners were a useful way to expose users to new products and services. Over time, many figured out that those long boxes located near the top of a homepage were indeed advertising, and they also decided that these ads distracted them from their goal. And as we have said before, web site users are highly goal-oriented.

Sooner or later, after consciously making the "just say no" decision about a lot of the banner advertising, many users learned to subconsciously block these ads from their view, as if they didn't even exist on the page. This happened about the same time some enterprising advertisers created banner ads that looked like they might be informative, enticing the user into clicking in the expectation of getting information—only to find himself in the middle of an ad.

Again, because users felt "duped," they strengthened their resolve to ignore banners.

Insight

Anything on a page that resembles an advertising banner is likely to be overlooked—if not purposely ignored.

The danger for designers, as a result, is to avoid making content or functionality look too much like banners. We have seen many good ways of emphasizing valuable content and functionality when site sponsors want to be sure they've gotten the attention of their users. Maybe they used bold letters in a long rectangular box somewhere near the top of a homepage, or maybe they used a page further into the site with animation and highlighting in a box off to the side of a content page. But users still seemed to skim over these. In testing, it became apparent that many assumed these "attention-getters" were banner ads, and, in their subconscious minds, turned them off.

The moral here, as we have said previously, is that users have come to expect certain conventions in web site development: the left navigation bar and a Home button to name but two. Along the way, they have also learned what to ignore.

The View from 30,000 Feet

Users process information differently based on factors like past experience, comfort with using the web, and individual learning style. We don't have the luxury of believing that all people are going to perceive and use instructions and content in the exact same way. The guiding principle is this: They don't need it until they need it.

A Few Hard Questions

- Are the benefits of processes like registration made clear before the user is actually expected to embark upon a process?

- Are all instructions presented in one format so the user has to read through a long list? Or can the user also get additional detail, as needed, at each step of a process?

- Does the user have a way to reference where she is in a process, as well as in the site, before moving on to the next step?

- Does your site provide a means of getting additional definitions within the process or content or in the left navigation bar, if not both?

- Is content presented first in relevant summaries, followed by an expanded version, with additional hypertext and related links for more detail?

- Is the Search option clearly differentiated from the Advanced Search?

- Are there any additional restrictions or other "catches," and are they presented in advance of a process so that the user is not expecting an impossible outcome?

Hieroglyphics Are Only Interesting When You Are Visiting the Pyramids

Icons and Language

Anyone who spends several hours a week on the web can report countless examples of sites that use icons or language that either have no meaning or are far from what the user might expect. Sites that force the user to traverse unintended paths because of unclear icons lead to user frustration and often rejection. Some of these points may be obvious to the reader—yet these are issues that arise throughout a surprising number of web sites, and they cause a great deal of missed opportunity for the web site sponsor. By that we mean that the site is ineffective because functionality and navigation that would have been extremely valuable to the user was a) not noticed and b) not understood.

Offline Metaphors Don't Always Translate Well to the Web

Developers sometimes assume that icons and functionality that are familiar offline (like the dashboard of a car or the control panel of a VCR) will make sense to users when that same functionality is displayed onscreen.

Consider, for example, a web site that wanted users to be able to make short videos using its software and then send them to friends and family via the web. The site offered an onscreen VCR panel that required users to hit "Record" as soon as they had the image they wanted to shoot. Faced with what designers expected would be familiar—a red button that indicates record on most VCRs—each and every user stopped dead in his or her tracks. When asked why they didn't make their videos, several commented that the Record button resembled a stop sign more than a record button, which communicated to them that clicking the button would stop the recording process, not start it.

This example indicates just how much we all have redefined our knowledge of icons as a consequence of being online. That is, icons that are second nature to us on the web ("Home," "Back," and so on) live only in our "web worlds." Similarly, icons that have meaning for us in an offline world lose that meaning when placed on a web page.

A similar example of interface confusion pertains to icons and functionality that many of us are accustomed to in a Windows world. For example, if you want to re-sort a column of data from ascending to descending order, you click the column header and voilà, the deed is done. If you prefer the data be sorted in some other way, such as in alphabetical order by subject or author, you just move over to the appropriate column and click on the header, and the column is alphabetized.

When a client of ours first set about introducing its wonderful site, which enabled users to get as granular as they wanted in locating a restaurant (that is, choosing Vietnamese food in Manhattan with an outdoor garden or a Sushi place in Piccadilly Circus that served on Sunday), they did some usability testing. One of their biggest challenges was to figure out how to inspire users to take full advantage of the site by sorting information according to a variety of available criteria—food rating, service level, neighborhood, price, and so on. As things stood, the interface required the user to click the column heading to sort the column.

Perhaps surprisingly, many users didn't think to do this at first. They saw only a column header that was underscored. To them, in "web speak," they were being told to click on the term that appeared underscored in the header to find out what it meant. After all, that is what hyperlinks do.

We had to work with test participants to figure out why it confused them to sort each column. Those that understood they could sort by clicking on the column header didn't understand why each column sorted differently, one alphabetically, one numerically, and so

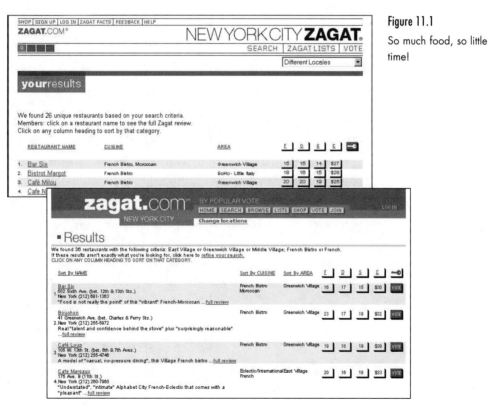

Figure 11.1

So much food, so little time!

www.zagat.com

on. This is what we call a "cognitive disconnect," or something that somehow stops the brain from "getting it." The designers of the site worked hard to write very explicit language to explain how to use the sort feature, and they re-emphasized the instruction by embedding it in each column head. Suffice it to say that "foodies" now take full advantage of the power of this site to find the perfect restaurant that meets each of their criteria.

Similarly, a good deal of the right mouse click functionality (which some have mastered on their desktop applications) simply doesn't translate to applications on the web that require the user to employ their right click. We've seen applications where the instruction to do so is given repeatedly and in context. Yet each time the user is faced with the need to right-click in order to move ahead as desired, they pause or forget. The action is simply not intuitive or natural when they are on the web.

These examples accentuate the fact that people have ingrained behavior around a number of online and offline functions, and web site designers must acknowledge such behaviors in order to deliver an intuitive and ultimately successful experience.

Here are some other ingrained user behaviors to note:

- PC and Mac users alike double-click on an icon to activate it. If your site cannot accept a double-click—or if it actually (and unknowingly) advances users two steps ahead as a result of a double-click—then you're in trouble!

- Most users expect that if they fill in data that is attached to one radio button selection, the radio button is automatically selected (that is, they do not expect to have to click on the radio button as well). Sometimes, they also expect that if they click on the text, the radio button becomes selected.

- Most people assume that placing a check next to a selection "adds" it. Therefore, checking it in order to request that it be deleted may well be a "disconnect" for the user.

- Many people think that pressing Tab or Return automatically advances them to the next field. They get upset or confused when their action does nothing or something other than what they expected.

- Likewise, many expect that hitting "Return" will serve the same function as the "Go" button. When it doesn't, they assume that the site is simply "broken."

Overriding such entrenched behaviors is near impossible, as we have seen in research. For example, we worked on a dating web site in which users were obliged to fill out a headline for their email (for example, "Sexy lawyer seeks his match"). Subsequently, they were asked to advance to an open field where they could write a message of any length and then email it to other visitors of the site by hitting "Enter." One after another, we watched people type in their headline and hit Return with the intention of advancing to the open email field to type their message. Each time, they would look surprised when they got a return message saying "Your email to Member ABC has been sent." Whereas they sought to advance to the next field, the site had other plans: It understood "Return" to mean "Enter."

The interesting thing about this was that even when the researcher explained to users how this function worked, they continued to hit "Return" and became increasingly frustrated. Observing this behavior during user experience testing enabled the developers to create a solution that did not allow the message to be sent without "reading" text in the open field.

Each and Every Icon or Button Can Have One— and Only One—Meaning

In many of the sites we review, we notice that the designers (perhaps inadvertently or perhaps out of sheer sleep deprivation that accompanies web design efforts) violate the basic rule of Consistency. Simply put, every major button, icon or navigational instruction, should have only *one* meaning. Moreover, only *one* word should be used to convey that one meaning. When this is done well, users quickly learn how to use a web site and feel a sense of mastery and ease. When it doesn't happen, confusion and frustration ensue.

A typical example is when "Next" and "Continue" are used interchangeably on a site to mean "Forward" to the next screen. Either of these terms is appropriate to convey this action—but not both. By contrast, "Enter" or "Submit" means you are actually telling the site to take action based on data you have entered or choices you have made. One of these words should be used to convey this action. If multiple words are used interchangeably within a site to mean the same thing, or if a single word is used in different contexts to mean different things, users become uncertain of how to proceed.

Alternatively, the user wastes countless valuable minutes attempting to understand what the possible difference in meaning could be between words or icons that, in the everyday world, "mean" exactly the same thing.

"What's Clickable?" Is NOT a Trick Question

Enough time has elapsed since the birth of the web that a majority of users know what they are looking at when they see the little hand emerge out of nowhere. That icon means that an element is clickable. If that rule is violated, so is their user experience.

People always expect to click on an image to navigate, and rarely imagine that it is there for aesthetic or decorative purposes. Likewise, they also assume they can click the image or the hyperlink *below* or *next to* icons just as easily and wind up getting where they want to go. If they can't, there is a problem.

We encourage designers to make all images clickable—that is, to design them to serve as navigational elements rather than window dressing. We also encourage designers to ensure that the graphic elements surrounding the image (which might be hyperlinks, bullets, or arrows) lead users to the same place on the site. In other words, different people have different habits when it comes to clicking: Some will click on the image, others on the hyperlink or caption below it, and still others on the little button at the left-hand side of the icon. The idea here is that designers should take into account and plan for these habits when they're building web sites so that each of these actions takes a user to the same place.

Emphatically, users should not have to resort to randomly moving the cursor around the page in the hopes of finding something to click. Nor should they feel like a bull in a china shop when they inadvertently select one icon or button only to find that it is the icon immediately below that they have selected.

The Many Sides of Online Meaning

One of the most fascinating things about user experience testing is to witness the myriad of meanings that people bring to an icon or word depending upon their profession, experience, and expectations. Marketers are the worst offenders with respect to assuming that their customers are familiar with their terminology. So basic to the language of a health care provider is PCP (as in "primary care physician") that it would never occur to them that for some patients, the acronym "PCP" refers to a narcotic—and not one they would choose to highlight in their plan!

Financial service companies will refer to their insurance plans or checking accounts as "products and services," often to the confusion of their customers and prospects.

As has been discussed throughout the book, those who live in a web world are convinced that the rest of the planet knows just what they mean by "FAQ," "Flash," "PDF," "thumbnail," and "DSL."

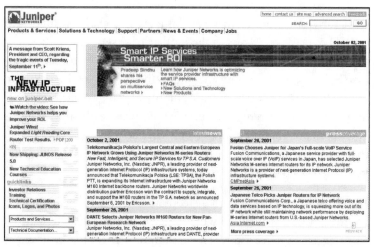

Figure 11.2

This homepage, for Juniper Networks, has some great information. But you certainly need to be familiar with the company's technical terminology to make use of it.

www.juniper.net

Aside from the fact that acronyms are to be avoided at all costs by designers, the point here is that the "rest of us" just want to find information, order products, see a big enough picture to know if we want to order the product, get a brochure, and so on. We have little, if any, interest in learning more about file formats, modem speeds, or browser technology. If we did, we'd have become web masters ourselves.

If Your Icons Need a Legend, You're in Trouble

To those in the food business, a little red heart icon means "healthy." We've seen the same icon used on different sites to mean "tell a friend," "add to favorites," and a variety of other things. Any experienced graphic designer will tell you exactly how long it takes for an otherwise obscure icon to become instantly recognizable without text to support it (for instance, the web browser "Back" button arrow—surely an instantly recognizable image—has retained the word "back" long after the necessity for it has passed. Everyone knows what it means. Imagine, then, how long users are likely to spend scrutinizing such icons for their intended meaning in the *absence* of such identifying terms? Perhaps for all of ten seconds, which is about the most time they will spend on your web site at all if they don't know what it is they're supposed to be doing!

We've seen a number of sites that deliberately design iconography to be interesting and to create curiosity about what is behind each one. The fact is, necessity is the mother of invention. Particularly on the web, people are in a big hurry and are less interested in using their imagination than they might be in the "real world." In other words, they can be extraordinarily *literal* in their interpretations. Users will attempt to unravel the mysteries behind icons as quickly as possible in order to reach their desired goal, but beyond that, the gig is up! After one or two "wrong answers," we find that it's "three strikes and you are out."

We've seen many designs where icons are defined on the homepage and thereafter are invoked willy-nilly throughout the site without any text to support them. The assumption is that somehow the icon will be so memorable, or the function so compelling, that

www.deborah.org

Figure 11.3
(Next three images)

Have a heart...as long as we know what it means!

www.udate.com

users will immediately perceive and effortlessly recall its meaning. Below are a few rules of thumb that we use to guide web designers on the design and application of icons:

• Before using an icon, check carefully to make sure it doesn't have another—perhaps conflicting—meaning to your intended audience (remember the "little red heart" example).

Figure 11.4

Where am I going with this? Are arrows directing me somewhere? Or are they being used instead of bullets?

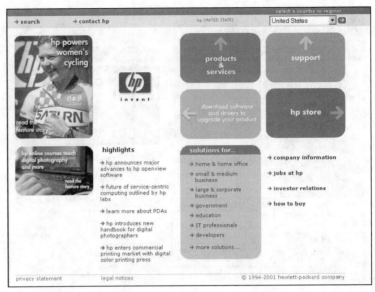

www.hp.com

- Always have text accompany your icon, or at least use a very easy-to-obtain rollover, the meaning of which is self-evident. However, be careful with rollovers. If the rollover does not appear in time (depending on the users' connection speed), it may be ignored.

- Whenever possible, avoid using legends. They imply more complexity than most web users want.

- If you do use a legend (such as "*" means "required information"), make sure you place it close to its icon so the user can't possibly miss it. Consider employing a striking color to draw attention to the legend and to associate it with the icon. Don't expect people to find the legend; point them to it.

The Design of a Site Is in and of Itself a Metaphor

When users arrive at a homepage, they quickly assess what they can do there: find information, buy stuff, compare prices, bid on products, get news, download music, and so on.

The overall design of a site is in and of itself a metaphor that communicates—sometimes unintentionally—what the site is all about.

For instance, we've seen sites that vaguely resemble magazines or which appear purely informational, and so fail to communicate that they sell products or what products that they sell. Conversely, many sites look so much like catalogues or store fronts that they mask the sometimes valuable information they have to offer.

We talk about this issue in more detail in other chapters when we discuss branding issues. For more detail, refer to Chapter 3, "Your Homepage Is a 30-Second Window of Opportunity: Don't Be Shy!" and Chapter 5, "It's Okay to be Different: Just Make Sure People Know What You Offer."

The Web Is About Putting Control in the Hands of the User

Perhaps most importantly, users expect to be able to stop anything they activate online instantly and without problems, including "splash" screens, animations, and demos. The prevailing logic is, "If I want it to start, I make it so; if I want it to stop, I expect it to stop—immediately! And (while you're at it), do what I say when I say I want to go somewhere else on the site!" So, for every "start" button or action, there must be a clearly defined "out": a way to stop or advance the demo, a way to close the window once it's been opened, or a way to minimize an image after it has been enlarged. Also, users should be provided with a simple means of navigating between a Flash site and an HTML site.

As many a trend analyst has noted, the web is the medium of the people, a place where users select their own paths and direct their own experiences. Unlike mass media—for which we are a captive audience having essentially the same experience—the web is an individualized place in which "control" is a central concern. Often, a misleading icon or word or the absence of a button to stop what one has started (or to get back to where one came from) is perceived as a loss of the control that is so crucial to the experience of using the web. In most cases, we've found that clear icons are an absolute necessity, even at the risk of being boring and passing up more intriguing iconography, labeling, or images. When it comes to unambiguous icons, be they ever so dull, the outcome is far more certain, and the goal of users is that much closer to being achieved.

The View from 30,000 Feet

Most of us respond better and faster to images and icons than we do to language—particularly on the web. Therefore, images should be used to both create interest and direct traffic, not to obscure meaning. And the web is a global medium: Icons certainly transcend language, but they can also lead to confusion, given the interpretation of certain symbols in other cultures.

Likewise, language needs to be direct and written from the vantage point of the person to whom it is intended. This is both more difficult (and at the same time more simple) than you think. It is difficult to step out of the shoes and language of marketers and web designers and into the words of users. (Writers and technical communicators need to play a role here.) Once that "switch" occurs, however, the process of writing to—and for—the intended users is quite intuitive.

The Hard Questions

- Do your images and icons retain their meaning on the web?
- Does your navigation require people to "unlearn" any involuntary behavior (like double-clicking) or "learn" any unfamiliar behavior (like right-clicking)?
- Does each and every button and icon have a unique meaning?
- Can the user guess what's clickable without using the cursor?
- Does the language of your site require the user to learn a new dialect?
- Do your icons need a legend?
- Consider your site as a visual metaphor: Does it communicate what you offer?

PART IV

Zeroing In

Site Design and Navigation

12 Give the People What They Want (and More),
or They'll Find Someone Who Can!   189

13 Functionality
Don't Just Lie There, Give Me Some Interaction   211

14 Whiz! Bang! Boom!
Graphics in Service to Content and Functionality   223

15 Search
*When to Keep Them in Your Playpen and When
to Open Them Up to the Universe*   235

16 Navigation
*You Know You're in Trouble When Users Look
for Your Site Map*   255

17 E-Commerce
If They Can't Find It, They Won't Buy It   271

CHAPTER TWELVE

Give the People What They Want (and More), or They'll Find Someone Who Can!

In Chapter 10, "When I Need Your Assistance, Believe Me, I'll Ask!," in which we discussed the importance of giving users control over the amount and type of information they receive, we looked at how this principle applied to content in terms of the use of summaries, links, and overall organization.

We often find that clients go to great expense and spare no amount of time to create content that enriches their offering. However, many frequently do so in a virtual "vacuum," without first finding out if their ideas would in fact add value or not. Others discover to their chagrin that, despite their efforts to develop a broad range of content, users actually have highly limited expectations for particular sites. Still other clients have learned, to their dismay, that much of their content is not needed at all, and that users would be just as happy with links to reliable and expert sources (that is, to sites that do the work for them).

Each of these problems poses a challenge for the web site developer. Therefore, this chapter focuses on content from the perspective of content sources and credibility.

Content: You Know, That Stuff You Usually Have to Read

If we are going to talk about content in this chapter, let's start with some examples of what we actually mean when we use that term. We generally think of content as one of the following:

- **News.** News generally includes quick blurbs that cover current events, much like what is encountered on a standard news or portal site. But more targeted sites also include even briefer news "bites," such as company-related or industry-related news.

- **Articles.** This content category includes speeches, editorials, position papers, columns, stories, and descriptive information, such as "how-to" information or travel destinations.

- **Product/Service Information.** Descriptions of features, functions, and benefits, as well as reviews written by others (for example, book reviews).

- **User-Generated Content.** This is a broad category, covering content that is contributed by site visitors or members rather than by the sponsor of the site. This can also include content that would fit into the above categories. Examples include message boards, product reviews, and articles on a variety of topics.

Oh Yeah? Says Who?

People are natural skeptics, and this is certainly true of web users. Throughout previous chapters, we have discussed ways in which this skepticism influences how visitors perceive web sites. It is hardly an overstatement to say that content is the one aspect of web sites that users are most likely to approach with caution, if not outright distrust. Articles, reviews, bulletin board messages, frequently asked questions, Q & A... content can either add a valuable layer of depth and perceived value to a web site, or it can undermine it—in the process doing more damage than good to that site's viability.

The motivation behind this skepticism is not necessarily directed at the developer, at least not initially. Instead, skepticism lies on the other side of that infamous double-edged sword. On one hand, users recognize that the web has a vast amount of information on virtually any topic imaginable, made accessible at a level that most of us never imagined would be possible, and generally free of charge. However, users have also learned that the freedom to access information is made possible by an equally significant freedom to post this information. For the most part, anybody can post at will, and most users have either heard stories about or have themselves been party to situations where online information seemed reliable but turned out not to be. As businesses continue to hungrily stake out their territory on the web, the inconsistent reliability of online sources begs an important question: To what extent can users be expected to trust such information? Many users have learned the hard way to question what motivates the dissemination of online information, particularly when it comes to sites whose clear objective is to make a profit or to grind one of a large variety of proverbial axes. This leads us to pose an additional question: If nothing is free, what is the ulterior motive here?

The end result is that users are primed to question your content even before they hit your homepage. Consequently, as they traverse through your site, they take the attitude of "guilty until proven innocent." It's up to you to prove that your content is worthy of a second look. That is certainly a challenge.

Insight

In many ways, the web is the world's largest "vanity press," and users approach all content with skepticism—even yours. Make content decisions with this skepticism in mind. If your content isn't credible, neither are you.

A Simple Rule of Thumb: Why Is It Here?

Before developers can answer the questions about content that are likely to be posed by target users, they have at least two important ones to ask themselves: What is the purpose of their site's content? And harder still: Do users even need it? These are critical considerations because expectations for content are high. Not only is it expected to be credible, but in most cases, extensive. If users get a big "build up" on a site's homepage, only to find that the article is brief and not especially interesting or useful, they may decide that your content wasn't worth the visit.

Exactly why is this content here? Web site visitors are going to ask this question. So should developers.

There are different ways to approach this question, beginning with whether developers represent an established and recognized brand, one that is less well-known, or something in between.

Established Brands
I Trust You, But Don't Disappoint Me

You probably remember your parents' warning you: "You are judged by the company you keep." This is certainly true when it comes to web site content. As we have noted, if it's well established, brand equity can take a company a long way on the web. While visitors will generally have expectations of a site based on their perception of the company behind it, they will also come to a site with an initial modicum of trust. If a company hasn't let the user down offline, why would it do so online?

From a content perspective, this means users will be highly receptive, at least at first, to whatever is being offered. They assume that if a designer selected the content (including articles and product information) for inclusion on a web site, it is trustworthy and truthful, and it can be taken and used at face value. They also assume that subject experts have written the content, that legal staff have evaluated it, and that the company and designer totally support it.

Moreover, even when they have no evidence that a company or web designer is doing so, users often take for granted that the sponsor of the site has reflected upon advice offered by users themselves, in order to be sure that unreliable or otherwise untruthful information is not being posted. For these reasons, established brands carry their full share of responsibility for ensuring that the content presented on their sites is up to snuff.

Let's take what is probably the most obvious example: financial institutions. This is an industry for which customers and prospects have such high (and rigid) expectations that employers seldom permit their staff the luxury of casual dress in the workplace. Imagine, then, what this disposition means for their web site.

We have interviewed users of numerous financial institutions and have frequently heard them give voice to such expectations. Users don't question who wrote the content of these sites because they expect that a given bank or investment company is sufficiently obsessed with maintaining their own reputation that they would never sell users a bum steer, to say nothing of a bear or a bull. Most assume that the information conveyed on that site can basically be taken as gospel.

For example, one large consumer banking institution offered a range of information on topics like planning for college, purchasing a home, and buying insurance. The areas of the site that dealt with each of these aspects were replete with articles and interactive tools, some of which were written by in-house staff and others by recognized experts. We found that, in general, users paid little attention to the name of the author because they assumed the bank was essentially "vetting" each article by including it on their site. Appearances notwithstanding, this was not necessarily a positive finding for the sponsoring bank because they wanted to offer their site visitors a range of opinions, not one "party line" to be swallowed whole. Consequently, as a result of the research, they chose to more clearly label the source of each article.

Other types of sites are likewise bound by this high level of expectation. For instance, imagine being the sponsor of a news site or portal. Users click on a blurb and assume that the information, say about a recent event or even one that is currently unfolding, is totally truthful.

Forbes.com illustrates this well. When conducting user experience testing, we heard many of their subscribers and site visitors tell us that they didn't even question the source of newswires, articles, or related links on the site. Why? Simply because the strength of the Forbes brand among regular readers—and even non-readers—was extended without question to Forbes.com. Again, this simultaneously proved a huge asset and a very tall order to live up to on a daily basis!

This high level of expectation, in keeping with the brand image, also applies to brands in other categories, such as retail and manufacturing. Imagine the high expectations that users must have for an old established retail brand!

Increasingly, web site content is being provided through links to other related sites. When these links occur on the sites of established brands, users also assume that this link (and any new information subsumed within it) has been approved by the original site.

Figure 12.1

The homepage for Lean Cuisine has provided its users with content that clearly matches their brand image. For example, the site provides nutrition and diet information, as well as health tips. What else would you expect from Lean Cuisine?

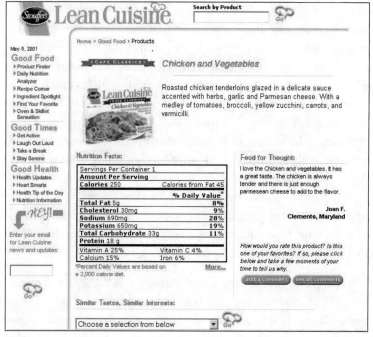

www.leancuisine.com

The Double-Edged Sword
Do I Want Content from This Brand?

The reputation of established companies precedes them, and although branding generally establishes an immediate level of trust among users, there is always the danger that notoriety and expectation can have unforeseen negative consequences for the success of a site. While established brands are generally associated with trustworthiness, there are additional aspects of a company's image to consider; among them, their actual and perceived social and political agenda (to the extent that there is one), whether they are (again, in perception or in fact) high- or low-tech, and so on. These factors are important insofar as they have a tangible effect on user expectations for web site content.

For example, we conducted research for a medical site that was sponsored by a major monthly publication. This venerable periodical has roots in the early twentieth century and is widely associated with family-focused content and conservative social views. So while they assumed that the content of the medical site was reliable, site visitors also approached it with an expectation that it reflected the perspective of the traditional medical establishment, and that it did not, therefore, give voice to alternative and/or holistic treatments. It was also assumed that, to the extent that they were addressed at all, topics like family planning and human sexuality would also reflect the publication's openly conservative views.

The developers of the site were thus faced with the challenge of satisfying the expectations of current subscribers of the publication, who are the most likely site visitors, while also attempting to attract a more diverse audience. Ultimately, they decided that current, rather than new, subscribers were their most likely target audience. Anticipating that these users were most likely to visit the site, they chose to offer more conservative content.

Next, let's take an example from the site of an HMO. Very few industries are viewed with as much skepticism as healthcare and, consequently, the content of HMO web sites is probably among the most likely to be questioned. We worked with an HMO who had developed their own site content, including articles about prevention and medical procedures. During testing, users were immediately concerned that the HMO had an agenda underpinning the content of its web site. Users anticipated that the site might steer customers toward those procedures that were least expensive for the company, thereby subjecting the health of customers to a clandestine cost-benefit analysis. Worse yet, the site might completely exclude coverage of editorial about procedures the HMO did not want to cover.

This comprised the bulk of the bad news. Fortunately, the HMO also learned that their customers expected the site to link them to a wide array of trusted (and hopefully objective) third-party sources that were experts on various specialties, procedures, and illnesses, rather than producing the content themselves. Not only did this remove the considerable burden of having to produce content, it also offered them a way of enhancing perceptions of their brand indirectly, by linking the user to "best of breed" content or content sources.

A web site sponsored by an encyclopedia has had a similar issue. They are also associated with family-oriented content. Developers wanted to create a web site that would provide numerous links to other sources throughout the web rather than offering any of their own content. Once users realized that the site was sponsored by this encyclopedia publisher (it was not immediately apparent in the URL), they also assumed that family-friendly content would be provided. When they discovered that links, rather than content, were offered, they also intuited that each and every link would be rated for general audiences.

Parents with children were comfortable using this site, based on the assumption that they could leave their children alone to explore it. In contrast, childless twenty-somethings and others seeking diversity of perspective or edgier material were not as happy. By and large, they were left with the sense that the site content was partial at best, and subject to censorship at worst. In order to satisfy the needs of the latter group, the sponsor was left with the decision of whether or not to (potentially) alienate a large, family-oriented target audience for the sake of being all things to all people. This proved a difficult line to tread, as the site's raison d'être was to function as a search engine. Developers were thus placed in the awkward position of having to accommodate contradictory web needs. On the one hand, they felt obliged to explore ways of filtering and labeling links to protect children, while on the other, they were equally committed to serving the needs of those customers for whom the presence of children was not an impediment.

In another instance, the bank to which we referred earlier, which offered its users guidelines for making decisions about mortgages, insurance, and other financial topics, also encountered skepticism. Some users wanted to know where the bank was getting this expertise. Maybe they had mortgage experts, but did they know anything about buying insurance? Moreover, just where were they getting all of those guidelines on planning for college finances? Did they also employ college scholarship experts? Users didn't necessarily associate this kind of advice with a traditional bank. Some questioned whether this was the best use of the site's real estate (yes, users have learned to use that term). The bank, on the other hand, insisted that it was simply attempting to offer additional value to visitors of the site, as well as to enhance its role as a full-service, customer-oriented financial institution.

For developers, it comes down to this: Do you want the content of your web site to mirror your brand image? If so, the process of making content decisions is one of finding or creating content that reinforces that image. If content is aimed at extending the brand image by perhaps moving it a notch or two off-center, you must carefully weigh that against the potential of alienating current customers. How far can the image be extended? This is a question that only customers and prospects can adequately answer.

Insight

If you have a recognized brand that is well-established offline, visitors to your site are going to expect its content to be just as high in quality *and* to be in keeping with the brand image they know. Don't shock them with content that is out of touch, both in terms of approach and quality, with how customers perceive your brand.

New Brands
Why Should I Believe What You Have to Say?

Content presents less established brands with both a challenge and an opportunity. On one hand, new brands try to establish both an image and market for their products and services. They can't be successful in one without making headway in the other, but carefully chosen content can be a double-edged sword. It can either help the process immensely, or derail it completely. On the bright side, the sky is the limit when it comes to new sites because where there are no expectations, any approach to content chosen by a developer is potentially the right one; there are no pre-existing rules or boundaries.

So, where does the web designer begin?

Even if the brand is not yet established, content needs to somehow be relevant to the target user. What type of person is this? What are his information requirements? What information does he really need, and what does he already have at his disposal? What content is it reasonable (and possible) for a given site to offer? Again, these are questions that only real users can answer. But we can make some preliminary suggestions based on a review of competitive sites.

Figure 12.2

Visualize.com does not have an offline presence, nor is it a widely known brand. To help establish their brand, they have used content to offer expertise in the art world through the "Articles and Ideas" section, which includes an online magazine.

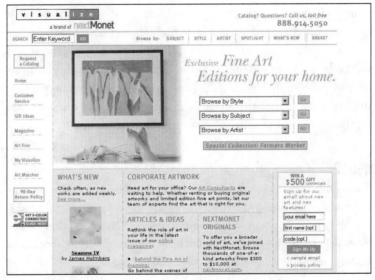

www.visualize.com

It is safe to say that credibility is a common goal among sites that lack established brand image. Without it, people won't visit, won't gather information, and certainly will not make a purchase. Judicious use of content can be a deciding factor in establishing that credibility and, by extension, brand image. And if, as the sponsor of the site, a site designer does not have a brand image, that means their content is immediately suspect. Users will take the attitude of "If I don't know these guys, why should I believe what they have to say? Where are they pulling this from?"

Insight
For a brand that is not yet established, content can aid in providing a voice and a personality. However, content needs to support a consistent and viable image.

Third-Party Content
A Judicious Solution

People generally love to hear from experts: talk show hosts, doctors, professors, celebrities, noted authors, columnists, politicians, industry pundits, weather-beaten veterans. Users, in particular, love to learn from people whom they imagine possess the attributes of expertise. Nevertheless, they do not always question the basis for expert knowledge—the credibility of such persons, if you will. Instead, they offer them unquestioning respect for having opinions that are recognized and respected in society at large. Indeed, professional experts are generally accorded more authoritative status than the companies that hire them.

Of course, the assumption of credibility does vary by category. We would probably not look to a celebrity for financial advice. Rather, we would look to someone who has either achieved certain credentials or is respected by people who have. This situation is not as cut-and-dried as it might appear, however, because people are frequently impressed when celebrities lend their names, and by extension their reputations, to retail web sites.

Here are some lessons we've learned about how to enhance web site credibility:

- Seek opportunities to bring outside content into your site. This includes articles or columns from experts. It will add depth and the potential of added value to your site.

- Leverage the image of appropriate celebrities and experts by announcing their presence on your site.

- Wherever possible, add links to other sites. These should be sites you trust, keeping in mind that your users are associating your name with these sites (again, the company you keep…).

Why take on the responsibility of developing valuable content, which must forever after be frequently updated? Portal sites, like Yahoo, have provided users with valuable links to other sites instead of developing their own, and non-portal sites also employ this tactic. For instance, healthcare provider sites offer links to the sites of government agencies like the Food and Drug Administration (FDA), as well as links to many medical information sites. In other cases, a manufacturing company's site offers links to related industry associations, and a music company site includes links to fan sites.

Figure 12.3

The homepage of *Salon*, an online magazine, includes a range of third-party content through the "From the Wires" section.

www.salon.com

Links deepen the user experience as well as increase the likelihood that a site will be "sticky." From the user's perspective, it makes more sense to go directly to a site that has valuable links than to start at ground zero with a standard search engine.

Links might be combined with third-party content that is available on your site. But heed this caution: Consider the source, because your users certainly will. Anybody can post. And as we said earlier, users have learned to be skeptical. Users assume you have read and approved any article offered on your site, so be sure to do that, or provide a clear disclaimer.

Also, with information created by outsiders, label both the author and the source clearly. Users have learned to look for sources and publication dates and, if the author is not known, some additional information about the author's credentials.

There is also an additional practical side to this issue. Do you have the time and the in-house expertise needed to generate all this content? Probably not. Especially given that users like to see content change often. Third-party content allows you to leverage your own resources while offering your users the potential of rich and credible content.

Insight

The rule of thumb is relatively simple. Whether your brand is established or not, third-party content has the potential to add depth, credibility, and value to your site.

Is the Hype Machine in Operation?
Overcoming User Skepticism of Articles and "Objective" Viewpoints

Whether from an established or a non-established brand, users have learned to expect to be sold something when they are visiting a web site. This concern has implications for how users approach content. We'll begin with articles.

Let's go back to our beleaguered banking site. Some of the users we talked to questioned the motivation behind the content, especially that which they perceived to be written by employees of the bank. If they were providing guidelines on what types of mortgages to purchase, was it possible that those types recommended most highly were also the ones that the bank "just happened" to offer? Was the bank also offering young parents the opportunity to start a college savings account in their bank? If so, wasn't this the purpose of the content? Ironically, others said that if they read an article that made sense, they would want to consider the bank as the provider of the mortgage or loan.

We have encountered similar opinions when it comes to healthcare sites, news sites, and pure play e-commerce sites. The questions are generally some variation on this: "Are you giving me this information to get me to buy something?" On the other hand, most users also ask whether they can indeed go ahead and spend some money if it turns out that they like what they are reading (for example, if they're visiting a car manufacturer's site and then they head for the car lot).

Remember that key word we keep using: control? Let's combine it with another word: honesty.

Users know that companies are in business to make money. If you have a product or service they want, and they want to buy it from you, they are open to at least having the opportunity to initiate this process through your web site. No problem.

But if you are giving them information along the way, they expect you to be honest. From a content point of view, that means you need to clearly identify the authors of articles you place on the site. Is it the staff of the jazz music department? The mortgage department? The long-term care insurance department? Clearly source the article, so they know how it might be biased.

Users are likely to be more skeptical if articles are located on one's own site—especially if they are penned by someone on your staff, rather than connected by a link from another site (we will discuss this later).

And do you want to offer them the opportunity to actually make purchases after reading an article? If so, make that an option so users feel they have complete control over this process. A simple button that allows them to get to product or service information should suffice. There is little point in automatically pushing product information; if the user is interested in buying something, he will click the button.

But I'm a Commerce Site, Right? Do I Even *Need* Content?

Users value the thoughts and opinions of sponsors of e-commerce sites. They suppose that if a company is actively selling products in this area, that company must know what it's talking about. We worked with a cosmetic site that users visited partly because they wanted to know more about cosmetics, such as which cosmetics to choose and when (or when not) to wear them. Likewise, visitors to a fashion site wanted (understandably enough) to learn more about fashion, such as what was in style and how to coordinate articles of clothing. Similarly, book and music sites generally offer users the opportunity to learn what's "hot" and why. Visitors of eBay are often there to view the merchandise, just as they might view Greco-Roman artifacts in a world-class museum. But unlike in any of the museums we know, they might also be enticed to place a bid on something that catches their eye. This is a really good example of user-generated content that is truly *perceived* as content.

If you take the time to offer your users appropriate and useful content, they may decide you know so much they had better buy from you while they're there.

Providing Product Information and Reviews
First, the Challenge

Earlier in this chapter, we told you that users are naturally suspect of all content they encounter on a web site, including whether the information is reliable and what the motivation behind offering it is. On the other hand, they come to the web for information, and they want as much as possible. They certainly use the web to make buying decisions. If they like what they read on your site, they might even stick around long enough to purchase, or at least to include you in their decision process.

This rule of thumb is also applicable to information about your own products and services. We will discuss this topic in Chapter 18 when we cover e-commerce, but it is also pertinent to this investigation of content. Visitors often go to a site for information about products and services. They want to hear what a company has to say about their features and functions, terms and conditions, benefits, and so on. Of course, they know this information is coming from the company itself and is, therefore, biased. Still, we have found that the company perspective is nonetheless desirable for users. Maybe this is the case because there is a perception that the company only plans to offer information, and that products and services are not offered through the web at all. Or perhaps they are, but not exclusively. Alternatively, maybe the web is the only way to obtain what a company offers, and users are obliged to visit the web site if they want to learn anything at all about a given product or service.

The control issue is again the guiding principle here. Sites like Amazon provide descriptions of books with a button off to the side that allows you to initiate the buying process. Dell does the same thing. Other sites allow you to click a button that takes you to a list of dealers.

Either way, the user is in control and doesn't find himself in the middle of an order form or shopping cart simply because he wanted to know what something was.

And Now the Opportunity

But let's examine the broader issue. What else do people—not just web users—consider when they are making a purchase decision? For one thing, they find out what other people think. We will deal with that later on in this chapter. They also look at product reviews and ratings. We'll tackle that here.

Web users who are in a shopping frame of mind have learned that the web is a great place to gather product and pricing information for the purpose of comparison shopping. They have also learned that the web is a great place to find out how products are reviewed and rated.

Some of these reviews and ratings will come from other users. We'll talk about that in the next section. But reviews and ratings are also offered by third-party sources.

If you have been reviewed in an industry publication or on another web site, and the review is one you want to share with your users, the value of showing it to them on your web site is obvious. You get permission from the source, copy it, put a nice frame around it, and feature it on your homepage. And you display the name of the reviewer and the source—or do you?

Think about the natural skepticism users have concerning anything that might even remotely be associated with hype. Suppose that they come to your site, and they read this review or an article that includes a series of product ratings that just happens to include a high rating. Even with the source displayed prominently, the purpose behind the inclusion of this review/rating is transparent: The move is self-serving, even if the original review is from a third party. That leads to skepticism.

Therefore, it's better to let them gather this information directly from the source if at all possible. Yes, include a blurb on your site, summarizing the review and the source. Then let your users read it for themselves. Offer a link to the exact spot on the other site where they can read more. Yes, they could get it from your site (and they know you wouldn't make it up), but they still want to get it from the objective source. Lend them a hand in getting there.

Insight
Third-party sources are most trusted if they are obtained directly from the third party. While you might consider summarizing a positive product review on your own site, also provide a link so that users have the assurance they really are getting the whole story. The user remains in control.

Figure 12.4

At the Compaq web site, users are alerted to the availability of product reviews and are linked to an independent source, *Review Board Magazine.*

www.compaq.com

Another Solution
Content as Community Through User-Generated Content

Although users value the objective opinions of recognized sources, they really want to hear from one another. They want to exchange ideas and tips, and hear success and horror stories. They want support, and they want to know that someone out there is experiencing the same thing. They want to network, make professional and social connections. And, they want advice—on resources to tap into and products and services to purchase.

What does that mean to you? It means your users are not only your content consumer; they can also be your content *provider.*

User-generated content has the potential to make your site the nucleus for people who might otherwise have a hard time meeting. Dating sites, like match.com, are the most obvious examples here. Other sites that fit into this model include sites focused on wine, books, and technology. On Amazon, for example, bibliophiles can review books they have read and even provide their lists of favorite books within a specific topic, like Zen. Web users often tell us that they go to sites like Amazon primarily to hear what other book lovers are reading.

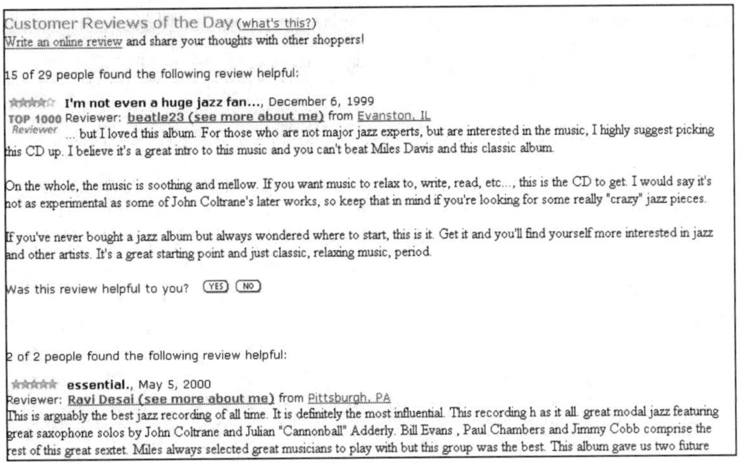

Customer Reviews of the Day (what's this?)
Write an online review and share your thoughts with other shoppers!

15 of 29 people found the following review helpful:

I'm not even a huge jazz fan..., December 6, 1999
TOP 1000 Reviewer Reviewer: beatle23 (see more about me) from Evanston, IL
... but I loved this album. For those who are not major jazz experts, but are interested in the music, I highly suggest picking this CD up. I believe it's a great intro to this music and you can't beat Miles Davis and this classic album.

On the whole, the music is soothing and mellow. If you want music to relax to, write, read, etc..., this is the CD to get. I would say it's not as experimental as some of John Coltrane's later works, so keep that in mind if you're looking for some really "crazy" jazz pieces.

If you've never bought a jazz album but always wondered where to start, this is it. Get it and you'll find yourself more interested in jazz and other artists. It's a great starting point and just classic, relaxing music, period.

Was this review helpful to you? YES NO

2 of 2 people found the following review helpful:

essential., May 5, 2000
Reviewer: Ravi Desai (see more about me) from Pittsburgh, PA
This is arguably the best jazz recording of all time. It is definitely the most influential. This recording h as it all. great modal jazz featuring great saxophone solos by John Coltrane and Julian "Cannonball" Adderly. Bill Evans , Paul Chambers and Jimmy Cobb comprise the rest of this great sextet. Miles always selected great musicians to play with but this group was the best. This album gave us two future

www.amazon.com

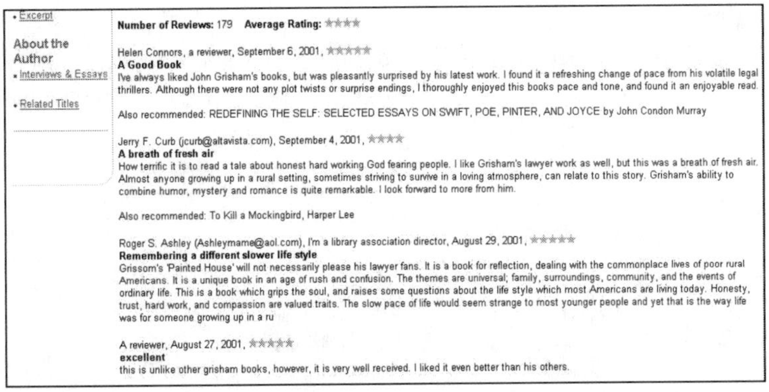

• Excerpt
About the Author
• Interviews & Essays
• Related Titles

Number of Reviews: 179 **Average Rating:**

Helen Connors, a reviewer, September 6, 2001,
A Good Book
I've always liked John Grisham's books, but was pleasantly surprised by his latest work. I found it a refreshing change of pace from his volatile legal thrillers. Although there were not any plot twists or surprise endings, I thoroughly enjoyed this books pace and tone, and found it an enjoyable read.

Also recommended: REDEFINING THE SELF: SELECTED ESSAYS ON SWIFT, POE, PINTER, AND JOYCE by John Condon Murray

Jerry F. Curb (jcurb@altavista.com), September 4, 2001,
A breath of fresh air
How terrific it is to read a tale about honest hard working God fearing people. I like Grisham's lawyer work as well, but this was a breath of fresh air. Almost anyone growing up in a rural setting, sometimes striving to survive in a loving atmosphere, can relate to this story. Grisham's ability to combine humor, mystery and romance is quite remarkable. I look forward to more from him.

Also recommended: To Kill a Mockingbird, Harper Lee

Roger S. Ashley (Ashleymame@aol.com), I'm a library association director, August 29, 2001,
Remembering a different slower life style
Grissom's 'Painted House' will not necessarily please his lawyer fans. It is a book for reflection, dealing with the commonplace lives of poor rural Americans. It is a unique book in an age of rush and confusion. The themes are universal; family, surroundings, community, and the events of ordinary life. This is a book which grips the soul, and raises some questions about the life style which most Americans are living today. Honesty, trust, hard work, and compassion are valued traits. The slow pace of life would seem strange to most younger people and yet that is the way life was for someone growing up in a ru

A reviewer, August 27, 2001,
excellent
this is unlike other grisham books, however, it is very well received. I liked it even better than his others.

www.bn.com

Figure 12.5 (Next two images)

Amazon and Barnes & Noble are primary examples of sites that have employed user-generated content. In both, users have the opportunity to add their own reviews to the site. This adds value to users, many of whom are avid readers who want to know what other avid readers think about a book. Furthermore, this helps to create a community of readers with shared interests in specific books and authors.

From an e-commerce perspective, as we alluded to earlier, user-generated product reviews and ratings satisfy users' needs for independent confirmation. Suppose you wanted some obscure object, like a Tibetan rug. Don't have any friends who have purchased one lately? A visit to the right web site might tell you everything you need to know, ranging from history, to what to look for in a dealer, and on to which dealers to do business with. Returning to the museum metaphor, the fact that eBay comes back with 63 results when you type in "Tibetan rug" or 28 results when you type in "Tibetan tiger rug" is content in and of itself. What antique store could you walk into that has so much inventory—along with a dealer rating—and so much information about each product? And you don't even have to speak to a salesperson!

Think of user-driven content this way: Each person has something unique to say. If you are providing your users with an opportunity to exchange information, they are more likely to perceive your site as offering valuable content. You might offer bulletin or message boards; reviews with easy-to-complete and post forms, along with a standard rating procedure; or even chat rooms. Regardless, users often tell us that it is the opportunity to hear from one another that is most likely to bring them back to a site. Most of the other content they can find in a book, in a magazine, or on TV.

There is an additional benefit to offering user-generated content: As your users build relationships with another, they also build relationships with your site.

Insight

User-generated content offers two primary benefits: a consistently fresh source of information and an established user community within your own site. Users want to know what other users have to say, and they want to network with one another. Your site may be the only vehicle for those purposes.

Are Other Users Always Credible?

Of course, user-generated content is not without its downside.

For instance, here's a question that arises in relation to user-generated content. Am I supposed to take the word of other users, when they may very well have an axe to grind or, in the case of eBay, a product to sell? eBay overcomes this concern by rating sellers. On the other hand, stock sites have not yet resolved this issue, as evidenced by recent stories in which bogus stock tips have been placed on message boards. Who is to say that the same anonymous person (or people) whose judgment you are accepting isn't serving his own interests by a positive (or negative) review? Or, for that matter, how do you know they aren't actually less knowledgeable than you?

Where possible, we advise that you build into a site a means of establishing credibility among users, perhaps through a rating system. Realistically, some monitoring of user-generated content is also recommended, as is the case with stock sites.

Delivering Content
The Power of Letting the User Opt In

Web site sponsors often make the following lament: Users say they love what they see, but they subsequently forget to return to a site in order to discover exactly what's there. Users, too, bemoan this situation. There is a lot of great stuff out there, but they can hardly visit every site every day. If a site is not foremost in the user's mind, chances are he won't even remember it. So, what's the harm in collecting email addresses and sending users a reminder note every one or two days? In a word: spam. Users hate to find their inbox filled with unwanted messages. If you do that to them, they'll hate you, too.

A compromise is possible. Offer email lists that users can opt into. For example, users do not want to hear from a music site every day, but they might be interested in hearing about their favorite musicians. The same goes for health insurance customers who don't care about everything you offer, but might be interested in anything specific to parents or to people with certain medical conditions. A car owner might not care about buying the next model, but he might want to hear about parts for the model he owns now.

The way to get users to come back and give your content another look is to let them tell you what interests *them*. Most sites do this through a subscription form that users complete, generally by clicking on a list of topics. If you have something that is of interest to them, they might even tell you something about themselves, like age, occupation, or special interests. If you give them valuable information, you just might get valuable information about the kinds of users that are most interested in your site. In short, it is better to give *and* to receive!

While this doesn't give you carte blanche to start contacting users for reasons beyond what they have indicated an interest in, it *does* provide you with a way to make sure your content is meeting the needs of the people you should be targeting.

The *New York Times* web site, for example, does a great job of convincing users to specify the type, and amount, of content they want to receive. Some users may want the "Circuits" section, while others are more interested in "The Arts." Amazon also does this by letting users choose to receive email related to specific genres.

Research Tip
Talk with both your current customers and your prospects. What kinds of content do they associate with your brand? Show them what you are planning and find out if they are likewise interested and, if so, whether they want it from you.

The View from 30,000 Feet

Content can add value to your site, but it also has the potential of being perceived as superfluous or even a distraction. If you have an established brand, content needs to be consistent with your brand imagery. If the brand is new, appropriate content can help to establish it.

Users are naturally skeptical about content, so the source should be clearly identified. Wherever possible, adopt quality third-party content for use in your site. This can enhance its credibility as well as provide a means of including in-depth content without burdening your own staff resources. User-generated content, in the form of message boards, articles, and reviews, offers the added benefit of providing users with a community forum.

A Few Hard Questions

- Does the content offer information that your target users will use and appreciate, or is it filler?

- Is the content consistent with your brand image? With the image you want to create?

- Are the author and source of the content clearly identified? How about the date it was created?

- Have you investigated the possibility of including in-depth content from other sources? Links?

- Are you providing a forum for your users to generate their own content?

CHAPTER THIRTEEN

Functionality

Don't Just Lie There, Give Me Some Interaction

Even in today's development environment, many sites offer users very little interactivity. Sites that enable people to see what their favorite car would look like in fire engine red or what their ideal computer would cost with just their desired bells and whistles truly engage users and keep them coming back.

When you're building a site, it is important to brainstorm ways to interact with customers and, in so doing, build rapport and a relationship with them. This can take the form of surveys, downloadable screen savers, coupons, self-tests, questionnaires, contests, configurators, and so on. But you need to keep one thing in mind when you ask users to supply information: Make sure you give them something in return so they know what is in it for them.

People Like to Play Games, Even When They're Not on a Game Site

Let's start with a guiding principle. People like to play games on the computer—even people who never actually play computer games, or board games for that matter. These people would strenuously deny even the slightest interest in computer games, and in reality, they are telling the truth.

Yet, people have an undeniable attraction to games if you define them in the broadest sense: filling out a form or otherwise revealing something about themselves and getting something in return. They get little insights into themselves.

Human beings also love quick answers: "If I do this, that will happen." This is especially true when the answer is personal, somehow tailored to them.

The key word here? Personal.

What does that mean for you? No, it doesn't mean you need the latest version of Tetris on your site, or a self-test revealing one's ideal spouse. What it does mean is that interactivity rocks, especially when it provides your user with some piece of information that is hers alone.

Build that into your site—make it relevant to your brand and your mission—and you have given your site visitors one more reason to stick around, if not to return.

The Dell Configurator
The First Lesson in the Value of Interactive Features

"Can I Get One With My Favorite Bells and Whistles?" Ask the Configurator.

The product configurator is a web site feature that has truly revolutionized shopping. It has created an opportunity for companies to reach out to prospective customers with personal assistance that often isn't available either in retail stores or on the telephone.

The product configurator has made its most profound impact in the personal computer marketplace. Although we have never worked on the Dell site, we would call their configurator the gold standard.

First, let's think about why configurators work so well. As prospective buyers make purchasing decisions, they have to ask questions that are perfectly suited to being addressed through a web site:

- Which of the models is best suited for me?

- Can I get the features I want on that model?

- With those features, what's it going to cost?

Configurators allow users to essentially try a product on for size. In the Dell site, for example, users can go through a whole list of available features, clicking on one drop-down menu after another, until they have their ideal PC set up exactly the way they want it. Then they can see the potential price and go back and make adjustments from there.

Ultimately, each visitor to the Dell site ends up with a PC that is perfectly suited to him, or as close to perfect as possible.

Figure 13.1

The Dell site shows a prime example of a configurator.

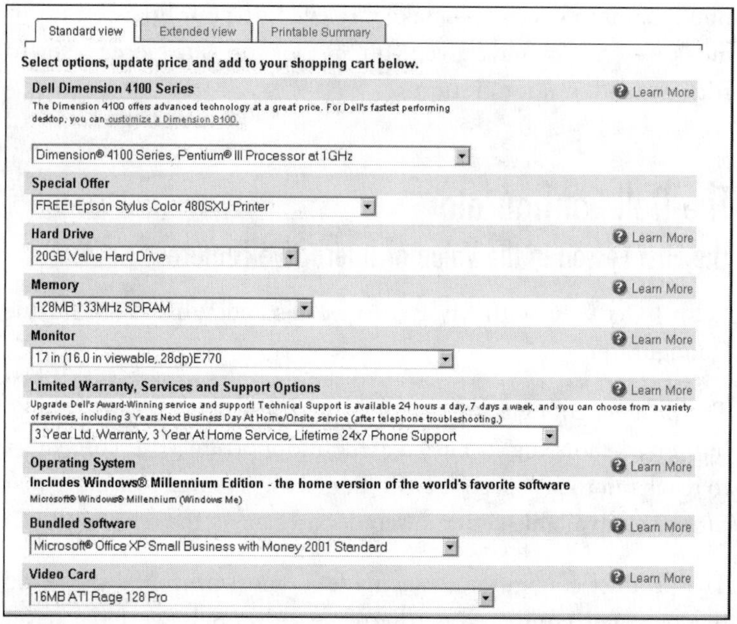

www.dell.com

Clothing sites that provide the user with an opportunity to essentially step into a virtual dressing room and try on an outfit (after choosing a body-type that approximates their own) provide another example of how interactivity can add depth to the web site experience. The Betsy Johnson web site is a good example of how clothing sites have adopted interactivity; you can even view a dress from the back!

What does this mean for you? Configurators and virtual dressing rooms are a major undertaking, and actually might not be feasible or necessary on your site. But their success does speak volumes for the value of interactive features on a site. The Dell configurator is both useful and intriguing to users, and they come back again and again.

Insight

Interactive features provide two key elements of web site "stickiness:" intrigue and personalization.

Self-Tests
Why Do You Think Horoscopes Are So Popular?

Therapists, doctors, and computer experts all get button-holed at parties by other guests who are hoping for some insight and a bit of free advice. Similarly, the daily horoscope in the newspaper or on a web portal is read by both true believers and those who don't live their lives by it but think, "well, you never know." More to the point, mainstream magazines are filled with articles that include small self-scored questionnaires, offering personalized insight into everything from the perfect spouse to the perfect vacation spot.

We're always looking for ways to get insight into ourselves, as well as advice that is somehow specific to who we are and the questions we have—especially from sources that have some credibility.

Self-tests on a web site are another way to attract users. They offer the following benefits:

- They intrigue the user to explore further.
- They save the user time by pointing them to relevant information or products.
- They offer a sense of personalization.

Self-tests can be used simply to offer an element of fun. For example, a site of a sporting goods manufacturer has a self-test for users that helps them choose their ideal sport, based on factors like lifestyle, age, and geographic location. It was developed in conjunction with an authority in this area. Totally reliable? Probably not, as most people who take the test would agree. Yet, it's fun, and it certainly offers another opinion to those who might be seeking the activity they are best suited for.

Self-tests are, by their very nature, personalized, which is a way of further connecting with users. At the most basic level, self-tests help create a relationship between you and your user. The user tells you something about himself, and you give something back in the form of advice or insight. That is what relationships are about.

Figure 13.2

A self-test sample from eDiets.com. Note that asking for the user's email address in the first field has the potential of scaring off users.

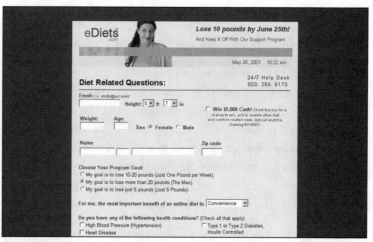

http://www.ediets.com

○ ○ **Insight**
○ A self-test helps you build a relationship by essentially creating a dialogue with the user, in which you share your expertise.

As such, a self-test can also be useful as a tool for encouraging users to register for your site. You might consider offering a self-test that requests that users provide their email address, as well as some personal information such as demographics. Users will accept this trade-off under certain circumstances:

● As long as they understand their information is being collected by the sponsor.

● If they are told how the information is being used.

● And, perhaps most important, they must perceive that they are truly getting back information that justifies their time spent.

Self-Tests Can Also Help You Connect Prospects to Your Products

A self-test could simply end with a score and an insight or two. But a self-test can also end with an invitation to take the next step in becoming your customer. At the end of the test, results might also include suggestions for products to buy on the site. This can be a potential bonus to the user, not to mention the sponsor, as long as further exploration is optional.

Banking and financial services sites often do this. For example, we worked on a banking site that offered users the opportunity to take a self-test that would essentially assess their willingness to take financial risks, as well as whether their goals are long- or short-term. Along with the results, the users were provided with the opportunity to explore funds and other banking products that were in keeping with their level of risk aversion and financial goals.

As long as users felt in control of this experience, that is, the products were not pushed at them but were instead offered through a list of links that could be clicked—or not—users found this useful.

Travel sites have also used this approach. We worked on one that included a self-test in which users could essentially choose among options that described their ideal vacation based on their preferences for factors like night life, adventure, structured versus unstructured activity, beaches, and shopping. Once they completed the self-test, users were presented with a list of suggested vacation locations. They could then explore these locations further and, once in a location, choose to look at vacation packages available through the site or through offline resources.

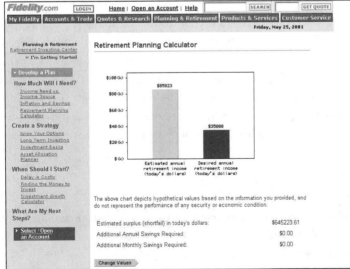

Figure 13.3

In this page from the Fidelity web site, users are shown in graphic form some of the results of their calculations, and they are given options for developing a plan with Fidelity in the left nav bar.

http://www300.fidelity.com/

Interactive Tools
Another Variation of the Self-Test

Interactive tools also engage the user in a web site. The most obvious example is the mortgage calculator you find on many banking sites. Interactive tools are first and foremost fun, especially if they offer something that isn't found on a range of other sites.

Here's an example of a really interesting use of interactive tools:

The MetLife site has an area called "Life Advice," which includes value-added information on a range of practical topics. Included in this area are two interactive calculators—one for figuring out how much paint to buy when you are painting a room, and another that helps you figure out how much wallpaper to use.

How many times have you wished you could have avoided that extra trip to the paint store, not to mention the extra gallon you have stored away somewhere that the store wouldn't take back?

On the MetLife site, interactive tools accomplish a second purpose. They also provide an element of surprise for users that are probably expecting page after page of details on insurance products. Essentially, their traditional brand image is extended through tools like this, made livelier and helpful. Although you wouldn't necessarily go to the MetLife site to make paint decisions, this feature makes sense within the context of home improvement in their "Life Advice" section.

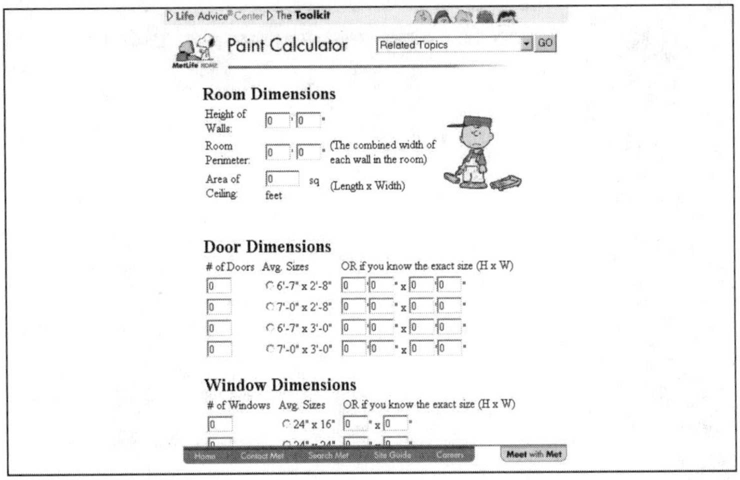

http://www.metlife.com

Figure 13.4

This interactive paint measurement calculator is featured on MetLife.com.

Polls Also Pull Them in, as Long as the Results Are Instant

We all love to know how we compare to other people. Do we think with the mainstream, or are our opinions somehow out-of-step? Pollsters have been exploiting our curiosity for years, so its only natural that web sites have jumped on the same bandwagon. It's a strategy that seems to work: How many times have you taken a poll lately?

Polls are often found on portals and news sites, but they are also effective on brand-oriented sites. We have worked on consumer brand sites, for example, that used polls to great advantage. One was oriented toward teens and provided them the opportunity to register their opinions on a range of topics from dating to the latest heart throb.

We have also seen polls used on more specialized sites. Here, users not only have their natural curiosity piqued, but they are further intrigued by the opportunity to learn how their opinions compare to those of people who already share similar interests or even their profession. As such, polls also reinforce a sense of community.

Association web sites often use polls, as do professional and hobby sites. A site for people seeking information on literary agents,

Figure 13.5

The homepage of
agentresearch.com.

www.agentresearch.com

www.agentresearch.com, is effective at using polls. On the homepage, users are exposed to a poll that tackles an issue site visitors are not only likely to have an opinion on, but also likely to be looking for the consensus of others with similar experience.

One selling point of web-based polls is instant gratification. Users can have the sense of effectively taking the pulse of the community, but only if the results are *instant*. They won't come back in a week or two to get the final results; it's the quick snapshot they want. Polls can become habit-forming. On one hand, it means users may come back often to check out the next poll. On the other hand, the polls need to change frequently or, once users figure out that the polls don't change, your site will look outdated.

Insight

Polls add intrigue and help build a sense of community. For them to be effective, they need to be relevant to your target audience, the results need to be instantaneous, and they need to change often.

Screensavers and Other "Give-Aways" Also Invite Return Visits and Build Your Brand

Who doesn't like something for free? Web users certainly do. Screensavers, while not exactly interactive in and of themselves, are essentially interactive because users pick and choose from a selection and then download it (don't forget to make those downloads totally hassle-free for your user).

A small software download, such as a calendar or other productivity tool, serves the same purpose as a screensaver. Coupons might also fit into the give-away category. For example, once the user completes a self-test, you might offer him a coupon for a discounted purchase within your e-commerce area, or at your retail outlet, or through a partner's site or outlet. To enhance the interactive aspect of coupons, you might allow users to choose from among various options in terms of products or outlets, and you could also ask users to register their coupons (collecting some demographic information, if not an email address, at the same time).

As another alternative, you might consider offering some kind of giveaway as a reward for registering. Giveaways, like other interactive features, keep users on your site for another moment or two. As with any free gift, users will likely remember the giver. Furthermore, giveaways can create further good will for your brand.

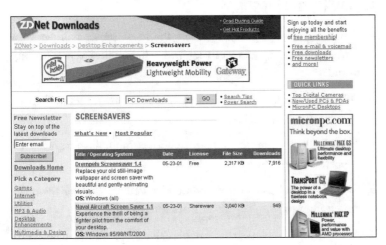

www.zdnet.com

Figure 13.6

ZDNet offers users the option to download screensavers.

If the giveaway is somehow "branded," (for example, with a company logo somewhere in the screensaver), then so much the better.

◔ ◔ Insight
◔ Giveaways are a means of thanking your users for stopping by and visiting your site. As such, they engage users and help create mind share for your brand.

◔ ◔ Research Tip
◔ Show users a range of interactive features that you are considering. Let them tell you which ones are perceived as most unique and intriguing.

The View from 30,000 Feet

Interactive features enhance the user experience. They offer intrigue and entertainment, might impart a useful bit of knowledge, or can reward the user for spending time on your site. Interactive features also build your brand by reinforcing what you are about while also creating a measure of good will.

A Few Hard Questions

- Which interactive features make the most sense, from both a time and money perspective? And what makes sense for my brand?

- Does the interactive feature meet a need of my target audience? In other words, is it relevant?

- Can I build an interactive feature with enough flash to meet the expectations of users?

- Can I keep polls instantly updated as well as rotating them often enough to keep repeat visitors interested?

- Am I using giveaways that are perceived as valuable to my target audience?

CHAPTER FOURTEEN

Whiz! Bang! Boom!

Graphics in Service to Content and Functionality

As much as people want to be entertained and visually stimulated on the web, it is very much a transactional medium. Until the advent of broadband—and perhaps even then—users will not want graphics to get in the way of the path they are travelling. On the other hand, if a graphic helps articulate which choice to make, gives the user a sense of which product to buy, or serves to make navigation more intuitive, that's great.

However, if a graphic has no apparent purpose or meaning, or worse yet, if it looks appealing and is not clickable, users will have very little tolerance for the time it takes to load or the space it takes up on the page. This chapter looks at how users evaluate and assimilate graphics and the relationship of graphics to content and functionality.

The First Rule: The Web Is a Visual Medium
Users Want Some Color

A few chapters back, we talked about the homepage and what works and doesn't work in terms of "sexy" colors and graphics. Basically, we said that users expect to see some color and personality on the homepage, but they don't want to sit through a three-minute download. Moreover, they don't want to be driven to distraction by dancing bears and strobe lights. In a later chapter, we also discussed the problems associated with requiring plug-ins like Flash, which users may neither understand nor feel comfortable downloading.

Having said all that, now let's focus on graphics (whether or not they move around or are colorful) in relation to what happens on the site beyond the homepage.

The basic rule? If there is one at all, it is that users expect graphics and color throughout the site. Beyond that, many factors determine what is right for each site.

Users Expect Consistent Use of Graphics and Color Throughout the Site

Before we move past the homepage, keep in mind that users have high expectations for it in terms of design and organization. We have worked with clients who understood that but also assumed that users were relatively forgiving once they got into the site. Unfortunately, we have not found this to be true. Thus, although the other pages in a web site may not be as flashy as the homepage, web sites are quickly criticized when these things are true:

- Homepage design elements and color are not reflected at some level in the inside pages.

- Not only do the inside pages not reflect the design elements of the homepage, but they reflect different elements and even different colors.

Users orient themselves to your site from what they see on the homepage. That obviously includes labeling and navigation paths, but it also includes design and color. When images and color schemes change drastically, users often assume that your site is in different stages of development, or that the departments in your organization are not talking to one another.

We have worked with companies that have recruiting sections within their sites. A professional services firm, for example, was concerned about appearing up-to-date to the recent graduates they wanted to attract. To help get beyond what they feared was a staid image, they considered a hip design, with flashy colors and photos of twenty-somethings involved in outdoor activities to appeal to that group. The recruiting area of the site would, as a result, not feature the conservative, tasteful colors used in the rest of the site.

Rather than serving to update the company, user experience testing revealed that their prospective employees were instead "jarred" by the sudden change in tone of the recruiting site. Furthermore, they said they feared that the recruiting department was out of step with the rest of the company. Finally, they said they were exploring professional services because they wanted to work in a conservative Blue Chip environment.

So much for switching art direction gears in recruiting.

As changes in graphic elements and color have a negative effect on the user experience, so does the other extreme, which is to ignore the need for graphics within the site. We have seen sites that did not reflect the homepage design, but also did not seem to have been art-directed at all. Instead, they incorporated a variety of hyperlinks, lists, and columns of text. This is most often the case on sites that were developed with a limited budget. One e-commerce site, for example, had a graphically interesting homepage but absolutely no graphic elements beyond it. The developers were hoping to get users excited about shopping and then, after making some money, redesign the internal pages to make them more attractive. Users weren't buying.

If your budget for art direction is going to be consumed by the homepage, rethink your strategy and try to spread it out over the entire site.

○ ○ Insight

○ Graphic elements—images, style, and color—need to be used consistently throughout a site. For example, consider the following tips:

- If you're using Greek columns, airplanes, or igloos on your homepage, users expect to see that theme reflected on other pages.

- Style should also be consistent throughout: black and white photography, abstract images, or illustrations, for example.

- Users expect your basic color scheme, primary colors, and so on to be carried throughout the site.

Your brand also plays a role here. Graphics and color are an integral aspect of your brand, whether you are already established or are en route to being established. When the graphics change drastically from what is normally associated with your brand, users get confused.

Users Don't Want to be Delayed by Graphics

As we have said repeatedly—and say repeatedly to our clients—users do not want to be delayed by heavy graphics. They might not wait for your graphics to download. Although we have used this warning the most in relation to the homepage, it also applies to the rest of your site.

We worked with a financial site that featured an animated graphic on the homepage. It was a cartoon character that moved around while introducing users to the site. It was cute the first time, but users got tired of being delayed by it. In addition, there were eight major sections within the site, and each of those sections was introduced by a similar cartoon character who also gave a brief speech, introducing the user to that specific section of the site.

On one hand, the characters complemented one another because they were consistent in terms of their design. On the other hand,

www.ew.com

Figure 14.1

Articles on
Entertainment Weekly's
homepage have tiny
headshots for illustra-
tion. They download
quickly, and they get
the point across—
appropriate to an enter-
tainment site.

they were also consistently annoying. They increased the download time and added further delays (as the user fumbled around
looking for where to click to turn them off).

We recommended that the graphic be made smaller to hasten the
download. We also recommended to our client that they lose the
sound or at least include a cookie so that users only heard it the
first time they clicked on that section.

Insight

Users can back out of a site a few pages into it just as easily as they
can back out at the beginning. Use graphics efficiently. In other words,
keep them small, static, and quiet. After the page is downloaded, the
user can opt in for further Flash and sound.

A Guiding Principle: If It's Not Needed, Get Rid of It

There are no magic formulas for creating the optimal web site. As we have often said, brand, target audience, and purpose all come into play. Each site is an entity unto itself, and it should be, in spite of the conventions that have emerged in site development.

You are probably thinking, "Great. Where does that leave me now? I've got a whole team of art directors who want to show their hands in the site. But didn't you already say that users don't want to be over-stimulated or bored out of their gourds?"

The answer is yes and no. Users don't want to be bored, but too much is simply too much. So an important question is this: When do you know it's time to pull back on graphics?

Actually, the answer to that is simple. Use a "litmus" test for each graphic element on your homepage, asking yourself this: "Do I really need it?" Let's break that down into smaller questions:

- Does it highlight a feature on the page so that it is brought to the user's attention? (However, you don't want it to highlight all the features so that the user doesn't know what's important.)

- Does it make a feature more useable, for example, illustrating how to use a specific function?

- If associated with content, does the graphic enhance the user's understanding, similar to the way photos are used with articles?

- Does it reinforce the brand—again, without overpowering the actual features on the page?

These are questions you can answer, at least as a first cut. Ultimately, they are questions your users need to answer for you.

Here is an example that illustrates why it is so important to answer these questions as you develop your site.

E-commerce sites are easy to pick on. Especially the pure play sites that have had to create their own brand identity along with their market. But here is another example that illustrates the use of graphics.

A site that featured a wide array of gifts wanted to create an aura of opulence. One version of the homepage was heavily designed with Greek columns (we weren't kidding when we referenced Greek columns earlier in this chapter) and other Classic imagery, along with dark, rich colors. Wouldn't this rich imagery transport users to another world and really put them in the mood to spend money?

As you might guess, the other pages in the site had the same design—lots of Greek columns, ships on the Aegean sea, ornate gilding everywhere. Product descriptions and other options were buried in the clutter. Product photos clashed with the dark backgrounds.

Users wanted to swim to the surface and take a deep breath.

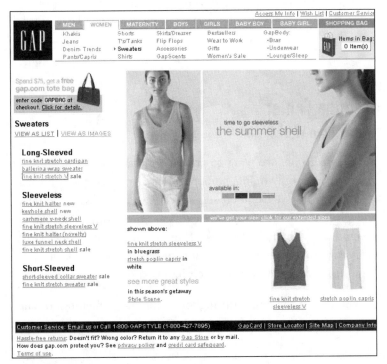

www.gap.com

Figure 14.2

Gap's main Sweater page features only one sweater, with a list of links to other sweaters. Users who want to see thumbnails of all sweaters at once can click the "View as Images" button.

The developers of this site took a deep breath and asked their users to help them figure out what graphics were really needed in the site. In user experience testing, people suggested that clean lines and lots of white space felt classy and sophisticated. More importantly, they were there to buy a gift and get on with their lives, not descend into the lost continent of Atlantis. They didn't need to be put in the mood to shop; that's what brought them to the site in the first place.

The solution: Go back to the basics. What are you trying to accomplish? If you don't have an answer to that question—for each graphic element on a page—then cut your losses...and the graphic.

Insight

Graphics can get in the way of, rather than enhance, the user experience. Each page in your site needs to be focused on what users can learn and do on that page. Graphics need to support content and functionality, to highlight it and increase usability. If graphics are not doing this, they are probably obscuring your content and functionality instead.

Lose the Clutter
White Space Works

Before we go on, we want to emphasize a guiding principle that holds true not only on the homepage but also throughout the site: Users like white space. It creates a feeling of openness and control and gives them breathing room to look around and familiarize themselves with their options. They are less likely to feel that everything on the page is competing for their attention like a roomful of first-graders all raising their hands at once.

As you design the pages throughout your site, remember the importance of white space.

Another Big Question: Is This Little Picture Actually FOR Anything?

Let's talk about another aspect of graphics. Users like to click on them. They don't always scroll over a graphic first to see if their cursor turns into an arrow. They simply assume that if it's there, it must work like an icon. Even if the graphic has a label next to it that is clearly hyperlinked, they still want to click on the graphic.

More often than not, we face the question of "to click or not to click" with the sites we work with, and we generally recommend that all the graphics be clickable. Why? Because users can become so determined to click on a graphic that even when nothing comes of their efforts, they have been known to click a graphic over and over. Frequently, not only do they not intuit that there is nothing to click, they also assume that something must be broken. Yes, even if the label next to it gets the user to the next step, the graphic should still be clickable, despite its redundancy.

However, you can also use clickable graphics to your advantage.

We worked with a photography site that had a large, visually intriguing graphic—an abstract photograph—on its homepage that did not add appreciably to the download time. It was simply there to enhance the attractiveness of the page; it *is* a photography site after all.

This design element was carried throughout the site. The opening pages to other areas of the site also included interesting abstract photographs, though not as large.

During testing, users repeatedly tried to click on these photos, both on the homepage and on subsequent pages, even though all were organized with adequate white space and clearly labeled, clickable icons. Still, users invariably clicked on the graphic first. Why?

We asked them what and where they expected the click to take them. Some wanted to know the name of the photographer. Others wanted to know exactly what object had been photographed (again, the images were abstract). Still others wanted to know how they could create a photo like that. Furthermore, the question

Figure 14.3

These decorative arrow images look like icons, causing confusion. Nothing happens when you click them.

www.time.com

arose as to whether the photo had been taken with the sponsoring company's photography products, and if so, with which ones?

Our client viewed these questions as an opportunity—and did indeed make the photo clickable. After clicking it, the user was presented with the background of the photo, answering all the questions he might have about it. He was also presented with a link to information about the specific products used to take the photo, as well as tips on how to take a similar kind of photo. Over time, users were informed of a contest, for which their own photographs might be featured on the site.

Consequently, a clickable graphic became a doorway to both value-added as well as product information, depending on where the user's curiosity led him.

Insight

Users do not make a distinction between graphic elements and icons. If it's on the page, it must be clickable. Give them that capability. Clickable graphics can provide an opportunity to provide the following:

- Additional background on the company or the site
- Value-added information
- The beginning of a product path that can lead to an e-commerce transaction

A Final Caution: Are You Sure the User Is in Control of the Experience?

In this, as well as previous chapters, we have emphasized the importance of allowing the user to remain in control of the web site experience. To reiterate that point within this context, users want to click on anything that catches their attention, including graphics. And, as we said, a clickable graphic can be an opportunity for you to provide value-added information or an e-commerce option. However, "opportunity" is certainly the operable word here.

Clicking on a graphic should lead to either a pop-up window or a separate page, where the additional content is presented in a succinct manner. Don't forget that the user may be in exploratory mode or may be quite intent on moving to the next step of whatever he is doing. If exploring, the user will want the option of going deeper or moving in another direction. Don't divert him, such as by throwing him into a product information path, unless he first has the option of indicating his interest in going that way. If the user is more directed at that moment, he might have clicked on the graphic by mistake. He definitely does not want to be diverted without opting in.

Insight

Sometimes users click on a graphic for the wrong reason, or for no reason at all, or something in between. In any event, don't bury them with content or, worse yet, divert them in another direction. For example, if you're giving them further background information, such as the source of the graphic, keep it brief. If you're offering more value-added content or product information, definitely allow them the option of exploring further or simply returning to where they were.

Research Tip

Research is an invaluable tool to use when making development decisions about graphic elements. Even before the site is operational, users can provide input on the kinds of imagery they associate with your brand and/or market. Users can also evaluate potential graphical themes and colors as design decisions are being made. As the site becomes operational, at least in prototype stage, users can also provide their reactions to specific graphical elements as well as their expectations of the role and purpose of graphics.

It is a matter of soliciting their expectations and reactions.

The View from 30,000 Feet

Graphics certainly make web sites more attractive and intriguing, and after all, the web is a visual medium. However, the web is about getting things done, and graphics that get in the way of this process quickly detract from the value of the site. Ultimately, graphics are judged by how well they contribute in a supporting role, in service to content and functionality. Furthermore, graphic elements need to be consistent with brand identity.

A Few Hard Questions

- First and foremost, what is the purpose of each graphic? Does it support content or functionality on the page?

- Is there a consistency among the graphics throughout the site in terms of color and style?

- Are graphics consistent with the brand image?

- Is each graphic as efficient as possible, without interfering with the download time?

- Are graphics clickable? And do they lead to pop-ups or separate pages that offer users the option of exploring further?

CHAPTER FIFTEEN

Search

When to Keep Them in Your Playpen and When to Open Them Up to the Universe

The Search function is one of the most important aspects of your site. It is also one of most the problematic elements of web site design for a number of reasons:

- Most search engines are unforgiving of errors in spelling, grammar, and so on.

- Most search engines do not make it clear what the frame of reference is that is being searched, for example, the site, a subsection of the site, or the entire web. Therefore, users are often disappointed by the results.

- Advanced search capabilities often are far more complex than users want them to be, and people often feel like they need a Ph.D. to use them effectively.

This chapter discusses these and other challenges you'll face when developing an effective Search function. In addition, it tackles the issue of when to keep users searching within your domain and when to take them outside of it.

Don't Assume Search and Browse Are Mutually Exclusive

Let's start with a truth about our fellow human beings. People are basically good. But they can be a bit lazy. Okay, maybe they are simply in a hurry most of the time. Now, what does this imply for search functionality within web sites?

We find that most people would rather look at a list of links, beginning with categories on the homepage, and click on the one that sounds closest to what they are looking for (or that interests them). Ideally, they would then be magically spirited to whatever they wanted and wherever they wanted to be. By "magically," we mean that the links you provide for your users would include the exact items they are looking for, based on the appearance that your site has the ability to "read minds." In the absence of such an unlikely gift, users will click on a homepage category, maybe burrow down a page or two to a list of subcategories, and then, within another click or two, arrive at the page or area they want to explore.

That's what most people do on the web, at least historically. However, we are noticing a few new emerging truths that relate to the use of search. These are covered in detail in the following subsections.

Search Engine Jocks

Some, but not all, web-savvy users have become search engine jocks. These users are distinguished by the fact that they go directly to the search engine, secure in the confidence that they know how to use keywords and can probably get what they want faster than you could ever possibly get them there using the links you have provided.

Browsers

Many browsers will explore the site by going from one link to another, backtracking, skipping around, maybe ending up with what they came to your site for, or simply getting a feel for what you offer. Others will browse by using your search engine, typing in a keyword (maybe a very broad one), and seeing where that takes them. Gradually, they will refine their search from there.

Browser/Searcher Combos

These users may begin with a list of links and, a couple of pages into the site, decide that they want to narrow down their search by using a search engine. They might want to search within the category they have arrived at through the links (for example, "New York"), but not want to use keywords to search further (for example, "restaurants" in New York).

Or maybe the user selects "Lawn and Garden" from among the choices in a drop-down menu, is transported to that area of the site, and then decides to look for lawn furniture. The user locates the search box on that page and types in "Furniture," expecting this to narrow the search. However, the results might include all kinds of furniture, including armoires, which one would never put out on the front lawn (unless it was for sale).

As you can see, after a point, it all starts to get really complicated.

The Only Consistency Is Inconsistency

The ultimate challenge: Users are inconsistent. The same user might approach one particular site as a search engine jock but approach another as a browser. And the same user might change his approach, on the same site, from one day to the next.

Insight

Users are not at your site to flex their information-gathering muscles. They want to find information easily, but they all have different ideas of exactly what that means. Let's simply say they want to do it their own way—whatever that is. As much as possible, your site needs to be able to accommodate as many approaches—and combinations of approaches—as possible.

Lose the Boolean Logic
Nobody But Statisticians Cares About Probability

During the heyday of mainframe computing, say, the early- to mid-1980s, corporations were enamored of the ability to create large databases, which employees could then search and from which they could create elegant reports (elegant for that time, meaning rows and columns) through the use of fourth generation languages. These languages were based on something called Boolean logic, which basically means developing a string of search criteria by connecting keywords with qualifiers like "and," "not," and "or." Basically, you had to have taken advanced logic in college (or at least a few statistics courses) to use this effectively, although it was certainly easier than FORTRAN or even BASIC.

We've come a long way since then, haven't we? On the other hand, maybe not.

Their anachronism notwithstanding, we continue to encounter search engines on web sites that require the use of this same logic. For example, a business-to-business site in financial services provides the user with a separate search page that he can reach only after he clicks on "Search" from the homepage. The user is thus obliged to begin the search process with an additional click.

On this search page is a typical search field and, in fine print underneath, is a set of instructions that basically provides the user with a crash course in Boolean logic. The user is told to use "and" and "or," for example, as well as to use quotation marks around words that belong together.

Keep in mind that this is the basic search, not an advanced search or even a special search for those who are still attached to Boolean logic. Couldn't the user simply enter a string of keywords and then get back results that show various directions that, based on combinations of those keywords, provide a range of options for further refining the search? After all, rumor has it that computer programs actually operate behind the scenes.

Back to our initial premise: Users are in a hurry. They don't have time for Boolean logic, even if they do know how to use it. Instead they want a field where they can dump words that will at least get them started in the right direction.

Insight

- Users often want to begin searching from the homepage. Provide them with a clearly labeled open field to begin this process. (They will also want to search from subsequent pages and will expect a search field on these pages as well.)

- Users do not want to learn Boolean logic to search your site. If it's provided at all, Boolean logic should be an option beyond a standard open field search.

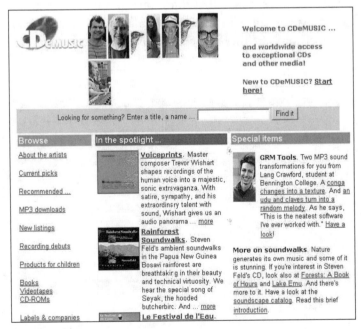

Figure 15.1

The CDeMUSIC site has an ideal way for users to get started searching. The Search option is clearly labeled, and it has a wide open field.

www.cdemusic.org

Spelling
Don't Be So Picky—This Isn't English Class

Few things are more frustrating, at least in web site usage, than being 100% certain that a page, area, or virtual object exists, and then to search for it with confidence in your assumption, only to be told by the site that it "doesn't exist" or that your search "failed." Yet, you know that it exists, not only in the world but also within that web site. Maybe you've even encountered it before, but you forgot to bookmark it the first time around.

Here's an example: Suppose you are interested in finding the newest CD from Jane Olivor. You go to the Amazon site and type "Jane Oliver" in the search box. You know who you mean, but you forgot about that "o" rather than "e" in Olivor. Low and behold, you are told that your search has failed. How could it fail? After all, she has recorded numerous albums. Well, if you didn't think to try an alternate spelling, you might assume that maybe Jane has been a figment of your imagination all these years. Or, you might assume that Amazon simply did not carry her music.

Remember that earlier comment about users being in a hurry? Unless they are in an especially calm frame of mind, users are not likely to experiment with spelling when a search fails. Of those who do, chances are they will choose an alternate spelling that is

Figure 15.2

The results from an Amazon search for "Jane Oliver," in which her last name, Olivor, was misspelled.

www.amazon.com

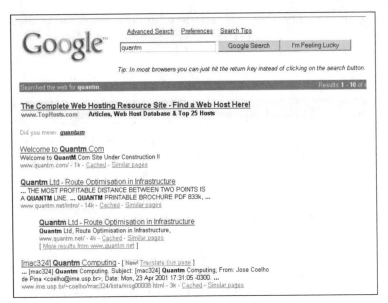

www.google.com

Figure 15.3

Notice that in this
Google search, the user
is given a chance to
correct a spelling error.

similarly mistaken and come up empty handed yet again. In all
likelihood, however, users will assume that what they want simply
does not exist on your site.

We have seen this phenomenon in a range of situations. Tennessee
with a missing "n" or "s." Or Tennessee referred to as "Tenn" or
"TN." Any of these slight variations can lead to a dead-end search
as well as to frustrated users who, in their mounting eagerness to
track down their quarry, move rapidly to locate sites that are somewhat more forgiving of their lexical impediment.

The moral of this story is obvious: To the extent that it is possible,
create a search engine in your site that accommodates alternate
spellings of words, as well as terms and product names. You may
never get it perfect, but users will appreciate if a missed letter here
or an incorrect letter there does not result in messages that inform
them, time and again, that their search has failed.

Some sites have a layer of "forgiveness" built into their search engine, which includes sub-fields with various instructions, such as
"includes these words" or "starts with." This allows the user to
search without having to know beforehand the exact spelling or

the complete phrase. The Zagat restaurant site, for example, uses "begins with" and "contains" in its detailed search option.

Insight

Your search engine should be as forgiving as possible. Alternate spellings need to include misspellings, and incorrect or alternate abbreviations need to be accounted for. And remember that in the world of the web, proper grammar is pushed aside in favor of speed.

You Say Tomato, I Say...

There are a lot of different ways of saying the same thing, depending on factors such as region of the country, frame of reference, age, and simply who you've been talking to. What does that mean for the search capabilities on your site? It means your users might surprise you with the words they throw into their search.

Let's start with your product names. Suppose you have one widget you call the Widget Lite, and another one called the Widget 400e. A visitor to your site who doesn't know exact names and spellings may simply enter Widget and get back a list of all your Widget products (we'll talk about that more later in the chapter). Or a user might enter Widget Light, or Widget 400 instead of 400e, or 400 with a space before the "e."

Users can also use different words to mean the same thing. A sofa can also be a couch, if not a loveseat, and back in the '70s, a "pit group." A personal computer can also be a PC (if not a pc), as well as a desktop, laptop, or handheld. PDAs can be referred to as handheld devices if not by established brand names like Palm.

We have also seen this issue arise at the international level. For example, the recruitment section of a large consulting firm's web site was developed by a team in the U.S. Users in the United Kingdom went to the site in search of positions like "managing director," which are not often used in the U.S. Consequently, British users assumed that these positions did not exist, rather than searching for an equivalent term like "executive director" or "executive vice president."

Don't forget that users will not have the same background as your development and marketing staff. They may come up with terminology you haven't even heard of but that is equally appropriate.

Insight

Effective search engines can handle multiple variations of product names (even if they're incorrect) as well as alternate terminology.

Was That "Lemon" Candy, Candles, or Body Lotion?
Understand How Your Users Want to Search

You gotta love individual differences. That's what makes humans interesting. Who knew that we would all have such unique perspectives on how to gather information? For those of us trying to build web sites (and especially search functionality), those unique perspectives can begin to drive us up the wall. Can't we all think alike?

So far in this chapter, we have talked about how we differ in things like spelling, terminology, and abbreviations. Now the mud starts to get deeper. Purpose comes into play. What do we want to do with the information we are searching for? The following paragraphs outline an example:

Let's say you have built a site that includes a wide array of cosmetics and personal bath products. One site visitor simply has a thing about lemon. It doesn't matter what form it's in. Lemon candy. Lemon candles. Lemon body lotion. Lemon soap. Lemon perfume, if you happen to have any on hand. This one is going to search for lemon and wants anything you have. Another user is looking for candles. Preferably citrus. Lemon preferred. Lemon candles. Don't tell this user about lemon body lotion unless you can stick a wick in it and burn it for hours. But a citrus candle (or orange or even pineapple, if that exists) might work.

We find that most of our clients haven't thought through all the permutations or products, services, and content their site visitors might come up with. And users, with their limited patience, quickly get frustrated. Especially when the word "lemon" leads to a long list of everything imaginable that has the aroma or flavor of lemon. "Candle" includes results of peppermint, vanilla, and bayberry, yet the combination of the two words yields an error message.

It's even more frustrating when the search doesn't work and the user is not told why, beyond being advised to refine his criteria and try again. Refine it how? What keywords?

The search engine called Dogpile is a good model here. If the user types "Lemon," the results begin with a question that essentially asks the user what they mean: Lemon law? Lemon pie? Lemon grass?

Insight

When searches fail, error messages that simply restate the obvious (such as "Search Failed" or "0 results found"), serve only to add to the user's frustration. The user already knows the search failed. What advice do you have regarding the next step?

How do you handle this in your site? The first answer is to provide an open field that can handle multiple keywords.

Figure 15.4

The romanzagifts web site offers two options for a search for "incense sage." One is for "incense sticks/ cedar & sage" and the other is from "incense sticks/tumbleweed."

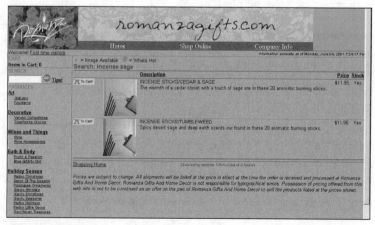

www.romanzagifts.com

Insight
Your search needs to take into account that users have their own ways of categorizing what they are looking for. Consequently, it needs to be flexible to handle keywords and combinations of keywords.

And if that first search doesn't work, if it yields everything but the kitchen sink, or if it could be refined just a bit more, users need to be provided with an alternative. We will get to that next.

Advanced Search
Your Last Resort...

Advanced search can be a fantastic option. It can help users zero in more quickly on what they are looking for, while also subtly educating them on what your site contains. They may come to your advanced search page, for example, and see categories of products, services, or content they had never associated with your site.

Still, here are a couple of common mistakes we see in how advanced search factors are presented to users.

First, all too often, we see a large open field, labeled with the word "Search" on the homepage. To this extent, there is no problem, because this is precisely what users expect. Underneath the word "Search," however (or buried somewhere under the open field), is an additional link called "Advanced Search." In testing, we generally find that users don't even notice the "Advanced Search" link. It's often too small. And if they are searching for the first time, they don't even know if they need an "Advanced Search" or whether a regular search will do.

To complicate matters, after users have embarked upon a search, even if it fails, they might not have spotted the "Advanced Search." If this happens, you might as well not have bothered creating one in the first place. What we have also found is that users don't see the purpose of "advanced" searching until they have done a "beginning" search. They don't intuitively perceive it as an alternate to the open field search.

We worked with a large computer manufacturer that followed this pattern. They offered a large open field with a nice big "Search" label and a little tiny "Advanced Search" link. The search function was located in the banner and essentially followed the user throughout the site.

The standard search was good (it allowed multiple keywords), but it still had limits. A couple of broad keywords could get users a long list to scroll through. Too many keywords got them nothing. Yet the advanced search option—which was well-designed, with drop-downs for hardware, software, even price-range—never got used. In fact, the link was often ignored, even though it was always on the page.

A few chapters back we talked about how users don't need information until they need it. This is also true for advanced search. They don't need it until the standard search engine fails to get them exactly what they wanted.

To illustrate this point, here's what we recommended to our client:

- Lose the Advanced Search link that was half-hidden under the Search field.

- Let users begin the search by using the open field.

- When the search results are displayed, also offer the user the option of further refining the search, whether or not the initial search actually yielded results.

With this approach, the advanced search becomes added assistance that the site offers users, either to refine a search that may have yielded too many results, or to help the user when a search has failed. Users remain in control because they began the search the way they wanted to, and they can accept the advanced search if they choose.

Insight
Users don't need an advanced search until they actually need it. Offer it as an option, but only after they have made the initial attempt.

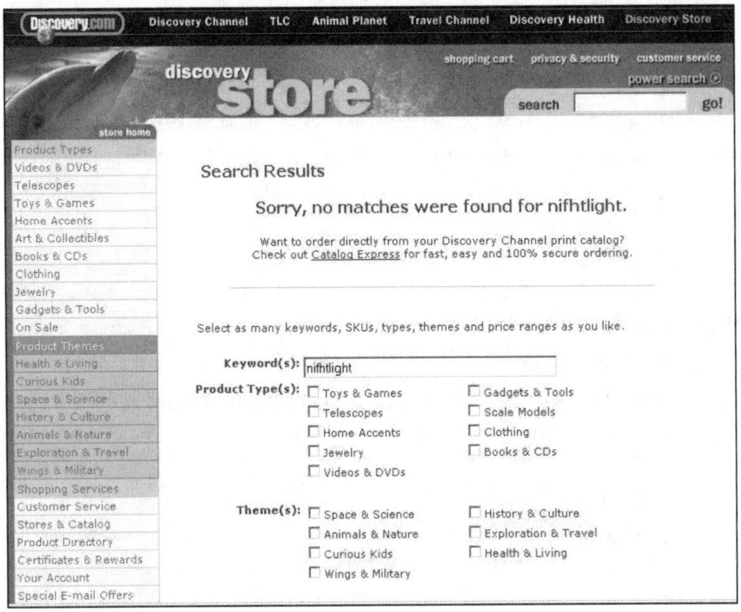

www.discovery.com

Figure 15.5

After searching for a misspelled word, the search feature in the Discovery site offers users further assistance through what is essentially a more advanced search.

Beware Multiple Fields
Relationships Are Assumed Where They May Not Exist

We've all been there. You're on the site of a major retailer, looking for a lawn mower that you can pick up locally and that won't cost you an arm and a leg. In the open field, you type "lawn mower" and your ZIP code. The search fails, but you're not too surprised. And the site provides you with an advanced search page that includes a few drop-down lists. So far, so good.

One of the drop-down menus lists major product categories, including "lawn and garden." The other is a list of state abbreviations. Not perfect, but worth a try. You click on "lawn and garden" in the first drop-down list and click on the abbreviation for your state in the other. There is a "Go" button next to each drop-down list. You click the one next to "lawn and garden."

The result is a listing of the products available within the lawn and garden category. Yes, it does indeed include lawn mowers. On the other hand, the state you live in has been ignored. Maybe you go back a page. This time you click on the "Go" next to your state.

Sure enough, you get back a list of all the retail outlets in your state. But there's no mention of lawn and garden.

Yes, you guessed it, as would your users. A relationship was assumed. After all, it is an advanced search. But there was no relationship.

Let's take another look at the example we used earlier on, the one about the lemon candles. We have seen advanced search functions that included drop-down lists for categories like "scent" and "product." If a user clicks on "lemon" and then "candle," be assured that she assumes she is going to get a listing of lemon candles, and not simply a long list of lemons.

In short, users expect multiple search fields to be related to one another. It is as simple as that.

Very few things are more frustrating than a search page that appears well laid out, with fields that seem logically connected, but that turns out not to be. This is especially true when a single keyword would have been no more effective, but at least it wouldn't have compounded your frustration by promising a means of zeroing in quickly.

We also see sites that offer multiple search boxes but only one "Go" button. The site assumes that the user will choose only one of the drop-down lists, rather than try to use them in combination. In contrast, the user assumes that they work in conjunction and clicks "Go" as well. The result is a close (but not close enough) approximation.

This same expectation will hold true when a user is offered an advanced search. Here's an example. A user is on the web site of a newspaper, searching for articles on the Civil War. The user types "Civil War" into the open field. The results include articles about "Civil Rights," "Civil Ceremony," and "Civil War." The page also includes an open search field. The user assumes that the search can be further refined.

If "Civil War" resulted in all these different "Civils," then typing "War" into the open search field should be a way to go a level deeper. Right?

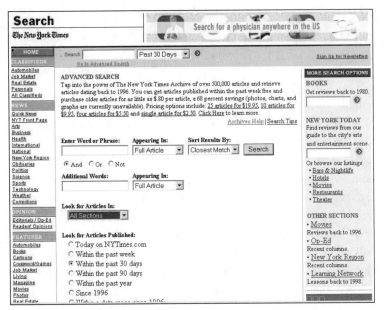

Figure 15.6

The advanced search page in *The New York Times* web site includes multiple search fields and drop-down lists, all clearly related to one another.

www.nytimes.com

This time, the search results include "War Room," "World War I," World War II," and so on. Yet again, it's time to start over. That's not fun when you expected to be advanced to the next step already.

Insight

Users expect multiple fields to work in conjunction. That's the best case option, but it's not always the case. If they don't, the labeling should clearly identify the limitations.

Inside the Playpen or the Whole Web?

Just when you thought you knew every possible complication that might occur with your search functionality, another one zooms into focus. Users are going to have different expectations about whether your search is covering:

● The whole World Wide Web

● Your entire web site

● A specific area within your web site

Earlier on, we discussed the web site for an encyclopedia company. In this site, users were being provided with links to a wide range of information, as well as links to other web sites. All they had to do was type a keyword or two into an open field labeled "Search."

Sounds simple enough. But it wasn't. The Search reminded users of what they might see on a standard search engine or portal site like Yahoo or Excite!, but it asked if they would be searching the entire web. Some thought this would be great because of the sheer number of sites they would see in the results. Others were concerned about—you guessed it—the vast number of sites they would see in the results. After all, weren't they coming to the site of an encyclopedia to limit the number of links they would see? Still others were concerned that the site might limit the sites they had access to unless the Search did indeed include the web. Parents wanted this "selectivity" for their children. Twenty-somethings called it censorship.

In the meantime, what all users agreed on was that they wanted to know exactly what the site's search would be searching. In turn, we recommended that the site offer two search options: one to include only information and web sites that had been evaluated by the encyclopedia company, and the other to include the entire web. Parents then had the option of restricting children's access to this search.

We also ran into this issue on the site of a large manufacturing company. A few layers into the site, users found themselves within an area of the site dedicated to a division of the company. This division manufactured a certain line of computer hardware. There was a whole lot of information within this area of the site, and when users searched it, they wanted to be assured that they would not be searching within the entire company (let alone outside of it).

Again, when the search was simply labeled "Search," users were afraid to use it. We recommended that it be clearly labeled in such a way that the user would know exactly what was being searched before using it.

Figure 15.7

In the cnet site, users can cast their searching net as wide as they want.

www.cnet.com

Insight

When users search your site, they want to search only within your site. When they search within a specific area of your site, they want to know whether they will be searching that area only or your whole site. Preferably, users should be provided with both options, clearly labeled.

Search Results
How Much Is Too Much?

In case you haven't guessed by now, users love to complain about search functionality. Admittedly, they are hard to please. Furthermore, these complaints do not stop at the moment when your site returns the information they have been searching for. Often, they don't like the way in which that information is served up either.

What they complain about most are search results that basically consist of lists of titles of articles, or links, that require a lot of scrolling. This can be overwhelming, not to mention hard on the eyes. If the print is small and the titles are close together (so close that the user can't be sure which one she is clicking on), a bad situation is made even worse. And if these titles or links are nothing more than links, with no explanation as to their presence or purpose, users also complain that they are forced to click on each one and wait for the next page to download, only to find it wasn't what they wanted. With link after link, this can be a very long process.

Many of our clients provide a brief summary along with each link. This can be useful because the user gets a chance to understand what the article or link is about before clicking on it. On the other hand, here is what happens with the summaries:

- Some of them are overly long and rambling, while others are too short to offer useful information (or they simply repeat the first few words of the article).

- The summary can sound like a sales pitch rather than describing content.

Summaries are useful, and almost anything is better than nothing—almost. However, if upon close examination, the summary is no better than not having a summary, it simply adds to the annoyance factor.

Figure 15.8

The search engine for *The Atlantic Monthly* site provides results with a brief description of each article. Notice that each description is roughly the same length and format.

www.theatlantic.com

Insight
Here are a couple of guidelines for what to provide in the results of a search:

- The results should include no more than approximately 10 links per page.

- Type should be large enough for the user to read comfortably so he knows exactly what he is clicking on.

- Each link should be accompanied by a succinct, yet informative, summary that gives the user a good idea what she is getting before she clicks.

The View from 30,000 Feet

Users love to use search engines—either at the beginning of or sometime during the process of finding what they want from your site. They are expecting your search to work like the best of the search engine/portal sites. That's the standard, and an admittedly high one. What is most important is that your search be clearly labeled as to what it searches, for example, your whole site or an area within the site. Expectations for keywords need to be clearly defined, such as whether one or more keywords can be used. Multiple search fields on the same page also need to be clearly labeled so that users know whether or not they can combine them. Basically, if users can't search your site, they will assume that what they are looking for simply isn't there, or that your site isn't quite ready for prime time. Either way, this can have implications for how your brand is perceived.

A Few Hard Questions

- Is it clear to users whether your search includes only your site, an area in your site, or the whole web?

- Is your search logic flexible enough to accommodate a range of approaches?

- Can a user search your site without prior knowledge of probability theory and Boolean logic?

- Is your search forgiving of an occasional misspelling?

- Is advanced search offered to users after they complete their first search attempt, or is it an alternative that may be ignored?

- Are multiple search fields on the same page clearly labeled as to whether or not they are associated with one another?

- Are results well-organized? Do they appear in adequate type size? And do they have informative but concise summaries?

CHAPTER SIXTEEN

Navigation

You Know You're in Trouble When Users Look for Your Site Map

This chapter will discuss some of the common navigational problems that get in the way of an intuitive experience. And it will highlight the elements of successful sites in which users always know where they are and how to get back to where they've been.

Several years ago, it was acceptable for users to take one look at a site and head for the site map. With the competitive environment web marketers face today, this is no longer the case. Although some users will bookmark a particular page on a site in order to get there quickly, sites should not force them to do so just because they can't remember how to get there on their own. Yet this is the experience that many web savvy users report.

By the way, while we are on the subject of bookmarks (again, which some of us *do* use to simplify navigation), make sure that if you change your site navigation, you create default links to new pages so that users don't encounter the infamous "File Not Found" message when they select one of their favorites.

Now that we have digressed a bit, let's get back on track. In this chapter, we approach the subject of navigation, by identifying those principles that can make or break a site.

Let Your Homepage Be Your Guide

We can't overstate the fact that one of the major benefits of doing research upfront—that is, at the concept stage—is to find out what is most important to your users. This saves countless dollars you could spend developing features and functions that are super-fluous, features that users don't expect or want from your brand or site.

More importantly, this research helps you understand the hierar-chy with which users access the information you offer and how they want to access it. It also teaches you the language they use to

Figure 16.1

When you change your site, don't make users work to figure out where you've gone, or worse, make them feel like they have made an "error."

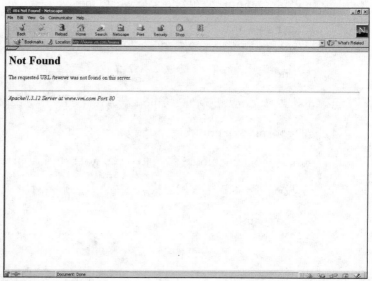

www.vm.com/tewrwr

describe a site and the visuals they associate with each area. This learning should translate to a clear directive as to what to offer on the homepage and how to label it. For example:

- When people are researching a medical condition, do they want to search by area of the body, disease type, or both?

- When shopping for clothing, what is the hierarchy of choices that makes most sense? Style? Color? Gender? Fabric? How about for furniture? Cars?

- If your site serves prospects and customers, what are the main options sought by either group?

- For sites that serve consumers and the trade (as do sites for computers, healthcare, and banking), how do you create pathways on the homepage that clearly announce the relevant path for each distinctive group of users?

- Moreover, with what level of security does each group feel confident that others (particularly their customers) can't access information, like pricing, that is perceived to be confidential. This is true of doctors, decorators, computer resellers, and so on.

Each of these questions should be explored at the very outset to make sure that your target group(s) can easily navigate the homepage to get exactly where they want to be. By learning what choices are of greatest importance to people, developers avoid a mistake committed by many homepages on the web: namely, offering so many options that key pathways are obscured. "Busy," "cluttered," "disorganized," and "overwhelming" are the adjectives most test participants utter when asked to give their overall thoughts about such homepages, frequently followed by a terse "I don't know where to go first." When this happens, it's a safe bet that their next stop is the competition.

To avoid this predicament, we encourage site developers to do their homework on day one—before anyone on the team is too heavily invested in site architecture or is too in love with a particular way of presenting key features or pathways. Generating great ideas is terrific. It is just as important to have a "reality check" from your target audience(s), in order to find out the following things:

- The key features and content that target users seek and the language they use to describe it.

- If users think of the content you offer in sequential steps, precisely what are those steps, and how should they be labeled? For example, when using a courier service, users may see the process unfolding in the following order: Order supplies, Create a label, Get cost and timing, Track delivery. If this is indeed the expectation, we believe this is how you should present the steps. (Don't forget graphic elements here.)

- The highest level of information by which users want to browse.

- How to bring each target group to the pathway designed for them.

On the Airborne Express site, the popular drop-off locator and shipment tracking features are located in prominent positions. In addition, the link to the tracking feature has an intuitive user-friendly label, "Track a Shipment," even though the feature itself is called "Airbill Tracking."

Anything that serves to simplify the homepage is good. A simple homepage subconsciously communicates to the user that the site

Figure 16.2

Airborne Express understands why customers visit their site and what language they use.

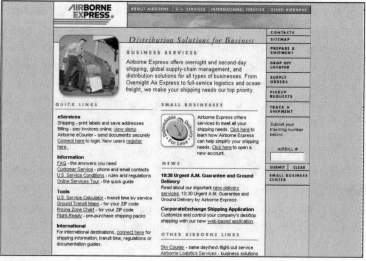

www.airborne.com/

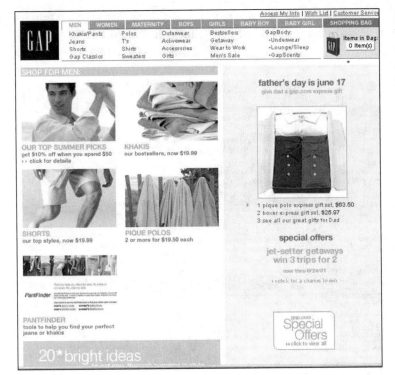

www.gap.com

Figure 16.3

The men's clothing page in the Gap site effectively directs users by offering few choices.

will be easy to navigate. Most users would rather click three times than to be presented with three times the amount of choices that should be on the homepage (or any other page).

Be Persistent in Your Navigation

We feel strongly that the left nav bar (or wherever the main navigation resides) should be present and accessible on every page. The reason for this is simple: The nav bar allows people to exit any path they didn't intend to follow or that otherwise fails to deliver "the goods." Having omnipresent navigation (that is, navigation that never deserts the user) is the guarantor of escape when one is needed, and the mere presence of persistent navigation has a subconscious effect on the user: He knows he can back out if he wants. We think that knowing where they are and where they've come from provides a sufficiently ample comfort zone for people to forge ahead more easily.

Following this logic, it is very important that secondary and tertiary levels of navigation be clearly delineated. The following examples illustrate good—and not so good—uses of persistent navigation.

**Figure 16.4
(Next two images)**

The *Washington Post's* left navigation bar changes as a user navigates through the editorial section.

www.washingtonpost.com/

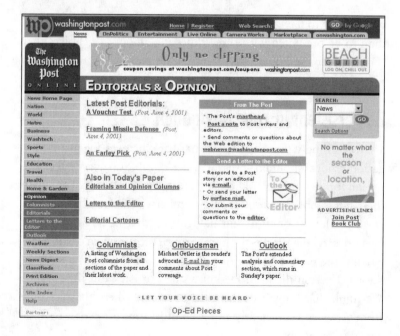

When it works well, users know what secondary or tertiary level they're in and can easily backtrack or leap to another primary choice, no matter how deep into another main choice they've clicked.

A Trail of Bread Crumbs

If you don't want your users to feel like they are foraging aimlessly through the forest, it is critical to offer them very obvious "bread crumbs" that show them the road they have already traveled. When this is done creatively, it can actually add visual interest to the page. Nevertheless, it is presumptuous to believe that users know exactly where they are after spending only a few short minutes there. In fact, as with the ubiquity of navigation bars, just knowing that a bread crumb trail is available gives users the courage to click with abandon, secure in the knowledge that they can always get back to a place they've been before.

Below are several interesting uses of bread crumbs to help provide perspective on the importance of a bread crumb trail to make navigation seem effortless and intuitive.

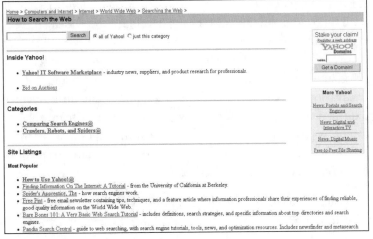

www.yahoo.com

Figure 16.5
Yahoo's bread crumbs are clear, concise, and informative.

Figure 16.6

Eddie Bauer's bread
crumbs help ensure that
the user always knows
where he or she is
located.

www.eddiebauer.com

The Customer Is Always Right
"Invalid Entry" Is Not an Option

A funny thing about most web sites is that they assume users will
both follow the path intended by the developer and understand exactly what information to enter on each and every page. The fact
is, sites should be built to allow users to navigate and enter data
fields intuitively. Some users, however (smart people and not-so-
smart people alike), will inevitably take a few wrong turns or enter
data in a fashion not intended by the development team. Therefore, it is just as important to create error messages that are intuitive as it is to build the "success" path. Here are some tips on how
to do this gracefully and effectively:

- Assume the customer is always right. Never use language that
  is accusatory (for instance, "invalid entry").

  In fact, the very term "error condition" suggests the customer
  is wrong. How about "unexpected condition" or "recovery"?

- Help the user recover by taking him right to where he needs to
  be in order to change his entry, and give him several tips to help
  him out.

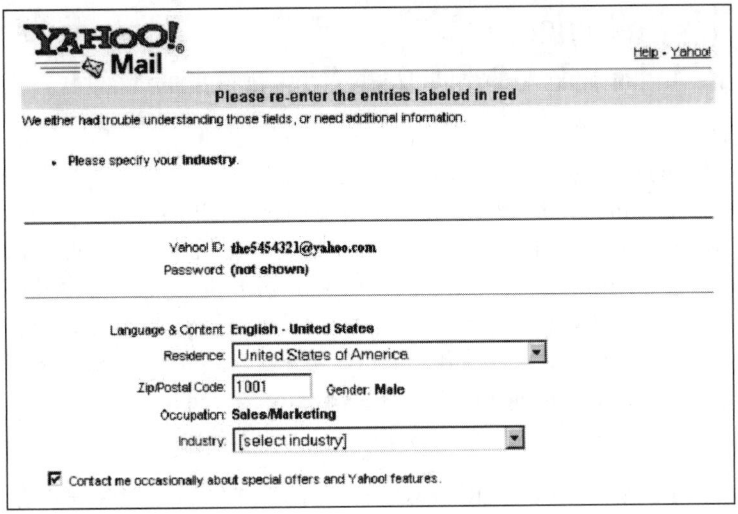

Figure 16.7

Yahoo makes it very clear which fields the user needs to re-enter.

- If users loop around three times after being told "invalid phone number" or "social security number" or "password," connect them to a customer representative, or supply them with another solution that addresses the frustration they are undoubtedly experiencing.

- If there is more than one pathway you want people to consider (for example, current customer/subscriber/member versus new customer/"want to become a member," place the options side by side. Face it, most of us have a Pavlovian response to entering data: When we see an open field, we are conditioned to fill it. Protect us from ourselves, and the fact that most of us don't read. Offering alternative options side by side makes people question their actions ("which side am I on?") before entering a field. Such visual constructs convey more meaning than many a lengthy paragraph.

- Allow people the option to "get there" from multiple places. By offering multiple opportunities to get to a desired feature, make it clear that there is no such thing as *the* right path. Instead, there are several possibilities. No matter how much you do usability testing, you'll never get all the people to travel the same route.

This Isn't Print
Use Anchor Links to Provide Quick Access to Multiple Choices

There is nothing more annoying—or more likely to lose your audience—than making them read through an entire paragraph or two in order to get to the next choice. The trick is to give people just enough information to get them interested and a simple way to find out more. The web is designed for surfing, grazing, or skimming. Therefore, you are doing people a favor by offering a clear way of obtaining more information—be it an anchor link, a picture, or a clickable headline—if they are interested in doing so. The goal is to get all main choices above the fold.

Because people are likely to use your anchor links freely, persistent navigation and bread crumbs are critical to their success.

Silos Are for Hay, Not Web Sites
Don't Make People Go Back to Go Forward

Few things are more frustrating than following a lengthy product path (for example, to find the perfect cell phone or PDA) only to find that you have no choice but to return to square one in order to learn the price, get the perfect cover, or find out what batteries you'll need. Conversely, when the web works wonderfully, you are offered each of the choices that you want next, just like magic. So if you just received your checking balance, wouldn't it be nice to have the option to pay bills as well? If you've picked out the perfect computer, wouldn't it also be nice to be shown advertised specials for printers, scanners, or disk drives that are compatible with the PC you've chosen? In this case, advertising is far from annoying, rather it actually provides welcome information. The experience should be "Gee, they can read my mind. How did they know I'd want X or Y or Z?"

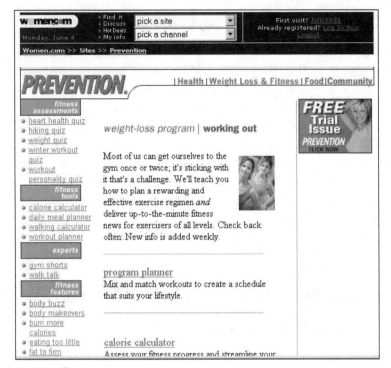

www.prevention.com

Figure 16.8

A free issue of *Prevention* is an appropriate and non-intrusive promotion for Women.com. It offers something valuable rather than just a "hard sell."

Research Tip

The best way to find out the multitude of "next steps" users want at any point in time is to ask them. Use focus groups (or ethnography) to have people walk you down the pathways they want to be able to travel. And it goes without saying that not all users will find the same set of options intuitive. The goal is to design your site so no one has to go back to go forward.

Insight

You can create the feeling of personalization by simply using the (not so) unique data a user has input to offer her other items she might like.

Use Images to Show People the Way

Having established that people don't read on the web and that a picture is worth a thousand words, it goes without saying that your visuals should work hard to serve as a source of navigation. Without saying a word, graphics, photos, and illustrations offer a compelling, creative, and intuitive means of getting people where they want to be. By the same token, images that are vague or downright confusing can create just the opposite effect. Worst of all, images that aren't clickable or which are used as mere wallpaper can be deadly. Aside from taking up real estate and adding to load time, they can confuse users who try hard to read into them meaning that doesn't exist or to apply them (without success) to navigation.

Offer Critical Instructions in Such a Way That They Cannot Be Missed

It still amazes us how often sites provide a button that takes users down an important path before supplying all the information needed to make an informed choice about which path to choose in the first place. More often than not, this information is never seen because users logically assume that any information required to make a choice would precede that choice.

How many times have you been on a site where some key piece of information needed to protect you from making an undesirable choice is written in hard-to-read "mice" type or is buried in a long introductory paragraph that you are guaranteed to gloss over in your desire to get to the next action step? If truth were told, the majority of us skim most of the text on a page and travel from empty field to empty field, headline to headline, "action" button to "action" button, and link to link. This is what we've been conditioned to do when surfing the web, and in fact, it's what we've been told is so wonderful about it; after all, when you're online, you—the user— shape the experience.

In order to deliver on this promise, take a look at your site from the perspective of a "skimmer" or "skipper" and see if you get lost or derailed. If you can navigate this way without fail, you've created an experience that will accommodate most of us—and ensure our success.

◯◯ Insight
◯ One of the best ways to offer critical instructions is to embed them in the actual navigational device, for instance, a link or button. Accordingly, among the surest ways to protect us "non-readers" from ourselves is to make the text that we must read glaringly obvious (displayed in red and bold type) and place it so that it clearly modifies the action step associated with it.

Don't Force People to Commit Before They Are Ready

Just as it's important for the user to be able to control what he reads and what he skips, researching web use has taught us that customers don't want to commit to anything until they're good and ready. We've witnessed the success of "wish lists" that are repositories for items *not yet* chosen for purchase, of "portfolios" that keep track of items the user might want to purchase (pending a second opinion), and of configurators we can use to design our nirvana PC that can be printed and taken to CompUSA to get a better bid or a second opinion. All this freedom of choice has led to a fair amount of suspicion of sites that attempt to force the user to do anything he is not ready to do. For example, don't ask the user to do the following:

- Register or provide any information he's not comfortable giving.

- Hit any button that is labeled "Buy" or "Send" or anything that is a step ahead of what he is ready to commit to.

And, given that most of us are commitment-phobic on the web, here are a few ways to keep people navigating toward the outcome you want them to achieve:

- Offer an incentive to register or a benefit to providing information.

Figure 16.9

Mapquest gives an excellent array of "final steps" for using their directions. The user sees immediately how to print, download to a PDA, email to a friend, and so on.

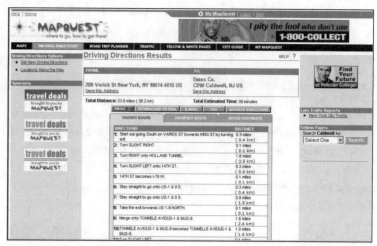

www.mapquest.com

- Avoid terms like "Buy" or "Send" in favor of the less commit-tal "Add to cart," "Get more information," or "Next."

- Use confirmation screens at key points so people are aware they have a way "out."

- Always offer an exit path via "Delete," "Go back," and so on.

Scroll at Your Own Risk!

Time and again, we've heard users in the lab tell us that the more important information or choices appear first on the page. Just as a newspaper article is structured with the most important stuff first, so, if you bail, you'll have gotten the high points. Users reason that web pages are configured the same way. If information was really important, why would they place it below the fold? What these users don't know is that content is often placed well below the fold, not because it is trivial or of secondary importance, but for the simple reason that it just didn't fit above the fold. And it might be that the developer's screen was much larger than the laptop that many site visitors are using.

Most problematic of all is the obscuring of key navigational elements like the "Submit," "Next," and "Buy" buttons. How many of us have totally missed critical information because the fold just happens to coincide with what appears to be the end of the page, the bottom of an image, or a horizontal line that is part of the page design?

Here are some tips for how to overcome the perils of scrolling:

- As mentioned before, use anchor links to reduce page length.

- Test your site on all sorts of monitors to make sure that natural break lines cannot obscure key navigation at any time.

- Make sure nothing that is critical to your site's success—features, content, or navigation—is below the fold. For if you place it there, know that many visitors will either never see it or will assume that it must not be very important.

The View from 30,000 Feet

In sum, don't force visitors of your site to hunt for and/or bookmark pages of which the location should be intuitive. Conduct research on what users want and expect so that, from the homepage on, your site will be easily understood in terms of how to access various kinds of information throughout its pages. Don't overwhelm them with disorganization and clutter, but don't underwhelm them with minimalism, either. As a rule of thumb, keep it simple. If users in your category already think in terms of a sequence of steps, try to replicate this on your site. Alternatively, provide multiple options for accessing the same information or pages.

Also, where possible, keep the nav bar in view on all pages so visitors have that extra sense of security about where they are on the site and (just as importantly) what they're doing there! We have found that bread crumbs, anchor links, and clickable images are often useful in this task. Again, provide the most intuitive assistance possible, and when opportunities arise to cross sell and up sell, go for it, always bearing in mind that customers are more impressed with useful information (such as the right kind of printer to go with a new PC) than they are with superfluous advertising and gimmicks. Above all, don't create the impression that you're forcing any choices to be made or paths to be followed. Remember, you can lead a horse to water, but you can't make him think...er, drink.

A Few Hard Questions

- What hierarchy of choices makes the most sense for your site (for example, should pathways be created that focus on gender, fabric, style, and so on)?

- Is your homepage intuitive with respect to the pathways that are available?

- Does the navigation bar appear on every page throughout the site?

- Does your site have bread crumbs that can assist users in navigation when necessary?

- Are your error messages helpful and instructive, or do they frighten users away?

- Can visitors access the information they want from multiple locations, or are they restricted to a narrow pathway?

- Does your site seem suspect because it forces users to commit to particular pathways before they're ready to do so?

CHAPTER SEVENTEEN

E-Commerce

If They Can't Find It, They Won't Buy It

S hopping on the web is about convenience and saving time. Whether the user wants to browse or go directly to the desired product, the site has to accommodate both approaches. Many e-commerce sites are minefields of mixed messages and dead ends, any one of which can leave the user frustrated, confused, and ultimately, searching for a competitor.

The basics of web site design, including navigation and content, have been discussed throughout this book. The same principles hold for e-commerce oriented sites, or e-commerce areas of sites. Rather than unearth them again, we are using this chapter to present for you what we think of as the "Top 10" considerations in building e-commerce sites that really work.

Understand Current Buying Behavior

So you want to create web-based shopping functionality. This is nothing new for developers and marketers, of course, but where does one begin? With a series of basic assumptions about functionality. In fact, that's where trouble often begins—with that innocent sounding word, "assumption."

Paradoxically, those of us who develop the functionality for online shopping are not necessarily regular online shoppers. Without real, day-to-day experience (for example, buying mainframe computers, shipments of steel, or evening gowns), we are not likely to be in touch with what's important to prospects and customers. Even after interviewing the "insiders," such as sales and customer service staff, it is possible to miss the nuances that make for an optimal shopping experience. On the other hand, we might be extensive online shoppers who are still far from "typical" e-shoppers. What looks like a simple straightforward process may seem anything but that to a novice user.

Furthermore, even with an extensive "bag of tricks," site developers who lack an adequate understanding of the target audience run the risk of adopting a one-size-fits-all approach to the shopping process, creating e-commerce functionality that basically looks the same as, for example, Amazon, even when that approach does not quite meet the needs of the audience.

Insight
The first principle in developing e-commerce functionality: Assume you know nothing about the buying process.

So where do you start? We have had well-intentioned clients begin by trying to learn what users want to do on the Internet. "How do you want to shop online?" they ask users. This certainly seems reasonable, in that they are at least starting out with user input.

But guess what? Users don't necessarily know what they expect to see in an optimal e-commerce experience, even within their own categories. If they knew—*really* knew—what to expect, they would have our jobs.

So where does that leave us?

We recommend that our clients begin even earlier in the process. What did users do before they could buy online? They bought offline, of course. Consequently, we help our clients start with gaining real insight into what users do offline.

From *real* buyers in your category, find out the answers to questions like these:

● What are the steps in the product/decision-making process?

● What are the information needs at each step in the process?

● Where are the information needs being met, and where are there currently gaps?

● Where do buyers go for information?

● How do they ultimately decide which company/store to do business with? Which product/service to purchase?

As you are learning about your category, don't forget to also explore any nuances as they relate to your brand. Is there anything different about people who will buy from you? Alternatively, if your brand is not yet established, what lures prospects into trying something new?

Look at it this way: Buying online may not replace buying in a bricks-and-mortar setting or from a catalogue, but it is not really meant to. Nevertheless, if users are forced to relearn their basic assumptions (there's that pesky word again), to work with less information, or to otherwise completely disrupt how they are accustomed to buying, they probably won't take the next step.

Insight

Learn as much as you can about the buying process, both as it relates to your category and to your specific brand.

Figure 17.1

Talk about consistency!
The birders.com site
knows their audience.
They define it front and
center and offer unique
products, including
CDs, as well as the
opportunity to register
for prizes.

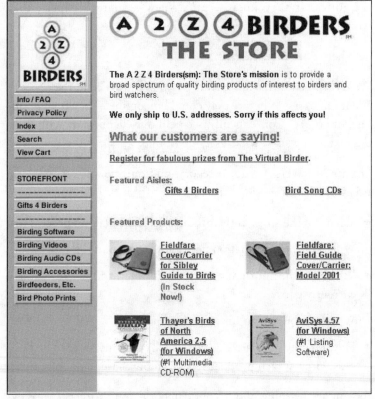

http://store.yahoo.com/a2z4birders/index.html

Don't Assume a Standard Approach to Shopping in Your Category

In the last section, we advised you to understand how users within your product/service category make purchasing decisions. So far, so good. But now, we're telling you that you shouldn't assume your users will take a standard approach. Doesn't this sound like we're contradicting ourselves? Yes and no.

Let's take clothes buying as a simple example. When someone buys a pair of pants, online or off, they want to see what styles are available. They want to look at texture and colors, and they want to see what it goes with. How will it look on them? Last but not least, they want to know how much it will cost.

These are basics of shopping for clothes—certainly much different, say, from purchasing a personal computer.

However, while you may have discovered the basics of fashion-oriented e-commerce, can you assume that buyers always think like you do? Consider the possibilities. Someone buying a pair of pants as a gift might start out wanting to know their price. Someone who is designer-conscious may want only a specific brand. The guy who got the royal blue sweater for his birthday may only want a pair of pants that matches it. And what about the user who has to get some kind of a gift purchased and delivered in two days?

Our point is that a variety of users, while requiring the same basic information, will almost certainly start in totally different places in the decision-making process. Accordingly, the steps they take in finding what they want and making purchases will also differ from one another.

What this means for your e-commerce functionality is that you don't have the luxury of developing a single shopping/purchase path on the assumption that each user will dutifully start at the beginning and traverse the path as you intended.

Insight

People are unique, but all want control of the web experience. Create e-commerce functionality that accommodates buyers regardless of their entry point into the decision-making or purchasing process.

Use Shopping Metaphors That Make Sense

Recall the title of Chapter 11: "Hieroglyphics Are Only Interesting When You're Visiting the Pyramids." This is certainly true in the realm of e-commerce: Users aren't going to give their credit card number based on what they think might be the correct interpretation of a hieroglyphic. They want to know exactly what your intention is each step along the way, to make sure that it meshes with theirs. After all, you will most likely be asking them, at some point, to open their pocketbooks. Let's examine that phrase, "most likely to," in a little more depth.

In previous chapters, we have discussed how many sites use terminology that is not only confusing but misleading. More than one, for example, provide users with a "purchase" icon that is actually going to take them to a list of retail outlets or resellers, instead of to the "Check Out." "Buy Now" is another metaphor that strikes fear in the hearts of users, especially novices. Generally, the sponsors of the site are using this to mark the beginning of an e-commerce path that will provide the user with a means of selecting products and features for which they, once satisfied, can enter credit card information. Users see this and fear that if they click it, they will suddenly find one or more items in their mailbox, along with an excessive credit card charge. This is one of those cases where the word "Now" is likely to be interpreted literally.

Over time, certain conventions have emerged in e-commerce, the primary example being the "Shopping Cart." Users have come to assume the ubiquity of a button that allows them to "place the item in your shopping cart." When they are ready to buy or "check out," they can go back through the shopping cart and make adjustments in quantities, as well as delete items, before committing themselves. Any variation from this approach, be it ever so slight, will result in bail-outs.

We've worked with sites that wanted to use a more creative term for Shopping Cart and came up with such uninventive handles as "Shopping Bag." In general, users complained of this new term because when they're shopping offline, they aren't provided with shopping bags until after they have made a purchase. Their items stay in the shopping cart until then. While this was a creative diversion, the term caused confusion.

However, the term "Shopping Cart" does not necessarily fit with the offerings of every e-commerce scenario (for example, luxury goods like jewelry, or services), and many sites have introduced terms like "Shopping Basket" and "Portfolio." Again, these terms resulted in initial confusion for many. At least until they were adequately explained, they were generally not intuitively understood.

Here is a good rule of thumb: For users, the offline experience is the frame of reference in the e-commerce world, but certain

Figure 17.2

The Starbuck's site is an example of a buying experience consistent with the category. Users can choose coffee and add it to their cart, either in whole beans or ground form. They can even "taste" it first, by matching the right coffee to their taste preferences.

www.starbucks.com

conventions are now universally popular in e-commerce (for instance, terms like "Shopping Cart" and "Check Out"). Deviate at your own risk.

Insight

In an e-commerce setting, not only are unclear metaphors confusing, but they can be misconstrued as an attempt to mislead the user. Users want to be totally comfortable when they are spending their money.

People Want to Know What They're Buying
Use Pictures and Descriptions

One of the biggest complaints users have about e-commerce is that they often don't feel like they know what they are (or might be) buying. Sometimes they are provided with an abbreviated product name as opposed to a complete name or brand name. At other times, the size, weight, or dimensions are missing, or they can't tell what it's made of. Alternatively, maybe they are shown a photo, but it's not big enough or shows only one angle.

Look at it this way: If users are forced to visit your offline store (or worse yet, someone else's store) before they can decide whether or not to buy it on your site, they may as well simply pick it up while they're at the store and ignore your web site altogether. Why not, after all, if that is the most convenient thing to do?

Don't forget to be consistent. Users tell us that another irritating aspect of product descriptions is when some products are explained very thoroughly and others aren't explained well at all, or when the language differs widely between products. Choose a standard and clone it across your product line. Each product or service description should have the exact same organization. Users tell us that, when looking at products or services, they appreciate first seeing a basic description with bullet points, as well as a thumbnail sketch if it is a product. Along with this basic description, they like to have the option to get more detail as needed, to view a larger photo or views from alternate angles, and to email in questions if they still have unresolved issues.

You may want to briefly look back at Chapter 10, "When I Need Your Assistance, Believe Me, I'll Ask." In that chapter, we addressed the issue of offering product information in layers.

And don't forget pricing. Users want to know the price of each item up-front, right along with the brief product summary. To hide the prices, or to be perceived as doing so, is to risk alienating prospective customers.

Insight

Users want product descriptions that provide the basic features of the product, and a photo if applicable, along with the option of digging a layer further for more detail.

And here's one more caution: As we discussed in Chapter 16, "Navigation," users may not even employ consistent terminology to refer to your products (for example, personal computer versus PC, pants versus slacks, couch versus sofa). Don't forget to keep that in mind, both when you label categories, as well as within your search function.

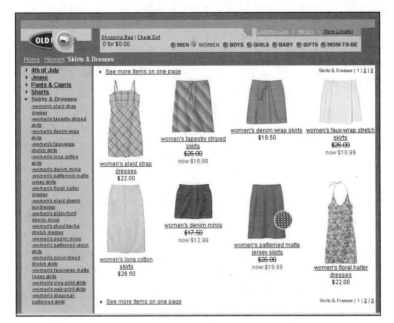

Figure 17.3

Old Navy provides short but succinct product descriptions, with a thumbnail that offers the user an additional point of reference. Pricing is clear. The user can then click on the hyperlink to explore further.

www.oldnavy.com

Track with the Buying Process

Here's a new wrinkle for you to keep in mind. Already in this chapter, we discussed the importance of understanding how your users go about purchasing products or services within your category, as well as the importance of not forcing them into a specific approach to purchasing, given that each may have a different starting point. Another important practice, even "guiding principle," for designers is to track with the customer's buying process. This is an organizational issue that bears on navigation and content.

To begin, the purchase decision process is multi-faceted. We told you before that the starting points differ among consumers. A related point is that their minds also work on different levels as they shop, meaning that they will want to access different levels of information as they go through this process.

Tracking with the buying process means having product information available at any point along the way. Suppose the user is trying to decide which digital camera to purchase. He or she comes to a screen with four models on display, each with a brief description and a thumbnail photo. Depending on his current level of familiarity, the user might want to

- Zero in on one specific model and get more detail.

- Look at the four models side-by-side and compare their features and prices.

- Find out the type of photography (for example, family picnics versus professional) each camera is suited for.

- Choose one camera and then compare it to the competition in terms of features and price.

Other issues arise as well. For example, a furniture site might offer the option of purchasing a couch (or a sofa) by style. But remember, not everyone knows what differentiates one style of couch from another. What are the differences between "traditional" and "modern" couches, anyway? Consequently, somewhere along the buying path, users will need to be able to see examples of furniture in traditional or modern styles to help them make this decision.

More complicated are products that incorporate aroma or the sense of touch as vehicles for familiarity. If, for instance, a "floral" scent means a combination of lilac and rose, you should provide users with that example. Although they cannot smell the object directly, the verbal comparison provides a frame of reference. Therefore, you can also follow one more rule of thumb:

- Provide adequate examples, in text and, where appropriate, visuals, to help your shoppers understand the terminology you use.

Our point here is that if your site tracks to the buying process of your users, they should be able to access any and all of this information *as they need it*, without having to drop what they are doing to move to another area of your site. In doing so, they might risk getting lost, or worse still, they might visit a competing site and abandon yours once and for all.

Figure 17.4

IBM offers server shoppers a range of options. Users can first get a basic idea of which server group they want to pursue further. They can also get recommendations and configure their own systems. Additionally, information on benchmarking, case studies, and promotions is available. And yes, the servers do get placed in a shopping cart.

www.ibm.com

Again, control is a key issue. This means putting buttons along the path with labels like "Compare Models," "Compare This to Competitive Models," and "Suggested Uses." If users can view this information within pop-up windows, that's so much the better.

Insight

As users traverse your purchase path, make sure they have all the information they need—in the form they need it—at their fingertips. In other words, give them all the tools they can use so they aren't obliged to leave your site to find them.

Offer Incentives

Everybody likes to get something for nothing, or at least for less than they would expect to find elsewhere. The quest for fulfillment of that promise brings us to a variety of stores and catalogs, so why not to web sites?

In the early days of the Internet, each and every new e-commerce site, especially the pure play sites, offered something for nothing—including discounts, free shipping, and free gifts. All of these served as incentives to get users to buy at their sites. These incentives also created an expectation that the good times would continue. After all, many users we speak to rationalize that, because retailers on the web are "avoiding the middlemen" (distributors, salespeople, and showrooms), these cost reductions should be reflected in pricing. Complicating the matter still further, in the competitive market, users also expect retailers to be competing for their business through strategic use of incentives as part of overall business strategy.

Profit margins being what they are, incentives are not always an easy thing to offer. However, you might consider ways in which you could offer your users the following incentive options:

- Frequent buying clubs to reward returning customers
- Discounts, especially for orders greater than a certain dollar amount
- Discounts for new customers
- Free shipping and handling
- Free samples, perhaps through agreements with manufacturers represented on your site, which offer the customer the opportunity to try new things (trial sizes, samples, or swatches, for example)
- Gifts or discounts for referring other prospects who actually purchase
- Digital coupons

We have also uncovered an additional reason to offer incentives. Users who shy away from trying new sites will often take that plunge if the incentive is high enough. Those who fear buying online have told us the same thing.

An old principle of direct marketing applies here. Incentives for first-time buyers do not necessarily build customer loyalty. They simply attract bargain-hunters. (You know the scenario: You buy

www.drugstore.com

Figure 17.5
The drugstore.com site is filled with incentives for new customers (such as free shipping), but it also offers incentives for returning customers (including promotions and pharmacy discounts).

one brand of discounted detergent in the grocery store one week, but buy a different brand that's on sale on your next visit, no matter how well the first brand worked.) New buyers may easily become regular buyers, but it helps if you offer incentives to keep newbies coming back. Don't neglect them, and they won't neglect you.

Insight

Incentives are effective for bringing in new buyers as well as building loyalty among current buyers. Everybody loves a bargain.

Can I Take It Back?
Life Is Mysterious Enough...

Users often describe the nightmare of making a purchase through an e-commerce site, only to discover that they didn't choose the product they thought they were ordering (often due to less-than-optimal product descriptions), or that the fit or style was not right, or that they simply received the wrong shipment. Inevitably, such annoying episodes are followed by lengthy accounts of having to re-pack the products, pay for return shipping, and deal with the fallout from ineptly handled credit card transactions and (adding insult to injury) payment for a product they never received. Moreover, users often describe the company as "three guys in a garage" who didn't have a system in place or, on the other end of the spectrum, a sprawling retailer who lost their package in a system that was overly cumbersome or bureaucratic.

Two things here that are worthy of mention:

- First, consumers have this concern about both pure play sites and those associated with bricks-and-mortar retailers.

- Even more intriguing, these stories are often semi-fictional, and even achieve the status of being "urban myths." When pressed, users frequently confess that this is an experience they fear they will have, or "something they have read about" happening to somebody else.

Perception is reality. If users fear not being able to return a product or get a refund, they will be inhibited when it comes to buying. Furthermore, users also tell us that they look for return and refund policies before they will shop at a site. Some have even followed the entire purchase path right up to the brink of entering their credit card number, in search of the return and refund policy.

From this, we have learned two important lessons:

- Users want to see the return and refund policy up front, and they complain when it isn't made accessible (they feel the company is holding something back on them).

- They are not likely to make any purchases until they have this clarified.

The moral of this story? Get your house, or at least your back-office, in order. Make sure you can efficiently handle any product returns that may occur, including giving proper credit to the purchaser. Moreover, make sure you are ready to offer complete refunds—no questions asked—just like the bricks-and-mortar stores and catalog companies do.

Furthermore, clarify your policy early on in the site. Some sites have a link in the left navigation bar that addresses returns and refunds, and some offer such a link within the Customer Service area. Others offer a link in the shopping cart so that users can review their purchases before proceeding to the check out. These are useful options, beyond which users shouldn't have to look in order to find simple information.

Other sites have taken the further step of providing a "return label" that makes returns easier for the consumer and also for the people who have to process them (at least these go to the right department). Some sites even pay for return shipping.

It is important to think about gift purchases here. Many web-based purchases are sent as gifts, and gift-buyers want to know that if the recipient decides to return the gift, this will be a completely hassle-free process. Return labels are especially useful for that reason.

Insight

Users want returns and refunds to work just like they do at the neighborhood shopping center. If you don't like the product once you get it home, simply bring it back to the store and get your money back. This information should be easily accessible and written in a clear and concise manner.

Use the Fulfillment Process to Cross-Sell

Do you ever find yourself in such a buying mood that you pick up a few extra items on the way out of the store? Retailers have been taking advantage of this tendency for decades. Clerks suggest a jacket to go with that shirt, a carrying case with that laptop, or a hunk of cheese to complement that bottle of wine. Shopping malls make you take the long way around when you are using the escalator, in order to make sure that before you ascend to the next floor, you get a look at whatever else they are offering on this one. Operating on this same principal, discount stores stock the areas around the check-out counter with items that you can toss into your cart on impulse before finally checking out.

This principle has also been used to great advantage in e-commerce sites. And why not? You've got people there who are open to the idea of spending money. Maybe they have searched for and found something specific on your site, and they're now ready to break out their credit cards. Still, they may not know what else you offer if they haven't done a lot of exploring, even though they might have some other products in mind for purchase, and might even need peripheral products they're unaware of.

We worked with a technology manufacturer whose product line included printers. Online purchasers would choose a printer and place it in their shopping cart. When it hit the cart, the site displayed additional products like cartridges (through a brief description and thumbnail photo) that the buyer should also consider for purchase. Users said they appreciated these suggestions because they might not have thought of them until their cartridge ran out.

Clothing sites have also incorporated this strategy into their web site design. The user selects a pair of jeans, and the shopping cart page (or one of the initial check-out pages) follows this up with a tee shirt or jacket that might look good with the pants. Talk about reflecting the offline buying experience! Not only do such features enhance the shopping experience, but if you can offer incentives, such as a discount on the additional products or reduced shipping and handling, you can build even more loyalty.

What users do tell us, however, is that they don't like a web-based hard sell any more than they like a pushy salesperson. Making suggestions in the shopping cart or on a checkout page is one thing; forcing them into a page they never wanted to see for the sole purpose of hawking a product is quite another. Offer the opportunity to explore the option of purchasing additional products, but don't grab them by the throat in order to do so.

Insight

Don't let buyers leave your site without gently suggesting additional products that might interest them.

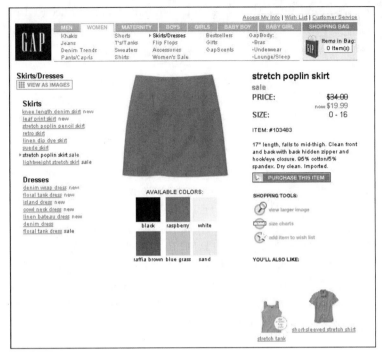

Figure 17.6

The Gap site cross-sells by offering items "You'll Also Like."

www.gap.com

There's another opportunity here too. People love to go to expensive stores and check out the sale rack, and we have seen that they like to do this on web sites as well. Use this as a draw to your site by allowing shoppers to look at "all sales items" and "sales items by category." As they place items in the shopping cart, use cross-selling to up-sell them on non-sales items or at least to get them browsing in another category.

Shipping and Handling? Don't Try to Hide It

Catalog buyers, as well as those who take advantage of those "special offers" advertised on television, have long been wary of shipping and handling costs. They have learned to be suspicious of great deals and deep discounts that are decidedly not so great once the shipping, and especially outrageous handling fees, have been added to the net cost. Unfortunately, the same has become true for the web, and more than one web merchant has been accused of using the same duplicitous tactics to eke a profit margin out of deeply discounted products.

The bottom line is that online buyers want to know what the shipping and handling fees are going to be before they make their decision to purchase. Note, this is not the same thing as saying that they don't expect to have to pay these fees at all, because they do. Reasonable people know there has to be a cost associated with all that convenience. In user experience testing, however, we have learned that users want to see the shipping and handling costs spelled out at the beginning of the checkout process rather than the end. This means that when they have added all they plan to purchase to the shopping cart and clicked the "Proceed to Checkout" button, they want to be presented with a page that shows the total cost of their purchase, including a clearly labeled sub-total for shipping and handling. Bear in mind as well that if the shipping expense can only be *estimated* at that point, then an estimated amount (clearly identified as such) needs to be provided.

We have also seen vendors offer a button on the Shopping Cart page that allows the user to update the total. The updated totals include shipping and handling fees. So much the better. On the other hand, some sites have provided shipping and handling amounts much further down the path, even keeping them hidden until after the credit card number has been submitted. What may simply be poor planning on the part of the site sponsors is assumed by the user to be an attempt at subterfuge. Not good.

Following up on our earlier discussion, here's another opportunity for a powerful use of incentives: Consider offering free shipping and handling to new or returning buyers or a discounted amount based on dollar volume.

Insight

In the minds of online buyers, shipping and handling are not an afterthought, but an important component of the total cost. As such, users want to see these costs included with the initial total purchase cost. Regardless of the truth, anything short of this is considered a deliberate attempt to mislead customers.

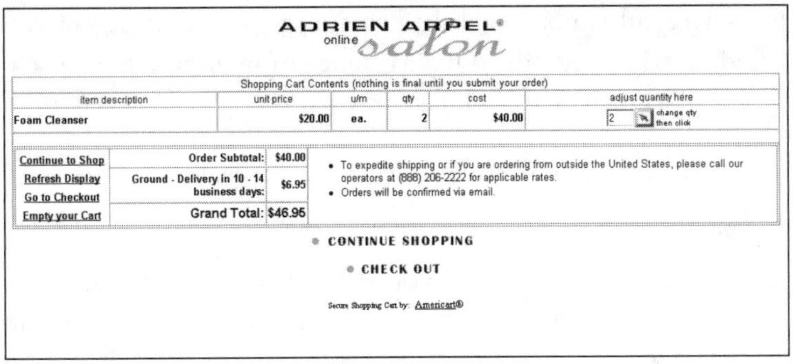

www.adrienarpel.com

Figure 17.7

In the Adrien Arpel site, the shipping and handling is provided on the first page of the shopping cart, itemized as part of the shopper's total cost.

Stay Consistent with Your Brand

This point goes almost without saying, but it shouldn't. Your e-commerce functionality needs to be totally consistent with your brand. With regard to this, are two important considerations to keep in mind, one obvious and one not so obvious.

First, the obvious: Offer goods and services that support your brand. Users are looking for a parallel between your site and your store, and shoppers have specific expectations about your products (color, style, logo, and so on), which they have developed based on your bricks-and-mortar store and through your advertising. Make sure your site delivers on these expectations and doesn't disappoint.

Some items may not lend themselves to the web. Others will. If some items are not going to be offered on the web, make that clear up-front so users know that although they can learn more about certain products, they will be directed to a retail outlet to buy them. For example, suppose Store X offers furniture as well as house wares. The web site, however, offers dishes and a few lamps, but not living room sets. This limitation needs to be made clear early in the site to prevent users from wasting their time only to be disappointed by the results.

Moreover, have a strategy behind how you advertise those products you do offer online. If the web is going to be used for sale items, clearly label them as such (again, incentives!). If you are targeting a certain segment of the population on the web (such as teens), make sure this is clear.

If your brand is not established, users will get an image of you based on what you offer. Quality, range of offerings, and presentation all contribute to an image of what they should expect from you.

Insight

Top-of-mind, if you are an established brand, users will expect to see the same products on your site that they do in your stores. Make sure that any discrepancies, in terms of offerings or availability, are clearly defined before the user goes down a purchase path.

We worked with a pure play gift-buying site that tried to be all things to all people, and which featured a wide range of products (from clothing to house wares to gifts) with an equally wide price range. The assumption was that the site would appeal to everyone. But it didn't. Mostly, users thought that the sponsors of the site didn't know what they were doing, or they complained that there didn't seem to be enough of anything. Some additional quirks in the organization and content, including a lack of consistency among product descriptions, further detracted from its image.

A not-so-obvious consideration that means everything to your brand is that the brand *is* the experience. Remember that mantra we keep chanting? Sites are judged by their e-commerce functionality, apart from the actual product mix. Poor functionality—which includes ineffective and/or confusing labeling, badly written product descriptions, hidden charges, broken links, and so on—all reflect on your brand. When the functionality is not ready for prime time, users wonder about your company. Do you know what you're doing in the 21st century? Are you committed to offering customers web-based e-commerce functionality and associated convenience, or is the web an afterthought?

Insight

The brand is the experience. Lack of clarity or organization, glitches in design, misleading product descriptions, all of these reflect negatively on the brand. The best way to enhance your brand is to make sure your e-commerce functionality is nothing short of perfect.

Research Tip
The best advisors on e-commerce functionality are your own customers. Talk to people who regularly buy your brand offline. You won't
learn much from people who aren't going to buy from you under any
circumstances. If you are not an established brand, also talk to people
who regularly buy in your category. Learn what they expect from you
and how they want to shop, beginning with an understanding of their
offline behavior. Later, put them in front of your site and let them talk
through the purchase process. What does and does not work will
quickly become obvious.

The View from 30,000 Feet

One size does not fit all in the world of e-commerce. The best starting place for understanding what users expect online is through an
understanding of offline behavior, both within the category as well
as the nuances related to buying your brand. Ultimately, what
users demand is well-organized e-commerce functionality, which
tracks with their buying process and offers clear and consistent information. They also want to know what all the costs are, including shipping and handling, and how to return something for credit.
Users may even want assistance in choosing the right gift for that
hard-to-buy-for person. In the final analysis, buying online is not
a whole lot different from buying offline.

A Few Hard Questions

- Does the buying process in your site make sense to people in
  your category, with terminology and decision-path organization that parallels what they do offline?

- Can they get the information they need, as they need it, along
  the buying path?

- Does shopping terminology in the site make sense?

- Do product descriptions offer everything the buyer needs to
  know, with availability of adequate detail and product photos?

- Is the return and refund policy clearly stated?

- Are shipping and handling costs presented at the beginning of the checkout process?

- Are you offering incentives for both new and loyal purchasers?

- Have you found opportunities to cross-sell without a hard-sell?

PART V

Back to the 30,000-Foot View

Your Site and Your Brand

18 The Challenges of Transferring an Established Brand to the Web
Top 10 Considerations 295

19 Business-to-Business
Challenges and Opportunities 311

CHAPTER EIGHTEEN

The Challenges of Transferring an Established Brand to the Web

Top 10 Considerations

When transferring an established brand to the web, you need to keep a wide range of considerations in mind, including image, look and feel, content, e-commerce, and other aspects of functionality. To overlook one function here or over-emphasize another there can result in a site that doesn't quite hit the right notes and, consequently, reflects badly on your brand.

As a point of departure (a theme that underscores the whole chapter), we'll once again beat our favorite drum: The experience is the brand. Or is it that the brand is the experience?

When we discuss this from the perspective of established brands, we are essentially talking about accomplishing the following objectives on your site:

- Reinforcing your brand image by extending it to the online world

- Enhancing your relationship with current customers to strengthen your brand equity

- Leveraging your brand equity in order to attract prospective customers

Users Expect Your Site to Look Like You

Users have very specific expectations from your brand, as we have discussed in earlier chapters. These include the following:

- What your building, showroom, and/or store look like

- What kinds of people work for you

- Your signage and logo and any distinctive packaging

- What kinds of people do business with you

- The products and services you offer

- The personality they associate with your brand, most likely expressed through the kind of customer service you offer

Users who come to your site anticipate that their expectations will be reflected in the homepage and throughout the rest of the site. We have worked with a wide range of established brands in industries like retail, financial services, and manufacturing, and we have discovered that users are amazingly consistent in this regard.

This is not, of course, to say that your job is all that easy. Sure, you know what your brand image is, and even if you don't, your ad agency or product managers can help you. Still, translating imagery to the web is a challenge, as we have talked about in various ways in previous chapters. The point we want to make here is that it is important to talk to your current customers and find out what they expect to see on your web site. How do they want to relate to your brand online?

We worked with an established financial services brand that viewed the web as offering the potential to reach out to a whole new audience of young, hip consumers who they felt they hadn't been able to impact in their offline communications efforts. So the company built a site with hip, edgy imagery and graphics. Both current and prospective users hated it. The current customers failed to recognize a company they believed themselves to be familiar with, and even non-customers tended to have the same expectations and image of the site as customers did. In addition to wondering what was going on, they found the tone somewhat forced, if not overly-hip. In short, the site didn't work for anyone.

In contrast, we have worked with a major retail brand that has a solid all-American image. Throughout the site are visuals that support that image: nice average people in family situations, young couples, older couples, children. Their customers and prospects come here, and they feel at home.

On the other hand, go to a site like MTV, and immediately you know where you are. It looks just like MTV and has the same energy.

The point is that if your brand is in the process of being established, or if it exists only on the web, users will most likely form an image based on the site. Visuals, look, feel, tone—all these elements contribute to overall image, along with the content and features. This means that your imagery needs to be consistent throughout the site. And while you're at it, make sure you understand how users perceive your brand, based on their reaction to these elements. If you don't like the image you're portraying, change it before it becomes too ingrained.

Insight

Users want to see a site that reflects their current expectations for your brand. This is what makes them comfortable. Although you can leverage your current brand and begin to move the image in a new direction, too much of a shift tends to create a disconnect with users.

Figure 18.1
(Next two images)

The homepages of
Charles Schwab and
Coca-Cola are excellent
examples of sites that
reflect the look and feel
of their brands.

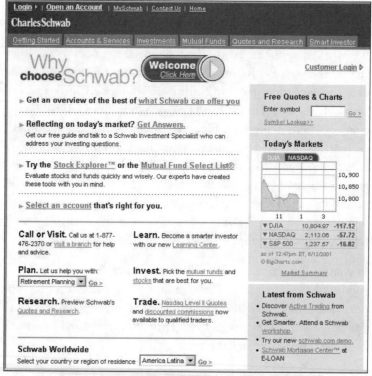

www.charlesschwab.com

www.cocacola.com

Your Site Should Be Organized, Just Like You

Think of the big bookstore chain that has a retail outlet in your neighborhood. What images does it conjure up? Most likely, you see a range of images, including books arranged by sections (fiction, travel, sports), as well as display racks with the latest bestsellers and gift ideas. Your favorite department store? Chances are that it also is arranged in sections, with emphasis on certain styles and price ranges.

One major retail chain is especially known for its tool department. Users told us they expected that web site's department to be featured prominently, so they could get there as soon as they entered the site.

What about the office of the insurance broker you do business with? Does it separate product lines, such as home, health, and retirement? And how about your bank? The auto dealership you bought your last car from?

What we are emphasizing here is that brand imagery has a very practical physical component. Customers walk into your business

Figure 18.2

The first page of a woman's area of the Saks Fifth Avenue site reflects the organization of the bricks-and-mortar stores.

www.saksfifthavenue.com

and immediately orient themselves based on the product or service they are seeking. They go to that aisle, that floor, or that office. Maybe they browse along the way, perusing the products in another aisle, or maybe they step into another department and grab a brochure or ask a question.

They expect the same thing from your web site. If your store has a tool aisle, users expect to see the tool aisle on your web site. Keep in mind, however, that your site should *not* be organized like your organizational chart, as we discussed in Chapter 4, "Understanding How Users 'Bucket' Your Space."

What Language Do You Use with Customers? Use the Same on Your Web Site

We have stressed the importance of clear labeling and logical navigation, all of which make for a valuable site experience for users. What we want to emphasize from a brand perspective is that, depending upon your category as well as your specific brand, you most likely have certain words and phrases that your customers are comfortable with. These should be reflected in your site.

Virtually any category can be used to provide examples here. In the music business, a "song" on a CD might be referred to as a "cut." On a book site, "browsing" has a special meaning. Auto buyers use expressions like "kick the tires" for taking a closer look. Computer buyers use terms like "peripherals." Stereo buyers say "components."

Insight

Reflecting your brand on your site goes beyond the look and feel of the homepage. The overall organization of the site, as well as terminology, also need to be consistent with what prospects and customers are familiar with offline.

And from a brand perspective, there is no better example than K-Mart and their "blue light special." It is so inherent to their brand that they gave it its own web site.

www.bluelight.com

Figure 18.3

Notice that bluelight.com focuses on the brand imagery associated with the "blue light special," and the K-Mart name is less prominent.

Sweat the Details (Down to the Last Tool)

The look and feel that your customers associate with your brand extends well beyond your physical plant. Think of all those little pieces of paper you hand out or send to your customers: receipts, statements, invoices, and so on. These also have characteristics that help define who you are and provide an added measure of comfort and familiarity to customers, who see the logo on the account statement and, even if subconsciously, know that it's you.

We often work with clients who employ functionality that parallels what they offer offline. Banks, for example, provide customers with the option of downloading and printing their current checking account statement. In the testing environment, users have told us that, although they appreciate access to these statements, they also expect them to look exactly like the ones they receive in the mail and are often surprised to find that those obtained through the site don't resemble the ones they get in the mail. Bank statements from the site, for example, may use a different font, have the columns in a different format, or be missing the logo.

These often seem like minor details to those of us on the development side. After all, isn't it enough that we are allowing consumers instant online access, something they have never had before? Nevertheless, consumers tell us that without the look and feel they are accustomed to, these forms simply aren't the same. Moreover, without the familiarity and the comfort level they associate with it, the crucial element of trustworthiness is missing.

Insight

Don't forget to offer consistency across channels. Telephone support, the web, and your branches all need to offer the same information, using the same language and tone. Provide your customers with the confidence that they are getting the same story—accuracy, timeliness, and depth of content—from each channel.

Sweating More of the Details
Don't Forget Site Quality

Yes, let's hit that gong again: The experience is the brand. We've discussed how the imagery of your brand needs to be reflected on your site. Now some additional details—big and small—need to be accounted for.

Throughout this book, we have emphasized the importance of providing users with a site that is usable, with respect to labeling, navigation, and organization. If your site is unusable, customers and prospects begin to wonder about your company. Are you disorganized? Behind the times? Unconcerned? Those are the big issues.

Now for the details at the micro level. For instance, is each and every word spelled correctly? We are amazed at the numbers of misspelled words we encounter, not only in prototypes that we are testing, but also in production sites, and not only in content pages, but also in major labels. And that's not to mention the occasional broken link that has passed unnoticed through lack of quality control.

Make sure that each and every word on your site has been read, proofread, and proofread again.

Insight

Even the tiniest typo or broken link detracts from your site and, ultimately, from your brand.

The E-Commerce Question: "How Does the Web Fit with My Other Channels?"

The implications of e-commerce for channel marketing is a complicated issue, and one that is still being sorted out as the role of the web as a buying channel continues to develop. Indeed, the topic stands alone as the subject of many books.

Many traditional businesses worry about how offering their services on the web will affect their retail sales and their channel partner relationships. Our research has shown again and again that there are powerful synergies between traditional retail distribution and web distribution. In many categories where people want to touch, smell, hold, or try on products, having a retail channel is a major strategic advantage. Consumers can try items on in the store and order them on the web. For example, customers at retail chains like the Gap initially shop in the bricks-and-mortar stores in order to get a feel for clothing items (including which styles fit best and which sizes are optimal). After that, they often go to the web site to buy additional items. Jeans are a good example of this. Most likely, fans of Gap jeans want more than one pair. Once they have found a style and size that fits, why not go directly to the web after that?

Here's another example. A retail company that offers car maintenance services obviously can't offer this service online. However, they do provide customers with a way to easily track their car maintenance and performance over the web, and when it is time for additional maintenance, the site also provides the customer with a coupon redeemable at the store.

The bottom line is that if you don't risk cannibalizing your sales on the web, you will be handing your customers over to other companies who are willing to take the risk.

Account Access
Encouraging Repeat Visits

Offering online account access achieves essentially two major purposes.

First, it is a value-added function that customers appreciate. We find that acceptance of online account access has increased dramatically over the past two years. At first it was a hard sell. There was, of course, the initial security concern, as well as fear that all opportunities for personal contact with the brand would be discontinued. Customers also added that they felt they were being jettisoned to the web in companies' attempts to increase profits.

These days, customers increasingly expect to have access to their accounts online. It saves them time, they can access it twenty-four hours per day, and they can print out the results. Compare account access to waiting for a telephone service rep or using voice response, and another benefit of online account access emerges. When customers are on hold for a phone rep, you can play music or maybe a few announcements. Therefore, a second purpose of having online accounts is that when your customers come to your web site to access these, you have a golden opportunity to provide them with a visual experience: sale items, new products, and other announcements.

Figure 18.4

The first page of the account access area in the Circuit City site offers the user a series of helpful options.

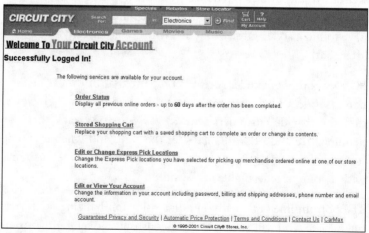

www.circuitcity.com

However, in order for either of these possibilities to be fulfilled, account access functionality has to work *really* well. It needs to be intuitive, secure, and fast. If it's anything less, it detracts from your brand.

Don't Disenfranchise Your Customers
Make Service and Technical Support Useful

Online customer service and technical support is still developing. In this section, we want to briefly discuss these functions from a brand perspective.

Through the years, we have seen online customer service and technical support offered in a range of formats, including FAQs, online support reps, email, and various online forms of help (such as context-sensitive help and online documentation). We even tested technical support that entailed dialing in for remote diagnosis.

Quite frankly, our current experiences can only be summarized in terms of user reactions, which have been decidedly mixed. To begin, customers hate to give up their telephones. They feel that, as your customer, you owe it to them to be available if they need you. After all, that's what they paid for. It is as simple as that. And whenever customers perceive that that support number is being somehow obscured, or worse yet withdrawn, they tend to get angry.

From a brand perspective, the risk in all this is that you might be perceived as dismissive of your customer's needs—that you might be trying to make a quick sale so you can move on to the next one. Most likely, this perception flies in the face of the equity you have built offline.

Here are some basic rules of thumb to follow:

- Online support has to be consistent with your brand. Reflect what you do offline, using the same terminology (for example, sales associates) that you do offline.

- Provide a phone number on each page of customer support and technical support.

- Emphasize to both online and offline customers the *benefits* of online service and support in communications.

We also recommend to our clients that service and especially support include an escalation path. If FAQs don't provide an answer, make sure the next step is clear. For example, consider a searchable database. Have a path in mind and take your user by the hand to get him started. Don't leave him with an unanswered question and nowhere to go, even if that means calling your support line. Again, your site needs to be embracing your customers, keeping them in the fold—not alienating them.

It is also advisable to train your phone support people to *gently* refer customers to online resources. This does not mean ordering them to go to the web first. Instead, train them to suggest online support as an option and to even offer to escort customers through this process.

If you can make your online support especially rich, for example, allowing staff to "push" web pages to the customer, your product will benefit.

Figure 18.5

The Customer Service Directory on the Whirlpool site is an excellent example of how to embrace customers. Notice that the page begins with a statement of purpose posed as a question: "Do you have a question or concern, or do you need assistance?" Also notice that the 800 number is displayed front and center.

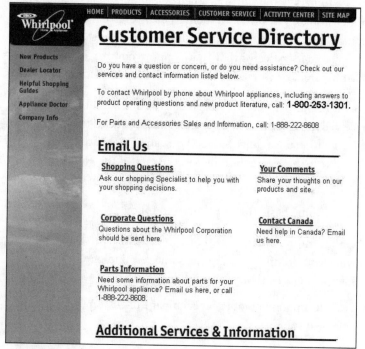

www.whirlpool.com

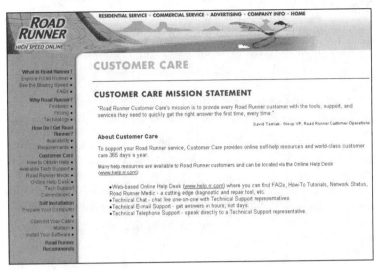

www.roadrunner.com

Figure 18.6

On Road Runner's Customer Care page, the Mission Statement clearly states the company's intention that online service be a means of offering enhanced service to valued customers. Also notice the list of options. By including the technical support number as the last option on the list, an escalation path is implied.

So what is the most important recommendation we can make? Online service and support need to work. That means testing and retesting to make sure that these build upon your brand image by being convenient, helpful, and useful.

Insight

Use online customer service and support to strengthen your customers' connection to your brand. Use features and terminology that support and enhance what you offer offline. Be certain that every aspect of these work, and don't forget to keep that 800 number front and center.

Consider Adding Premium Services for High-Value Customers

We often see sites that reach out aggressively to new customers or to current customers that want to make additional purchases. This is too often a missed opportunity to strengthen the relationship between your brand and your customers.

The site of a major telephone utility, for example, offers one advertisement after another, supplemented by assistance in adding new services. Yet the site offers minimal value-added content, such as features like "reverse look-up" or an online directory. Nor does it offer much in terms of service and support. And special offers for high-value customers? Non-existent.

Users often tell us that they don't even visit the web sites of the brands they do business with most often because they assume there is nothing there for them—unless, of course, they have a problem (and then they may hit the site long enough to get the 800 number).

Increasingly, the web is a brand builder. Think of the potential for further strengthening your connection with high-value customers. Collect the email addresses of your high-value customers. Reach out to them, offline, and ask for their email addresses, along with their *permission* to keep them abreast of offers that may be of interest. Also, ask yourself if it makes sense to provide high-value customers with a special area of the site, password-protected, which offers available only to them, additional account access, or a special newsletter.

Leverage Your Marketing Messages, But Don't Make Your Site a Commercial

Users often tell us they enjoy seeing current advertising reflected on the web, especially if this advertising is somehow intriguing to them. Some of the major consumer brands have done this effectively. Examples include major brands featuring current pop stars, additional content and photos about that star, and perhaps music clips on their site, as well as gift items (for instance, tee shirts and other brand-related merchandise). TV commercials or print advertising can be used to essentially drive users to the site.

On the other hand, users also complain that some sites are nothing but online commercials, with advertising plastered all over the homepage. If they are already purchasing the product or service, why do they have to be advertised to on the web site?

There is no rule of thumb here. What works for a consumer product brand, especially with a campaign that is reaching out to a certain group, like teens, will not necessarily work for a financial services company or even a department store chain.

Only you can decide the best way to integrate offline brand advertising with your web site. And who are your best advisors? Your users.

Research Tip

Use focus groups to gain an understanding of how users perceive your brand and their expectations for how your brand would or wouldn't translate to the web. Show them initial page designs, beginning with the homepage. Does this look like your brand? Does it have the functionality and content they would be most likely to associate with your brand? In a lab setting, explore reactions to functionality from a brand perspective, in addition to basic usability. Also, consider showing advertising at the beginning of a usabiliy interview. Then, explore how your site compares to the expectations generated by the advertising.

The View from 30,000 Feet

Your customers expect your web site to reflect the way in which they experience and perceive your brand. This means paying attention to not only the look and feel of the site, but also to overall organization, product and service mix, and labeling. Additional functionality (such as online account access, customer service and support, and premium services) can serve to further involve your customers in your brand. However, heed one caution: Don't shortchange your brand through poor usability. Test and retest until all typos, broken links, and other glitches are eliminated.

A Few Hard Questions

- Does the look and feel of your site reflect your brand in a way that has the potential of both strengthening and leveraging your brand equity?

- Is your site organized the way your customers think of your product line or retail outlets?

- Are you offering products and services online that are consistent with expectations for your brand?

- Is the language you use on your site consistent with how you communicate with customers offline?

- Are account access and online customer service and support areas designed in a manner that will enhance your customers' experience and, therefore, their relationship with your brand?

- Have you checked and double-checked all spelling and links and made sure the overall site usability is optimal?

CHAPTER NINETEEN

Business-to-Business

Challenges and Opportunities

Although a user-centered approach will enhance any web site, we think a "user first" attitude is best for any site geared to businesses. To reach a business audience, a site must be designed, built, and implemented with the user's viewpoint in mind from beginning to end.

Over the past several years, we have seen dozens of approaches to utilizing the web to reach out to businesses. Whether the goal is setting up a global supply and procurement system, or simply marketing a particular good or service, the complexities and idiosyncrasies of the targeted industry must be taken into account.

Successful business-to-business (B2B) web ventures don't move forward until the builders understand these key things:

- Internal approval and payment processes; levels of authority
- Language that is unique to the industry—including acronyms
- Differences in measurement and currency terms by country
- Arcane business rules and trading practices

Given how loath many industries are to change the way they do business, it is essential that target users be brought into the development of B2B sites to ensure that the transition to online transactions is as smooth and organic as possible. One of the best ways to do this is to identify and leverage the benefits the online world offers so the stakeholders in a prospective client company have the ammunition they need to sell the online business model up the line.

The following sections outline some general rules of thumb that we have found apply to all businesses, whether you trade steel, sell office supplies, or provide healthcare services.

Understand How Your Customers Do Business

Any business consultant that has spent a week or so getting to know a new industry will find that the way they do business is unique and at times inexplicable to outsiders.

In the financial services industry, for example, new account openings are the lifeblood of a firm and are generally given priority over existing account management. Advisors have just one chance to make a first impression with new clients. They are willing to do whatever it takes to ensure that new accounts are opened without problems. Unfortunately, they have many obstacles to deal with. Potential "deal killers" include the following:

- Poorly trained back office staff
- Indifferent custodial banks

- Former financial advisors of their new client who "accidentally" forget to transfer funds

- An arcane regulatory process

In addition, a host of other glitches could end a new client relationship before it starts.

This audience perceives a site as valuable only if it provides a solution to an existing problem. All else has little value. Consider then, the following examples of solutions to those problems:

- Although principals and accredited brokers usually initiate client contact, the bulk of the resulting paperwork is often done by interns and inexperienced staff. As a result, financial services professionals are generally more receptive to using sites that could be manipulated by a second-week trainee as easily as by a seasoned broker. This means a simplified interface with several layers of error recovery mechanisms.

- When an investor chooses a new manager for his money, the former financial advisors sometimes delay transferring funds. They have no vested interest in sending the money quickly and helping the new advisor appear competent. Therefore, advisors need applications that allow them to instantly track the progress of funds transfers. That way, if an irate client calls in, they can go online, check on the status of the transfer, and place the blame squarely on the shoulders of the former manager—all while the new client waits on the phone.

- The SEC requires that investors fill out certain regulatory forms annually. A client designed a site that stored client data and allowed them to easily retrieve it when generating such routine paperwork. In most markets, brokers were satisfied with the interface. However, advisors in the Midwest balked. The interface only allowed room for one address. Why would that matter? In cold weather states, well-to-do clients were likely to have a second semi-permanent address in a warm weather state. Brokers were used to dealing with two addresses and were greatly helped by a design that allowed them to toggle between the two. In other words, because of the way they conducted business, a "helpful" feature was useless to a large segment of the target audience.

This "know the industry" principle applies everywhere. The trick is to know the answers to several important questions concerning how business is conducted in the offline world:

- Who are the players? What are the priorities and potential obstacles faced by the audience?

- What is the division of labor within the prospective customer's company?

- What are the statutory hurdles and regulatory concerns?

The next step is to identify gaps in the current process. Where can you and your site meet an existing need? We have found focus groups among prospective customers to be the most effective method of identifying exactly what would make them consider adjusting their current practices in order to do business with you.

Research Tip

When you conduct focus group research, consider yourself an anthropologist. You are studying this unique tribe of members of a given industry. To help design the optimal online offering, you need to get beneath the surface and understand their business practices, concerns, and wish lists. Tell them you want to understand everything that is important to them. If you don't understand why something arises as an issue—or you don't understand their language—probe them for answers. Don't act as if you know what they mean if you don't.

Last, ask them to design an ideal online application that will replace what they are currently doing. Make sure you understand the ways in which it differs and ways it remains the same. They will welcome your interest.

Remember, Company Rules Exist for a Reason

One of the amazing things we find in working on B2B sites is the degree to which companies that create them fail to understand (or allow for) the levels of authorization required within large and small companies when it comes to commerce, banking, and even access to information. Consider the following:

- In most companies, some people have spending authority up to a certain amount, and others always need someone to authorize a purchase. Successful sites understand and incorporate such authorization procedures. If your prospective customer's current procedure requires "Lou on the 14th floor" to authorize all orders over $500, you won't even be considered unless your system does the same.

- In most companies, access to information is not shared equally. Your target audience's "need to know" policies must be adhered to. For example, if you want medium-sized businesses to use your financial management product, you'd better make sure that low-level employees can use the online bill payment feature, but that only selected staff can view the amount of direct deposit payroll payments. If this flexibility is not built into your site from the start, you might as well start over.

- Some companies have rules about how much money can be spent for shipping, couriers, and so on. If your service doesn't meet these guidelines (or if it exceeds them), your service will not be purchased.

These policies—the systems of checks and balances that exist in most companies—are created for good reason. Don't assume that your product or service is so phenomenal it will cause companies to ignore the way they do things. It won't.

To sum up, the rules for business sites are far different from the rules for consumer sites. When building a site for consumers, the object is to give the end user as many options as possible. When gearing a site to business, however, the object is to limit the end user's options to what higher-ups determine is appropriate. Period. End of story.

Your Client List Is Your Credibility

You know the expression "you're as good as the company you keep." We all know what this means. If I am interested in your service, and I go to your site but don't learn about your other customers—or I don't recognize any of them—why would I take a risk and do business with you? How do I know that your services are what you say they are? How do I know that you'll be around in a year when my project is over? How can I get references or see samples of your work?

In service businesses in particular, you are most definitely judged by the company you keep. The fastest way to check this out is to visit a company's site. On yours, you should make sure you provide easy access to:

- Your clients

- Your experience and your years in business

- Any case studies about or samples of your prior work

- The industries you serve (we all know that each industry finds itself and its needs unique)

Prospective customers are checking you out as we speak. Make sure these visits—most of which you will never know about—serve to enhance your credibility.

One of the most important things you can do if you are trying to expand your client base or the breadth of industries you serve is to approach a company you'd most like to work with and pitch them on a project. If necessary, offer to do it on spec or at a great

Figure 19.1
(Next two images)

Whether through a montage of business cards or a good outside quote, both sites have harnessed the power of a credible client list.

www.idealab.com

www.comw.com

discount so that you get the credentials. Let your client know that if they will let you do a case study, you will give them a discount, or offer to write it or link it to their site. This way you build off of their credibility.

By the way, the fact that you are doing business online is no reason to not establish your credibility offline. Offer to speak with them at an industry conference. Showing your work with them to an audience of their peers will enhance your credibility in their industry. It will also help to mobilize them to strut their own stuff. In other words, this process is a two-way street.

People Stick to Their Own Kind: Make Sure They Know You Are One of Them

Each of us pretty much knows the big shots in our industry and who the newcomers are. Those newcomers are frequently interrogated by prospective clients: Who are you? What do you know about the automotive parts industry? The investment banking industry? The printing industry? Who is your senior management? Do they come from the industry, or were they imported from a totally different one? Are they looking to just make a killing on the Internet and haven't a clue about the restaurant industry (or the healthcare industry or whatever)? Potentially, the questions go on and on.

If you have credentials in an industry, display them prominently in About Us or even on the homepage. Include in your bio all the experience you've had in the industry and all the players you've worked with. Prospective clients want to know that you know their industry, their language, and their needs. They don't want to think you are an opportunist who has built a product or service that may not meet their needs. As we have said before, if you need credentials, borrow them. Join industry associations. Speak at industry conferences. Include multiple mentions on your site about the industry experience your company or site brings to bear.

Figure 19.2
(Next two images)

Neither of these sites is the least bit shy about touting the credentials that will most intrigue their target audience.

www.studioscriptsales.com

www.mangroupplc.com

What's in It for Me?
Look for Allies Before Attacking a Market

One of the wonderful things the Internet has created is the opportunity to partner with certain players in an industry. By serving them well, a B2B site can create allies and a built-in sales force—preaching a site and a company's virtues to others. We recommend to our clients that they don't move forward until they identify all potential allies—that is, stakeholders who might benefit from association with their site.

Let's use the insurance industry as an example. When designing an interface for use by policyholders, the first instinct might be to focus only on the needs of end users, the employees who will hopefully use the site to check on claims, order lost cards, and find new doctors. Why not take into account other stakeholders as well? Benefits Administrators of the companies whose employees are policyholders are a perfect example. These people spend much of their time replacing lost or outdated employee membership cards, filing change of address forms, finding out about each plan's stipulations, and chasing claim forms. If a health insurance site can make the lives of Benefits Administrators easier by reducing their workload, the site can win critical allies.

Think about it. If your site makes jobs easier or provides faster or cheaper access to information needed on a daily basis, your customers will be very loyal to you. Heck, they'll even promote your site to employees, direct them to your web site, and tell them about new features you've added. If your site is good enough, it may push me, the customer, to recommend your plan over another competitor for whom these same tasks are very cumbersome. Time is money. And, if I have more time, I can attend to the really cool projects that might not otherwise have been possible.

Our research indicated that a substantial number of insured employees (potential end-users) turned to Benefits Administrators first when conducting routine transactions. We advised our client to make the Benefits Administrators "part of the team" and suggested that they create a printable "Frequently Asked Questions" page that directs users to the proper section of the site. Benefits Administrators could hand out these sheets to employees who came in the office with routine questions. The net effect is that Benefits Administrators could reduce their workload while driving traffic to the site.

Our approach is to embrace, rather than directly challenge, existing habits and relationships. The dotcom landscape is littered with failed companies who planned to "change everything" and "revolutionize the way" people obtain services. Why? The way we see things, you should focus on your objectives and hand a digital olive branch to anyone who can help you meet them.

Don't Forget That Your Customers Have Customers

In today's competitive environment, successful companies must be obsessed with pleasing their customers. We have noticed that sites that understand and incorporate this philosophy are usually well received, especially within service industries.

Our research indicates that "client-centric" audiences, such as insurance agents and financial planners, prefer to use sites that somehow enhance their image in the eyes of their customers. Often, the intended benefits of a business-to-business site, such as a reduction in back-office labor costs, are considered secondary to the benefits that directly affect the face-to-face customer relationship.

When developing a site geared to "face" businesses, be prepared to answer several questions:

- *How does the site/product help generate new sales opportunities?*

   A client designed a 401K site to allow employees to check their retirement account balances. They also offered independent brokers the opportunity to place their contact information throughout their site. Brokers who handled the accounts of companies with moderate-income employees (such as factories) felt as though giving out that information would be problematic, because it might well increase the number of routine calls to their offices.

Brokers who handled the accounts of companies with high-income employees (such as law firms and architectural firms) loved the idea. Phone calls could only lead to opportunities to sell other products to their well-off clients.

● *How does the site improve relations with a customer/client base?*

Another client, a large financial service client, assumed their site's killer app was that it reduced labor during data entry. What they discovered was that the greatest perceived benefit was that the site produced neat, professional-looking paperwork. This helped small independent brokers appear competent and tech savvy in the eyes of new clients.

An HMO site offered its physicians the ability to tailor patient information on different diseases with the physician's name, address, and logo. The ability to print these custom-looking materials off the site and create instant collateral materials and patient information was perceived as one of the most useful benefits of the site. Why? It made the doctors look good.

● *Does the site improve upon any process undertaken by your customer's customer?*

A business services site assumed that CPAs would be attracted to a feature of their site designed to offer information about reducing office costs. Interestingly, CPAs didn't want to use that section of the site themselves. They wanted to show it to their customers. Why? They knew that it would streamline an existing process for them.

Leverage Your Brand and Stick to Your Core Competencies

Over the past several years we have seen many examples of companies that tried to expand their product range and offer a wide variety of services and information online. Many assumed that the key to "stickiness" was to offer as many resources as possible, without regard to whether they were related to the brand's core strengths. This approach failed.

Interviews with businesses of all sizes indicate that no one is looking for the "web-site-o-matic." They don't need a site that "slices and dices" and offers every conceivable service or piece of information. They are looking for sites that meet key needs and offer credible solutions to their problems.

We have seen sites geared to small businesses that tried to establish themselves by offering everything from loans to postage stamps. Successful sites, however, leverage their existing credibility by offering services that are connected in some way. For example, some credit card sites hoped to become a one-stop resource for businesses. What small-businesses were actually interested in, however, was information related to the credit card companies' core competencies: transactions. They found real value in the sections of the site that offered fraud prevention tips and related information, and information on how to do credit card transactions online. The credit card company was the natural expert in this area, and these tips emerged as the site's key driver.

Be Careful Who You Set Your Sights On

We often hear B2B clients tell us that their target customer is the CTO of a Fortune 1000 company. First, we ask, how many CTOs or CIOs are on the web? Second, why do they need your site when they have hosts of "hunter gatherers" collecting information to bring to them?

The following questions need to be asked here:

- What size companies are going to use your site and its services, and why?

- What kinds of people in these companies are going to use your site, and why?

- What are the compelling benefits of using your site versus offline or online alternatives?

- Will they save time? Money?

- Will they get better record keeping as a result of placing their orders online?

- Will they get 24/7 access to information they can now access only during business hours?

Sometimes, we find that clients think the only answer is Fortune 1000 clients, when in fact, their services offer far more appeal to smaller businesses. Unfortunately, due to their lesser size, these also have lesser clout. Therefore, there are services that smaller companies don't have access to that their far larger counterparts already have covered.

One client designed a site that made copyright-free animated designs available to companies for use on their web sites and assumed that Fortune 1000 firms would be the most likely purchasers of the stock designs. What they found, however, was that Fortune 1000 companies were so brand conscious, they did not consider using stock animation.

Smaller firms did have a need for such products, but they didn't have the time or resources to create them. However, they wanted edgier fare than the stock animations that had been created with a Fortune 1000 audience in mind. Earlier research would have saved our client time and money.

Know the Difference Between End Users and Decision Makers

We are often surprised at how many developers are unaware of the need to position the product to different audiences. Many use a cookie cutter approach that touts the same benefits to everyone at a prospective company, regardless of his or her level within the organization.

We have worked with several clients who have designed highly technical IT-related applications for use by businesses. These clients, who tend to have technical backgrounds, often assume that the benefits of their service or application are so readily apparent that CIOs and IT help desk administrators alike will recognize their value. That is rarely the case.

Implementers—help desk administrators, LAN managers, and network security personnel—can easily recognize the value of a highly technical application. They understand why they would use a site or service, how they would use it, when they would use it, and where. Unfortunately, they are rarely the person holding the purse strings. That audience requires a different approach.

Decision makers have a different set of concerns. They are not interested in the technical intricacies of a product. They are concerned with how that product can make them better managers or how it affects the bottom line. In this case, we suggested that our client rewrite key content areas using a less technical approach.

The View from 30,000 Feet

B2B sites require in-depth knowledge of an industry, as well as the way business is conducted online and offline. The ticket to success lies in exploiting the web to enhance whatever activities you've undertaken online, without forcing users to radically change the way they do business or to break the rules that apply to their company and/or industry (for example, levels of authority or access to information).

A Few Hard Questions

- Have you studied the way target users currently do business both online and offline?

- Have you identified who, within a corporation, will champion your site? For instance, will it be benefits administrators who view online HMO claims checks as a way to save time and money?

- What other companies can you partner with to establish credibility and build business?

- Are you leveraging your current clients to reinforce your credibility?

PART VI

And the View from Outer Space

Staying Ahead of (or at Least Keeping Up With) the Speed of Technology

20 Step Out Of the Shadows and into Their Shoes
   The Power of Listening   327

21 Just When You Think You Know Everything,
   It Changes   335

Step Out of the Shadows and into Their Shoes

The Power of Listening

Many successful web marketers—large and small—make it an ongoing practice to bring target users into the development process prior to introducing any new functionality. They want to make sure not only that the new stuff works, but that it doesn't have a negative impact on the existing site.

This continuous exercise in listening enables marketers to keep a pulse on customer behavior and needs. Each time target users are given the experience of using a site, they not only identify potential problems, but also draw potential opportunities to the surface—features that add value and differentiate a given site's offering from that of its competition.

Throughout this book, we have talked about the importance of listening to the user, and in our "Research Tips" sections, we have given you some tips on how you can accomplish that. In this chapter, we want to summarize our thoughts on the importance of listening, as well as help you make the case for formalizing this process in your own development and marketing efforts.

Why Listen? Isn't the Answer Already Obvious?

By this point in the book, you have probably already formulated an answer to this question. We've been telling you and, more importantly, showing you throughout the book that the user's voice must be solicited and heeded.

By now we hope that you agree that it is much easier to ask the question than to answer it, and solutions are not always obvious. Users think, reason, and react in ways that never cease to amaze and mystify us. And we talk to them every day.

Nevertheless, you may have some lingering doubts. Maybe you think it's a good idea to listen to users when you're creating a site or when the first prototype is developed, but after that initial splash, you're planning to wing it. Or maybe you're assuming that the next steps will be self-evident. Maybe the web feels "cooked" at this point. So why do anything else to your site?

Alternatively, maybe you're totally on board with the idea of involving the voice of the user in your development process, but you aren't sure if your co-workers or management are equally convinced. So first, let us say this: The job of listening to the user is never finished. The only way to make sure the user is heard is to build his voice into every step of the process.

The User Dialogue Establishes the Foundation for Your Site

We have discussed at length the importance of launching your site from a foundation of strength—one that is based upon a dialogue with your users, a dialogue that addresses the following things about them:

- What they do offline, their processes
- What they expect and don't expect to do online
- The terminology they use
- Their expectations of your brand
- What they most need from your web site, or even the potential for "killer apps"

We have also discussed the importance of testing your site, with a focus on the initial prototype, including elements such as these:

- Navigation
- Labeling
- Functionality
- Look and feel
- Content

When addressing the usability of your site, we have frequently invoked the term "intuitiveness," which you might define as the ability of a user to achieve his goals on your site without you having to sit beside him and guide him every step of the way.

So, if you've covered these bases, is the task of listening to users finished? No, not when so many questions assert themselves time and again. A couple of these questions are covered in more detail here.

Is It Time for a Revamp? Only Your Users Really Know

You are familiar with your own schedule for modifying your site. But is it in sync with what your users are thinking? You may be considering a semi-annual, or annual, "refurbishing" of your site, at which time you will make a few adjustments here or change a link or two there. Your users may tell you, however, that certain aspects of your site are no longer useful, or even dead in the water.

For example, we worked with a technology products company that was planning to modify their shopping area... at some point. They decided to obtain user feedback, if only for "strategic planning purposes."

Guess what? In focus groups, users (who were also paying customers) told them that their shopping functionality was way behind that of their competitors. The users also said that, given the perceived similarity of the products offered by the two companies, they might just shop with the other guy.

Needless to say (almost), the schedule for changing the site changed drastically. The priorities were certainly clear.

What Do They Want Next? Anticipating the Curve

Although what users tell you is critical, so is what they don't tell you. Going forward, users will certainly let you know if they want to see something particular on your site. Often, it is not so easy to put a finger on what is needed, and they don't know how to answer questions about improving a site. After all, we—not they—are the developers and marketers. They just know that something is missing.

Listening to what they say and what they don't say (or can't articulate) is critical to the ongoing welfare of your site. This is where building a better web site gets complicated and more involved in questions of their behavior, online and off. For instance, what are they doing offline that they want to do online? What kinds of things are they doing on other sites that are useful or interesting? Could some of these features be added to your site?

Look at the history of chat, as some of our clients have done. Users were chatting online, at least socially. Clients got wind of this and began to look for ways to incorporate this feature into their own sites, especially when their users began to report that other sites were offering chat for business purposes, such as technical support and sales assistance. Users may not have suggested moving chat into some of these sites, but listening to them opened up a host of possibilities.

Checking the Oil
Creating an Ongoing Dialogue

Of the many things you have probably observed and experienced regarding the web, you will probably agree that the only constancy is change. We will discuss this in more detail in the next chapter. For now, we just want to stress once again that things move quickly online. What do you want and need to accomplish in your site as, for example, you adopt new features like online support or value-added content? What do users expect from one month to the next as the yardstick of expectations is constantly raised? Yesterday they were happy with email. Now, they want to watch movies.

That *is* what they want, isn't it? Oh, you mean you haven't asked them?

The only way to know what your users, as well as prospective users, really want from your site is to keep talking to them. We've examined various ways to accomplish that, most importantly focus groups and user experience testing (both of which are covered in the Appendix, "A Crash Course in Web Development Research"). What we want to emphasize here is that the process of talking to your users is ongoing. Not just pre- and post-launch.

We recommend that clients schedule research on a periodic basis, regardless of whether or not they actually have made changes or are even considering making them. Monthly research, quarterly research—it depends on how fast things are changing in your category. And if you are in an industry that is undergoing a transition (such as local and long distance carriers), or in which your competitors are suddenly rattling their sabers, you may want to step up the dialogue temporarily.

Insight
The world of the web moves at lightning speed. So your site is never really finished. Keep listening to your users to make sure it doesn't become outdated.

Some of our clients have established web site advisory councils. They have asked users to volunteer to provide them feedback on a regular basis, either in person, through a phone interview, or on-line. Such a council, which may be only a dozen or so people depending on how involved you want to get in this process, is generally comprised of users from a range of demographic backgrounds and levels of sophistication. Council members feel involved, and the sponsor of the site has a feedback mechanism that can be tapped at a moment's notice.

For business-to-business sites, the council can consist of major clients. They will be more supportive of your progress and forgiving of your mistakes if you make them part of your team.

Whether a council is formed or more formal research is conducted, seeking ongoing feedback is like regularly checking your oil. You gauge your current health—perceptions of the site, experiences, wants and needs, changing habits—and consequently anticipate when the next change is needed. We have carried this metaphor far enough, but by being proactive about gauging where your users are, you also avoid emergency maintenance.

You Can't Test in a Vacuum
New Features Versus the Whole Site

We work with a major financial site on an ongoing basis. They make frequent modifications to their site and engage us to conduct user experience testing each time they come to another juncture. Sometimes we see them every couple of months, and sometimes many months pass before we hear from them. The changes may be very minor (a tweak to a chart or graph, for example), or they may be major (such as a whole new content area).

The important thing about this client for the purposes of our discussion is that they don't feel comfortable making a move without involving their users. And reactions to the site reinforce the benefits of this testing.

But here's the point we really want to make: When we test a new function or piece of content, regardless of how small or how deep into the site, we begin the testing on the homepage. In the testing situation, we ask respondents, who are recruited from among current and prospective users, to begin at the homepage. We assess, or re-assess, their perceptions of the homepage. Then we create a task for them to complete, which involves whatever we are testing. In other words, we don't click on a page or function and say: "This might be in the site. Do you like it?"

Web site features, even new ones (and even those new for old users), are not employed in a vacuum. If the path to a feature does not begin on the homepage, even if there are a few steps in between, it is not going to be found. Also, if the feature doesn't make logical sense in the context of the whole site, it is not going to be used.

And that leads us to another benefit of testing new features. When we are conducting web site testing for this client, we also talk to their users about how they feel about the site. What is working or not working? What do they wish they could do? We also ask them about their web use in general. What are they doing more (or less) of online?

Consequently, our financial services client, by testing potential changes to their site in advance of implementing them, has devised a built-in "oil check" that keeps its motor running smoothly.

Insight

Test each and every new feature you add to your site. Find out what users (and prospective users) think. Moreover, conduct this testing within the context of the whole site and not in a vacuum.

No Matter How Sophisticated Your Site, Don't Underestimate the Role of the Offline World

As we have emphasized, the offline world continues to yield clues to opportunities online. Certainly, this makes sense when you are first building your site. Offline processes, and gaps in those processes, suggest both expectations for how online processes should work, as well as features that will be especially interesting to users. For example, knowing how users make product selection decisions, what kinds of information they need to do this, and what they have the most trouble obtaining, have implications for developing a winning web site.

But even after your site is built, the value of understanding the off-line world does not necessarily decline. After all, it continues to grow and change just as the web does. New sources of information—magazines and journals—spring up and find a place in the lives of professionals. Or they disappear. Likewise, the competitive landscape changes as companies come and go and buying habits adjust accordingly. New products come along, like wireless devices and new entertainment technology, that affect what consumers want and how they gather useful information.

Can users advise you as to what this means for your site? Probably not. But they can certainly tell you how they are being affected by developments in their world, what they're gaining, and what they're losing, all of which can sound alarms and present opportunities for your site.

All you have to do is listen.

Insight

Users may not be able to articulate what you should do next on your site, but they can certainly tell you what's missing in their lives. Their gaps are your opportunities.

CHAPTER TWENTY-ONE

Just When You Think You Know Everything, It Changes

The web is a moving target. This rapid pace of growth, in terms of both user expectations and technological advancements, keeps things exciting for those of us responsible for creating relevant, cutting-edge web sites and keeping them that way.

There are no rules.

But over the past few years, we have learned a few things we would like to pass on to you in this last chapter.

Adoption Patterns Do Not Remain Consistent

One of the amazing things about the web is the speed with which new features, navigation, content, and language are adopted by the growing population of web users. For example, of late many "newbies" who have just started using the web are e-commerce active. Why? Well, many became web users with a particular intent—to shop or trade. Hence, their e-commerce behavior does not mirror the slower adoption of e-commerce by their predecessors.

What this suggests is that rules and stereotypes have no place when you're defining how people use the web. Whatever principles apply today will not necessarily be true six months from now or after the next holiday season. Moreover, what is true for one web site with a specific architecture, brand, or industry is not necessarily true for another.

What remains constant is the importance of bringing users into the development process, early on and throughout the evolution of a site.

User Needs Grow, and Sites Grow with Them

As marketers and developers, we tend to see things through a relatively myopic lens. We have a specific vision for our own web site (functionality and content that we think makes sense for our target users), and we often doggedly pursue that direction. Generally, this is a strategy that works in the short-term.

But users are not visiting your site alone; they will also visit a range of others. While they are on these other sites, they frequently experience functionality that intrigues them, though much of it is irrelevant to your site. At least you thought it was irrelevant. But your users may think otherwise.

Here's an example from the realm of online matchmaking sites: At one point, these sites offered a means of meeting people to date in one's own geographical area. Users were happy being able to find someone of whatever sex they were seeking, in the same basic age group, within commuting distance. It was a good start, and certainly better than hanging out in singles bars.

Over time, however, users wanted more exact matching, according to a number of criteria—for instance, guitar player, graduate school, intense blue eyes, works out three times a week. After all, these users were experiencing some pretty sophisticated and advanced search features on other sites. Why not get narrower searches and avoid those dates that never get off the ground?

Subsequently, users began demanding that matching sites connect them not only to that special someone, but maybe to a pool of potential special someones, in the form of a group of like-minded people that could get together for casual events and take some of the pressure off the initial date. Again, they were modeling these aspects after some interesting community functionality on hobby and business sites.

More complicated still, if like-minded people are online at the same time, maybe they should also be able to chat while they are there. Matching sites responded with more community functionality, helping their customers to form groups and even adding functionality that made it easy to poll one another on what events the group members would most likely participate in, like travel or parties.

In the end, all this led in yet another direction. If users were forming groups and planning events, maybe the site should be sponsoring these events. This would both serve the primary needs of users and provide another source of revenue. Why not? Users were certainly accustomed to using entertainment sites to find events and register for them, along with paying with their credit card.

How did all of this come about? Most likely, the sponsors of matching sites solicited feedback from their users and listened to what they had to say. What's important is that these sites have continued to evolve along with the needs and sophistication levels of their users. Those that stayed "married" (if you'll pardon the pun) to their original business models most likely have been bypassed by the competition.

The Role of a Function Can Shift and Mature

Nothing stays the same. Functionality emerges within one category or business model and migrates to another. Here are just a few examples of functions that have changed from their first introduction to the present, after they have been embraced by users and have subsequently found their way to new applications and types of sites.

You could say that what goes around comes around. Or you could say there is nothing new under the sun. Maybe the point is simply that good solid ideas are applicable in a range of situations.

Chat

Chat started out as a way for online users to make social contacts, and it continues to serve this function. But it also has a business purpose. E-commerce sites now have online sales reps who are available to chat about sizes, styles, and technical requirements. Sites are also making online support reps available who can talk a user through (or "chat through") a solution.

Online Bidding

At one point, online bidding was limited to auction sites like eBay. Users caught on to the idea. Now standard e-commerce sites are providing the opportunity to not only buy new products, but also to bid on used products.

Message Boards

There was a time when entire sites were devoted to message boards. Some continue to thrive, but others have fallen by the wayside as users became less and less interested in spending time on sites that offered nothing beyond this capability. Yet, the idea of reading about what other people think, especially people with similar interests or experiences, continues to attract users. The message board concept is being used in e-commerce sites, news sites, content sites, and so on. Essentially, it creates a sense of community, offering people an opportunity to connect with kindred spirits they were previously unable to find. Amazon and Barnes & Noble are good examples. The message board concept is the basis for the users' ability to post their own reviews of individual books; this essentially creates a community.

Online Calculators and Worksheets

Financial services sites moved their questionnaires online, with the added benefit of getting answers without having to send them off for scoring or to score one's own. Now almost any site you can imagine, from cosmetics to small business to games, offers users a way to interact with the site. Some of the interactive tools are simply for fun, whereas others are vehicles for self-insight or are intended to help the user self-define and consequently get started on the most appropriate path through the site.

Video/Audio

Music, movie, and other entertainment sites pioneered the use of audio and video clips. Now it is rare to find a site that does not incorporate this technology in some way. Examples include product demos, introductions to employees or the CEO, and tours.

E-Commerce

Many of the pure play e-commerce sites came and went. The large bricks-and-mortar outlets and manufacturers gradually expanded their e-commerce offerings. After a few initial forays in which many were consumed by the fear that they might "cannibalize" their offline channels, developers learned that e-commerce served to add to their overall strength rather than diminish it. They also learned that consumers love sales, and that the web is a highly effective and cost-efficient outlet for discounted items.

The ability to shop online and return products to a local store has also been a major factor in swinging the e-commerce pendulum in favor of buying through the sites of bricks-and-mortar companies. Furthermore, the ability to get customer service 24/7 extends the footprint and the service levels of bricks-and-mortar companies.

The lesson here? It's one we've been emphasizing throughout the book. Keep listening for what they want, what they like, what they don't like, and what they wish they could do.

Insight

Listen to your users. Find out everything you can about them. Your site is not an island: Don't limit yourself to what they do on your site.

Morphing: First Web Sites, Then Complementary Technologies

You could almost say that a morphing process is occurring. Web sites were separate entities for a while, with companies creating web site groups that, seemingly set adrift from their parent companies, were sometimes even launched as separate businesses. Lately, this tendency has waned, and site design and marketing have been drawn back into the mainstream of company activity.

Business models mature and find a role in the company. And as we discussed in this chapter, functionality that has been successful in one type of site has found its way into others.

Features mature and evolve into new roles. Ultimately, other technologies spring into existence. Wireless, for example. But then, users are hooked on the web. They want to use it not only at their desktop, but when they are out on the street. The result? New challenges and opportunities that require synergy among technologies that did not previously intersect.

How did companies know that users wanted web access while they were on the go? They asked their users. And they listened to what users said. Now all they have to do is figure out how to deliver it.

They'll come up with some alternatives. And they'll keep asking users what they think.

Parting Words in the Form of a Reminder

Keep listening to your users, now and in the future. If you're looking for compelling reasons, here they are:

- You announce the most compelling messages on your homepage to attract new users and retain current ones.

- Your site is effectively building brand equity.

- New content and functionality add value and provide a competitive edge.

- Navigation and language are intuitive, which enables users to find what they want and successfully complete desired transactions.

- You can serve your users 24/7 and build an ongoing relationship with them.

- They will want to come back.

And ultimately, getting users back to your site—and continuing to build a relationship with them—is the real test of your site's effectiveness.

A Crash Course in Web Development Research

One of the main reasons developers tell us they don't conduct research is the simple fact that they don't know where to begin.

The goal of this appendix is to provide enough information about web development research to enable people who strategize, create, and market web sites to gauge how and when research can help to accomplish these goals:

- Shape the concept—from positioning the site to defining functionality and content.

- Expedite the development process.

- Create a site that is optimized—both with respect to its appeal and its usability—for the audience(s) it serves.

The purpose of this appendix is to address some of these questions and, in so doing, to empower development teams and to provide them with the requisite confidence to embark on a research project.

Which Method Do I Use?

This appendix focuses on two research methods, both useful and usable, that we've found to be invaluable in the development of web sites: focus groups and user experience research.

In both cases, we are advocates of doing research in person versus online. We recommend this because it has proven difficult to inspire respondents from a remote location or to converse at length with them about concepts or web sites. These and other benefits gained by doing research in person—with the development team inches away to observe the experience—are discussed here.

Focus Groups: What They Are and What They Do

Focus groups, as most of us who have been in one or who witnessed the last presidential campaign know, are round-table discussions that typically involve eight or ten carefully chosen people and are usually led by a skilled facilitator or "moderator."

In web development, the following variables are used to decide how to conduct focus groups:

- A desire to validate one's initial concept, and to know whether people are interested. If so, what emotional and rational benefits does the concept provide?

- A need to understand what a company has to offer customers, and how this might be preferable to what they are currently getting on- or offline.

- A desire to understand one's target audience. Developers may have unwarranted assumptions about taken-for-granted target segments that need further exploration.

- A need to know how target users "bucket" what is being offered to them: that is, what language and logic do users share that developers need to know about in order to create and label effective site architecture at a high level?

- A need for better insight into the expectations of target users while visiting the sites of *established* brands. What is the relationship between these and a developer's other channels?

Some Rules of Thumb

Having established the *raison d'etre* of focus groups, we now offer a few suggestions about the key points to keep in mind when actually beginning the process of conducting research:

- Look for research firms that have experience in the kind of work your company does. This will allow you to "piggy back" on their learning and will add value in defining your audience and your markets.

- Decide what target audiences you want to interview, as well as how they are to be evaluated behaviorally, attitudinally, and demographically.

- Don't try to mix target audiences that are very different by placing them in the same respondent group. Their experiences are in all likelihood very different from one another, which might, in turn, dilute the focus or momentum of research.

- Harbor no illusions about "global" testing. In most cases, statistically significant sample sizes are impossible to obtain, and attempts to acquire them are likely to be both costly and ineffective. Thus, we never do more than a total of eight groups for web site development, and often even fewer.

- Select a market or markets that represent your target audience. For example, if you think many of your likely visitors live far from a major metropolitan center, include such a market in your research.

How to Structure a Focus Group

While all projects are unique in that each is based on the intersection of particular concepts, industries, audiences, and stages of development, there are nevertheless some guidelines that are generally relevant to the effective structuring of focus groups.

- Start by discovering how target users set about accomplishing the tasks you provide them on your site.

- Find out what they like and don't like about the site as it is currently set up.

- Discover whether there are opportunities to improve upon what is currently available on a site.

- Ask respondents what features and functions your site could offer to evoke the greatest interest. *Tip*: Let users generate their own ideas *before* you ask them to react to concepts you've created. Exposing respondents to your ideas at a later stage will only serve to confirm their interest.

- Let respondents design their own homepage. This provides insight into how respondents themselves create, label, and use buckets.

- Have respondents describe the homepage they have created and tell you why they've designed it that way.

- Subsequently, expose them to ideas developed by you, the design team, and ask whether these generate sufficient interest to merit incorporation into the "ideal" site of their making.

- Having designed their ideal version of what you want to offer them, discover on what occasions they would visit such a site and what motivations they would have to do so. *Tip*: This input will provide valuable guidance about how to promote your site and how to describe it on your homepage.

- If you have screens that are more-or-less complete (even if they remain in rough form), present them for discussion and discover how they stack up against the group's expectations.

- If you have site names or taglines, present them at the end of the group. Then participants will be able to consider them in light of having been submerged in discussion of your site.

How to Make the Results of Focus Group Research Actionable

Although some development teams will conduct several rounds of focus group testing—primarily to refine the concept and shape high-level architecture—most do not have the luxury of an unlimited budget or amount of time in which to conduct the research. In light of these constraints, the goal of a round of focus groups is to come away with answers (however preliminary) to a small number of very basic questions. Developers should be looking to discover these things:

- The most compelling, jargon-free way to describe a site. This could be a tagline or a series of phrases that best communicates why people would want to use it.

- A strong understanding of the high-level architecture needed (that is, what buckets should appear on the homepage and how to label them). This will help you give users access to the functionality and content that is most appealing.

- A strong sense of the features and content in which to invest time and money, and the order in which this should be undertaken. We've seen focus groups enlighten developers about features that are extremely easy and inexpensive to build, but which nonetheless hold much greater appeal than others that are very costly. Focus group research saves enormous sums of time and money that might otherwise be spent building stuff no one wants.

- Enough guidance to create a prototype that target users may actually try out in user experience testing. Such prototypes can also be used to enable senior management and investors to "kick the tires" and buy into a concept that has been executed with target users and development partners.

User Experience Research: What It Is and How You Do It

Once a prototype has been built that is robust enough for target users to try out on their own, we suggest conducting research that enables them to do so. The reason we call it user experience testing—as opposed to, for instance, "usability"—is that this research is designed to have people experience your site. It is not sufficient in this competitive arena for a site to be merely usable (that is, navigation-friendly). Sites must also provide experiences that are compelling and that do a better job of delivering what they offer than other options available, be they online or offline.

We recommend conducting one or two days of research, which means 8 or 16 interviews, each of which should be roughly one hour in length.

The major concept behind user experience research is that individuals will be empowered to experience a company as intimately on their web site as they would in the real world. Accordingly, the goal during the hour-long interview is to see how a user experiences your site so that it can be refined in ways users will appreciate. If a user wants to search for a pair of pants and shirt that match as a gift, he should have the option of doing so. Likewise, if he would buy or sell steel on the site, he needs to be able to do that, too. The following are typical of the goals companies seek to achieve by conducting user experience research:

- Grab their attention with an effective homepage.

- Establish a tone and manner that is consonant with their expectations of your brand and your industry.

- Empower users to easily and intuitively travel the pathways of your site to accomplish their goals.

Some Rules of Thumb

Regardless of the approach you take in your research, focus groups or user experience testing, the following are some additional guidelines to keep in mind:

- Again, look for a firm that has experience in your company's industry because this will give you the benefit of learning from other people's experience. And while some companies are a bit nervous about doing so, we recommend it. Any firm that has worked on three other trading sites or several education or healthcare or gaming sites will have gathered a lot of wisdom in the category about how to define the target audience or structure the interview, and this can only be of benefit in the design and structuring of your web site.

- If you are not testing your current "live" site, try not to schedule research until you are certain you have a prototype that is robust enough not to "blow up" on users or frustrate them with its incompleteness. Even if they can buy only one sweater, permit them to travel the entire purchase path. Doing so will provide you with valuable insight into the shopping experience. In contrast, scheduling testing prematurely results in money wasted in cancellation fees, or in the testing of a site that is simply not ready to be viewed.

- This being said, understand, too, that the site need not be all but ready for launch when it is tested. In fact, if it is too polished, there may not be time or money to fix what testing reveals is broken. To be effective in testing, functionality should be the paramount consideration.

- Populate the site with enough content and functionality to simulate the experience you want to test. For an information site, this might mean loading the prototype with articles; for a finance site, it might mean populating it with a sample account so that users can see what their real account might look like.

- Try to make sure the entire team attends.

- Again, don't do 30 interviews (a clear case of overkill when it comes to user experience testing). We've found only three reasons to do more than eight (or at the most 16 interviews):

  1. If you have three or more significantly different target audiences: for instance, parents, educators, and kids, or brokers, doctors, and patients.

  2. If your development allows rapid prototyping, which enables you to make changes between days of testing and, therefore, rapidly enhance your site within a day or two of research.

  3. If your site has so much functionality that the number of pathways you need people to travel is more than can be covered in a day or two—even if the tasks you give people are rotated.

- Don't give people more than three to five tasks to accomplish. Remember, the goal is to simulate reality, not to create an endurance test.

- Phrase the tasks you give people in "plain speak," and be careful not to employ the same words used on the site. In this way, people understand what you are asking but are not led directly to the button you are testing.

- Unless you are AOL or an ISP that is targeting those who are new to the web, don't waste your time interviewing what some call "newbies." Those who have never searched or browsed are not going to give you much useful feedback about your site. Even if you are an e-commerce site, split your interviews between experienced e-shoppers and those who are merely open to the idea. We believe that you will learn a great deal about your site from those who have shopped on many other sites.

Structuring a User Experience Interview

While each project has its own unique objectives, we have developed a basic approach to the user experience interview that we use as a question flow for the interview guide. This basic flow, outlined below, is designed to gather initial impressions and expectations, as well as in-depth reactions, to content and functionality. And, of course, we've also built in additional probing on brand issues.

- Before even showing the homepage, ask the participant what his relevant experience is on- and offline. How does he currently shop for a car? Get information about a disease? Decide which play to attend? This will enable you to understand his expectations and interests.

- Gauge his gut reactions to the homepage. What kind of site does he think it is? Where do his eyes go first? What kind of people is the site for? Would he stay? And if so, where would he go?

- Ask some users to simply do something they've told you they are interested in doing—search for a car, buy a gift, or register for a prize. Leave the testing room and see what paths they travel. (We recommend videotaping the interview "picture in picture" so the development team can observe the user's facial expressions and, in some cases, hand movements, along with the screen they are using.) Simply watching where they go is very useful, especially if the site is geared toward searching or shopping. It shows you how they would approach the task and how intuitive or circuitous the process is.

- For others, drill down on each button and area of the home-page. Ask the user what he would expect to be behind the button. Learning that the button means five different things to different users, or that no one understands what the button means, tells you a lot.

- Give each user a series of tasks to do that are in sync with what he would do in real life. We suggest three to five tasks, which can be less or more depending on the complexity and length of the task. Make a list of every path you want users to travel. Write tasks that take them there. Then, rotate the tasks you give people based on their interests and what you want to learn from them.

- After (and sometimes during) each task, ask users what they are thinking. If they look confused, ask them how they are feeling. If they tell you they are confused, ask them to explain why and what might be different about the site (language, flow, place-ment, type size) that would mitigate this response and make the process appealing and easy. Ask them what words or images would make sense to them.

- When you wrap up the interview, ask about their overall opin-ion of the site. If you were a fly on the wall, would you see them returning of their own volition? If so, why and when? How would they describe it to a friend? What three things would they fix? (Usually, what people remember at the end of an interview *is* what most needs to be fixed.) If the site is for an established brand, find out if the site met with their expectations of the brand. If not, why? How could it be fixed?

Making User Experience Testing Actionable

First, and perhaps most importantly, we recommend conducting a debriefing with the entire team immediately following research. Almost every team we've met will retreat and make changes with-in 48 hours of testing. By debriefing right after the research—the minute it is over, in fact—the entire team is more likely to be focused on and agree about the major elements learned, and they will be able to brainstorm about what to fix and how to accomplish this. We often notice that the majority of fixes that come out of such *in situ* meetings are implemented within days of testing, even before the final report is complete.

Finally, and on this note, in designing a final report of research findings, we think what you learn from user experience testing can be divided into three broad sections:

- *Mindset of the User*. In this section, describe the perceptions or behavior that shape what users expect of your site. These often impact how people experience it and how they interpret the meaning of labels. These are important to understand when you're fine-tuning your site.

- *Strategic Findings and Recommendations*. In this section, describe the learning you come away with that impacts branding, positioning, or overall communication. These findings are often related to homepage design: how you describe your site, whether people think they need to register with the company in question, what they expect to do on your site, and so on. Making small changes on your homepage, such as reordering functions, changing the prominence of your logo, or using a visual metaphor to communicate what the site is about, can dramatically affect the way target users experience your site. As stated in Chapter 3, "Your Homepage is a 30-Second Window of Opportunity: Dont' Be Shy!," these perceptions drive interest—or dismissal—of your site.

- *Tactical Findings and Recommendations*. In this section, identify, page by page or task by task, any problems that exist with respect to navigation and nomenclature and how to fix them. We find that the more concrete these recommendations are—and the more informed they are by suggestions made by users—the easier the team can integrate them into Version 2.

Index

A

abilities of users, anticipating in order to retain user interest, 131
    adding plug-ins, 134
    back ups, 132-133
    enlarging or shrinking an image, 134
    manipulating Windows, 133-134
    upgrading browsers, 134
About Us (mission) (homepage anchor), 84
account access, transferring established brands to the web, 304-305
accountable research
    benefits, 15
        generating consensus, 16-17
        launching with confidence, 22
        learning to think like target users, 18-19
        saving time and money, 19-20
        selling up the line, 20-21
    defining and conducting web-related research, 13-14
    making research pay for itself, 22
        appropriate treatment of test participants, 26-27
        bringing the whole team into the process, 24-25
        distinguishing "can they use it" from "will they use it," 28-30
        interviewing people who use site, 27-28
        rapid prototyping, 25-26
        researching before spending big money, 23-24
    reasons to perform research, 14-15
acronyms, avoiding, 182
    homepage design, 58-60
advanced search option, 245-246
allies, business audience sites, 319-320
alternate spellings, search engines, 240-242
alternate terminology, search engines, 242-243
anchor links, navigation, 264

anchors (specific elements expected on all homepages), 84
    About Us (mission), 84
    bells and whistles, 84-86
    Contact Us, 84
    Customer Service, 84
    Home Button, 84
    Search, 84
anticipating
    abilities of the users, retaining user interest, 131
        adding plug-ins, 134
        back ups, 132-133
        enlarging or shrinking an image, 134
        manipulating Windows, 133-134
        upgrading browsers, 134
    user needs based on user dialogue, 330
application guidelines, icons, 183-184
articles, content, 190, 201-203
artistic design
    chaotic approach, 78-80
    minimalist art, 77-78
assistance features, 151
    balancing benefits and detail of explanation, 161-162
    banner advertising, 173-174
    content page, 167-171
    directions, 152-154
    highlighted benefits, 156-161
    links to information, 154-155
    orientation in the site, 162-166
    restrictions, 171-172
    search function, 166-167
audio, functionality changes, 339
avoiding acronyms, 182

B

banner advertising (assistance feature), 173-174
bells, obscuring homepage anchors, 84-86

benefits of conducting web-related research, 15
    generating consensus, 16-17
    launching with confidence, 22
    learning to think like target users, 18-19
    saving time and money, 19-20
    selling up the line, 20-21
bias of anticipating user needs, homepage design,
    66-69
Boolean logic, search engines, 238-239
borrowing credibility, brand affiliations, 39-41
brands
    affiliations, borrowing credibility, 39-41
    consistency, e-commerce sites, 289-291
    downloading, 149
    established brands, evaluating need for
        content, 192-197
    imagery, page design, making the site in sync
        with the brand, 88-89
    new brands, evaluating need for content, 198-199
    transferring established brands to the web, 295
        account access, 304-305
        customer service and technical support,
            305-307
        details, 301-302
        e-commerce and channel marketing, 303
        expectations, 296-297
        language of the customer, 300
        leveraging marketing messages, 308-309
        organization, 299-300
        premium services for high-value customers,
            307-308
        site quality, 302-303
"bread crumbs"
    navigation, 261
    orientation in the site, 165
browser/searcher combinations, 237
browsers, 237
"buckets," user language (homepage design), 54
business audiences, client relationships
    client list credibility, 315-317
    "client-centric" audiences, 320-321
    core competencies, 321-322
    creating allies, 319-320
    decision makers, 324
    displaying industry credentials, 317-318
    implementers, 324
    levels of authority, 314-315
    leveraging brands, 321-322
    target customers, 322-323
    understanding how customers do business,
        312-314

C

calculators, online, functionality changes, 339
categories, homepage, setting up categories
    according to organizational structure, 54-58

changes
    functionality, 338
        chat, 338
        e-commerce, 339-340
        message boards, 338
        online bidding, 338
        online calculators and worksheets, 339
        video/audio, 339
    listening to your users, 341
    morphing process, 340
    web as a moving target, user needs growth,
        336-337
chaotic approach, 78-80
chat, functionality changes, 338
clashing colors, 107
clickable
    elements, icons, 180-181
    graphics, 231-233
        user control, 233-234
client list credibility, business audience sites, 315-317
client relationships, business audiences
    client list credibility, 315-317
    "client-centric" audiences, 320-321
    core competencies, 321-322
    creating allies, 319-320
    decision makers, 324
    displaying industry credentials, 317-318
    implementers, 324
    levels of authority, 314-315
    leveraging brands, 321-322
    target customers, 322-323
    understanding how customers do business,
        312-314
"client-centric" audiences, business audience sites,
    320-321
color, graphics, 224
company logo, as Home button, 116
competitors
    learning from successes and failures of
        predecessors, 113-114
    static models, 109-110
        balancing originality and creativity, 110-111
        modeling online process with offline world,
            111-113
concepts for homepage design, staying in service
    to your concept, 44-45
configurators, increasing interactivity, 213-214
confusing icons in page design, 82
consensus generation, as benefit of web-related
    research, 16-17
consistency rule, icons, 179-180
consistent use of graphics, 224-226
Contact Us (homepage anchor), 84
content, 190
    articles, 190, 201-203
    delivery, 209
        optional email lists, 209
        subscription forms, 209-210
    evaluating need, 192
        established brands, 192-197
        new brands, 198-199

news, 190
product/service information, 190, 204
  reviews and ratings, 204-205
skepticism, 190-191
sponsors of e-commerce sites, 203
third-party, credibility, 199-201
user-generated, 190, 206
  establishing credibility, 208
  product reviews and ratings, 207-208
content page (assistance feature), **167-171**
control
  providing user control, 135-136
  site development, 89
controversial icons in page design, **82**
core competencies, business audience sites, **321-322**
creating allies, business audience sites, **319-320**
credentials, homepage design, **37-39**
  borrowing credibility, 39-41
credibility
  third-party content, 199-201
  user-generated content, 208
critical instructions for navigation, **266-267**
cross-selling, e-commerce sites, **285-287**
Customer Service (homepage anchor), **84**
customer service, transferring established brands
  to the web, **305-307**

D

decision makers, business audience sites, **324**
delays, avoiding with heavy graphics, **226-227**
delivery, content, **209**
  optional email lists, 209
  subscription forms, 209-210
description, e-commerce sites, **277-278**
design
  guidelines, 183-184
  homepage. *See* homepage design
details, transferring established brands to the web,
  301-302
development process, engaging target users,
  learning to think like your users, **6-7**
directions (assistance feature), **152-154**
displaying industry credentials, business audience
  sites, **317-318**
distractions on the homepage, **74-77**
  chaotic approach, 78-80
  minimalist artistry, 77-78
downloading, **137**
  brands, 149
  plug-ins, 138
    assisting the user, 143-145
    defining what a download is in your site,
      139-140
    necessity of a plug-in, 147-148
    reasons to download, 141-143
  rules, 150
  software, 145-147

E-F

e-commerce
  channel marketing, transferring established
    brands to the web, 303
  functionality changes, 339-340
  sites, web-based shopping functionality
    brand consistency, 289-291
    cross-selling, 285-287
    how consumers make purchasing decisions,
      272-273
    incentives, 281-283
    metaphors, 275-277
    pictures and descriptions, 277-278
    product returns, 283-285
    shipping and handling charges, 287-288
    standard approach to shopping, 274-275
    tracking the buying process, 279-281
effective use of homepage space, **41-44**
"entertainment," entryway of a site, **74-77**
  chaotic approach, 78-80
  minimalist artistry, 77-78
error messages
  managing, retaining user interest, 129-131
  navigation, 262-263
established brands, transferring to the web, **295**
  account access, 304-305
  customer service and technical support, 305-307
  details, 301-302
  e-commerce and channel marketing, 303
  expectations, 296-297
  language of the customer, 300
  leveraging marketing messages, 308-309
  organization, 299-300
  premium services for high-value customers,
    307-308
  site quality, 302-303
evaluating need for content, **192**
  established brands, 192-197
  new brands, 198-199
expectations of established brands, **296-297**

"floating" 800 numbers, **128**
focus groups, web development research, **344-345**
  conducting research, 345
  making results actionable, 346-347
  structuring focus groups, 345-346
functionality
  changes, 338
    chat, 338
    e-commerce, 339-340
    message boards, 338
    online bidding, 338
    online calculators and worksheets, 339
    video/audio, 339
  shopping on e-commerce sites
    brand consistency, 289-291
    cross-selling, 285-287
    how consumers make purchasing decisions,
      272-273
    incentives, 281-283

metaphors, 275-277
pictures and descriptions, 277-278
product returns, 283-285
shipping and handling charges, 287-288
standard approach to shopping, 274-275
tracking the buying process, 279-281

G

game attraction, increasing interactivity, 212-213
generating consensus, as benefit of web-related research, 16-17
getting information, 151
    balancing benefits and detail of explanation, 161-162
    banner advertising, 173-174
    content page, 167-171
    directions, 152-154
    highlighted benefits, 156-161
    links to information, 154-155
    orientation in the site, 162-166
    restrictions, 171-172
    search function, 166-167
giveaways, increasing interactivity, 221-222
"glowing" colors, 107
goals, serving strategic goals in homepage design, 45-48
graphics, 223
    avoiding delays with heavy graphics, 226-227
    clickable, 231-233
        user control, 233-234
    consistent use, 224-226
    desire for color, 224
    "litmus" test for each graphic element, 228-230
    white space, 230
guidance features, 151
    balancing benefits and detail of explanation, 161-162
    banner advertising, 173-174
    content page, 167-171
    directions, 152-154
    highlighted benefits, 156-161
    links to information, 154-155
    orientation in the site, 162-166
    restrictions, 171-172
    search function, 166-167

H

heavy graphics, avoiding delays, 226-227
highlighted benefits (assistance feature), 156-161
Home Button (homepage anchor), 84, 116
homepage design
    acronyms and insider terminology, 58-60
    anchors, 84
        About Us (mission), 84
        Contact Us, 84
        Customer Service, 84

        Home Button, 84
        Search, 84
        use of bells and whistles, 84-86
    brand imagery, making the site in sync with the brand, 88-89
    chaotic approach, 78-80
    credentials, 37-39
        borrowing credibility, 39-41
    effective use of homepage space, 41-44
    entrenched bias of anticipating user needs, 66-69
    how you serve your customers or prospects, 71-72
    icons, web site navigation, 86-87
    identifying audience and welcoming users, 49-51
    informing visitors of limitations, 51-52
    introduction of a product, 34-36
    minimalist artistry, 77-78
    questions to ask yourself, 52
    reducing distractions, 74-77
    rollovers, 61-62
    Russian dolls, 60
    serving strategic goals, 45-48
    setting up categories according to organizational structure, 54-58
    simplicity and control, 89, 256-259
    staying in service to your concept, 44-45
    team brainstorming, 69-70
    testing new features, 332-333
    trendy language, 60
    user language, 53
        how users identify with "buckets," 54
    web site minimalism, 63-66

I-J

icons
    clickable elements, 180-181
    consistency rule, 179-180
    design and application guidelines, 183-184
    literal interpretations, 182
    offline metaphors, 176-185
        ingrained behaviors of users, 178-179
    online meanings, 181-182
    page design, 82
        confusing icons, 82
        controversial icons, 82
        misleading icons, 82
        testing, 83
    putting control in the hands of the user, 185-186
    web site navigation, 86-87
identifying audience, homepage design, 49-51
images, 99-100
    navigation, 266
    slowing down the images, 97-98
    visual cues versus text links, 95-96
implementers, business audience sites, 324
incentives, e-commerce sites, 281-283
inconsistent searchers, 237-238
industry credentials, business audience sites, 317-318

information (seeking information), 151
    balancing benefits and detail of explanation,
        161-162
    banner advertising, 173-174
    content page, 167-171
    directions, 152-154
    highlighted benefits, 156-161
    links to information, 154-155
    orientation in the site, 162-166
    restrictions, 171-172
    search function, 166-167
informing visitors of limitations, homepage design,
    51-52
ingrained behaviors of users, interface confusion
    with icons, 178-179
insider terminology, avoiding use in homepage
    design, 58-60
instant gratification, interactive polls, 220
instructions
    navigation, 266-267
    written versus visual cues, 91-96
        images, 95-100
        literal meaning of instructive words, 100-101
        making instructions brief, 103
        making step-by-step instructions clear,
            104-105
        presenting high-level choices first, 101-103
        "print" media, 107-108
        readable text, 106-107
interactivity, 211
    game attraction, 212-213
    giveaways, 221-222
    interactive tools, 218
    polls with instant results, instant gratification,
        219-220
    product configurators, 213-214
    screensavers, 221
    self-tests, 215
        connecting prospects to site, 216-218
        encouraging users to register for your
            site, 216
    software downloads, 221
interface confusion, icons, 176-185
    clickable elements, 180-181
    consistency rule, 179-180
    design and application guideliines, 183-184
    ingrained behaviors of users, 178-179
    literal interpretations, 182
    online meanings, 181-182
    putting control in the hands of the user, 185-186
introductions
    product, homepage design, 34-36
    reducing distractions, 74-77
        chaotic approach, 78-80
        minimalist artistry, 77-78
inverse text, 107

K-L

keywords, search engines, 243-245
language
    customer, transferring established brands to the
        web, 300
    trendy, avoiding use in homepage design, 60
    user, homepage design, 53
        how users identify with "buckets," 54
launching with confidence, as benefit of
    web-related research, 22
left navigation bar, 114
levels of authority, understanding how customers
    do business, business audience sites, 314-315
leveraging
    brands, business audience sites, 321-322
    marketing messages, transferring established
        brands to the web, 308-309
limitations, informing visitors of limitations on the
    homepage, 51-52
links
    information (assistance feature), 154-155
    Search function, 236
    third-party content credibility, 201
listening, 327-328
    offline world, clues to opportunities online, 333
    user dialogue, 328-329, 341
        anticipating needs, 330
        creating ongoing dialogue, 331-332
        modifying your site, 329-330
literal interpretations
    icons, 182
    instructive words, 100-101
"litmus" test, graphic element necessity, 228-230
low contrast text, 107

M-N

managing error conditions, retaining user interest,
    129-131
marketers, listening, 327-328
    offline world, 333
    user dialogue, 328-332, 341
marketing messages, leveraging, transferring
    established brands to the web, 308-309
message boards, functionality changes, 338
metaphors, shopping, e-commerce sites, 275-277
minimalism, web site minimalism, 63-66
minimalist artistry, 77-78
misleading icons, homepage design, 82
modeling
    online process with offline world, 111-113
    site based on user dialogue, 329-330
morphing process, 340
multiple fields, search engines, 247-249

navigation
    icons, 86-87
    bars, leaving it in the left position, 114

issues, 255-256
    anchor links, 264
    "bread crumbs," 261
    critical instructions, 266-267
    error messages, 262-263
    images, 266
    "next steps," 264-265
    "portfolios," 267-268
    scrolling, 268-269
    simplifying the homepage, 256-259
    "success" path, 262-263
    "wish lists," 267-268
negative notoriety, established brands, evaluating
    need for content, 195-197
"newbies," 336
news, as content, 190
"next steps," navigation, 264-265

O-P

offline
    communication, retaining user interest, 126-127
    metaphors, icons, 176-185
        ingrained behaviors of users, 178-179
    world, clues to opportunities online, 333
ongoing dialogue, 331
    web site advisory councils, 332
online
    bidding, functionality changes, 338
    calculators, functionality changes, 339
    meanings, icons, 181-182
    worksheets, functionality changes, 339
orientation in the site, 162-166
overdesign
    chaotic approach, 78-80
    minimalist art, 77-78
    reducing homepage distractions, 74-77

page design
    assistance features, 151
        balancing benefits and detail of
            explanation, 161-162
        banner advertising, 173-174
        content page, 167-171
        directions, 152-154
        highlighted benefits, 156-161
        links to information, 154-155
        orientation in the site, 162-166
        restrictions, 171-172
        search function, 166-167
    brand imagery, making the site in sync with
        the brand, 88-89
    chaotic approach, 78-80
    creating pathways based on user profiles,
        116-118
        power of users to choose own categories,
            118-119
    Home button, 84, 116
    homepage anchors, 84
        About Us (mission), 84
        Contact Us, 84

        Customer Service, 84
        Home Button, 84
        Search, 84
        use of bells and whistles, 84-86
    icons, 82
        confusing icons, 82
        controversial icons, 82
        misleading icons, 82
        testing, 83
        web site navigation, 86-87
    instructions, 103
    left navigation bar, 114
    minimalist art, 77-78
    presenting high-level choices first, 101-103
    "print" media, 107-108
    readable text, 106-107
    simplicity and control, 89
    step-by-step instructions, 104-105
    visual cues versus written instructions, 91-96
        images, 95-100
        literal meaning of instructive words, 100-101
parallel functionality, how you serve your
    customers or prospects, homepage design, 71-72
pathways, creating based on user profiles, 116-118
    power of users to choose own categories,
        118-119
pictures, e-commerce sites, 277-278
plug-ins, downloading, 138
    assisting the user, 143-145
    defining what a download is in your site,
        139-140
    reasons to download, 141-143
polls, increasing interactivity, instant gratification,
    219-220
"portfolios," navigation, 267-268
premium services for high-value customers, trans-
    ferring established brands to the web, 307-308
"print" media, 107-108
product
    configurators, increasing interactivity, 213-214
    introduction, homepage design, 34-36
    product/service information, content, 190, 204
    returns, e-commerce sites, 283-285
    reviews and ratings
        including in product/service information
            content, 204-205
        user-generated content, 207-208
proven models, based on user experience research,
    118-119

Q-R

rapid prototyping, making research pay for itself,
    25-26
readable text, page design, 106-107
reducing distractions on the homepage, 74-77
    chaotic approach, 78-80
    minimalist artistry, 77-78

research
  benefits, 15
    generating consensus, 16-17
    launching with confidence, 22
    learning to think like target users, 18-19
    saving time and money, 19-20
    selling up the line, 20-21
  defining and conducting web-related research,
    13-14
  making research pay for itself, 22
    appropriate treatment of test participants,
    26-27
    bringing the whole team into the process,
    24-25
    distinguishing "can they use it" from "will
    they use it," 28-30
    interviewing people who use site, 27-28
    rapid prototyping, 25-26
    researching before spending big money, 23-24
  reasons to perform research, 14-15
  web development research, 343
    benefits of, 15-24
    focus groups, 344-347
    user experience research, 347-352
restrictions (assistance feature), 171-172
results, search engines, summaries, 251-253
retaining the interest of users, 124
  anticipating the abilities of the users, 131
    adding plug-ins, 134
    back ups, 132-133
    enlarging or shrinking an image, 134
    manipulating Windows, 133-134
    upgrading browsers, 134
  managing error conditions, 129-131
  offering offline communication, 126-127
  providing user control, 135-136
  strategies for recovery, 124-125
role of the offline world, clues to opportunities
  online, 333
rollovers, homepage design, 61-62
rules for downloading, 150
Russian dolls, homepage design, 60

S

Sachs Insights (SI), 8-9
saving time and money, as benefit of web-related
  research, 19-20
screensavers, increasing interactivity, 221
scrolling, navigation issues, 268-269
Search (homepage anchor), 84
search engines, 236
Search function, 166-167, 235
  advanced search, 245-246
  alternate spellings, 240-242
  alternate terminology, 242-243
  Boolean logic, 238-239
  browser/searcher combinations, 237
  browsers, 237

defining search within the site versus the World
  Wide web, 249-251
homepage links, 236
keywords, 243-245
multiple fields, 247-249
results, summaries, 251-253
search engines, 236
user inconsistencies, 237-238
self-tests, increasing interactivity, 215
  connecting prospects to site, 216-218
  encouraging users to register for your site, 216
selling up the line, as benefit of web-related
  research, 20-21
serving strategic goals, homepage design, 45-48
shipping and handling charges, e-commerce sites,
  287-288
shopping functionality, e-commerce sites
  brand consistency, 289-291
  cross-selling, 285-287
  how consumers make purchasing decisions,
    272-273
  incentives, 281-283
  metaphors, 275-277
  pictures and descriptions, 277-278
  product returns, 283-285
  shipping and handling charges, 287-288
  standard approach to shopping, 274-275
  tracking the buying process, 279-281
SI (Sachs Insights), 8-9
simplicity, site development, 89
site quality, transferring established brands to the
  web, 302-303
skepticism, content, 190-191
software, downloading, 145-147
  increasing interactivity, 221
  necessity of a plug-in, 147-148
space, effective use of homepage space, 41-44
spelling, alternate spellings, search engines, 240-242
splash pages, visual cues, 96
sponsors of e-commerce sites, content, 203
standard approach to shopping, e-commerce sites,
  274-275
static models, 109-110
  balancing originality and creativity, 110-111
  learning from successes and failures of
    predecessors, 113-114
  modeling online process with offline world,
    111-113
step-by-step instructions, homepage design, 104-105
strategic goals, serving strategic goals in homepage
  design, 45-48
structuring
  focus groups, 345-346
  interview, user experience research, 350-351
subscription forms, content delivery, 209-210
"success" path, navigation, 262-263
summaries, search engine results, 251-253

T

target customers, business audience sites, 322-323
team brainstorming, homepage design, 69-70
technical support, transferring established brands to the web, 305-307
terminology, alternates, search engines, 242-243
testing
icons, homepage design, 83
new features, homepage, 332-333
text links, 92
third-party content, credibility, 199-201
tools, interactive, 218
tracking the buying process, e-commerce sites, 279-281
transferring established brands to the web, 295
account access, 304-305
customer service and technical support, 305-307
details, 301-302
e-commerce and channel marketing, 303
expectations, 296-297
language of the customer, 300
leveraging marketing messages, 308-309
organization, 299-300
premium services for high-value customers, 307-308
site quality, 302-303
trendy language, avoiding use in homepage design, 60

U-V

uniform models, 109-110
balancing originality and creativity, 110-111
learning from successes and failures of predecessors, 113-114
modeling online process with offline world, 111-113
user confusion
chaotic approach, 78-80
minimalist art, 77-78
user dialogue
anticipating needs, 330
creating ongoing dialogue, 331
web site advisory councils, 332
establishing the foundation for your site, 328-329, 341
modifying your site, 329-330
user experience research, 347-350
making testing actionable, 351-352
mindset of the user, 352
strategic findings and recommendations, 352
structuring an interview, 350-351
tactical findings and recommendations, 352
user experience testing, 3
engaging target users in development process, learning to think like your users, 6-7
reasons to create user-focused web sites, 3-5
retaining the interest of users
anticipating the abilities of the users, 131-134

managing error conditions, 129-131
offering offline communication, 126-127
providing user control, 135-136
strategies for recovery, 124-125
user profiles, creating pathways, 116, 118
power of users to choose own categories, 118-119
user-generated content, 190, 206
establishing credibility, 208
product reviews and ratings, 207-208

video, functionality changes, 339
visual cues versus written instructions, 91-108
images, 95-100
literal meaning of instructive words, 100-101
making instructions brief, 103
making step-by-step instructions clear, 104-105
presenting high-level choices first, 101-103
"print" media, 107-108
readable text, 106-107

W-Z

web development research, 343
benefits of, 15-24
focus groups, 344-345
conducting research, 345
making results actionable, 346-347
structuring focus groups, 345-346
user experience research, 347-352
making testing actionable, 351-352
mindset of the user, 352
strategic findings and recommendations, 352
structuring an interview, 350-351
tactical findings and recommendations, 352
web sites
advisory councils, creating ongoing dialogue, 332
development, user experience testing, 3
engaging target users in development process, 6-7
reasons to create user-focused web sites, 3-5
minimalism, 63-66
navigation, icons, 86-87
web-based shopping functionality
brand consistency, 289-291
cross-selling, 285-287
how consumers make purchasing decisions, 272-273
incentives, 281-283
metaphors, 275-277
pictures and descriptions, 277-278
product returns, 283-285
shipping and handling charges, 287-288
standard approach to shopping, 274-275
tracking the buying process, 279-281
welcoming users, homepage design, 49-51
whistles, obscuring homepage anchors, 84-86
white space, 230
"wish lists," navigation, 267-268
worksheets, online, functionality changes, 339

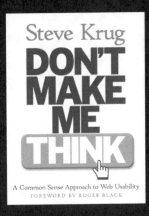

VOICES THAT MATTER

VISIT OUR WEB SITE

WWW.NEWRIDERS.COM

On our Web site you'll find information about our other books, authors, tables of contents, indexes, and book errata. You will also find information about book registration and how to purchase our books.

EMAIL US

Contact us at this address: **nrfeedback@newriders.com**

- If you have comments or questions about this book
- To report errors that you have found in this book
- If you have a book proposal to submit or are interested in writing for New Riders
- If you would like to have an author kit sent to you
- If you are an expert in a computer topic or technology and are interested in being a technical editor who reviews manuscripts for technical accuracy
- To find a distributor in your area, please contact our international department at this address. **nrmedia@newriders.com**

- For instructors from educational institutions who want to preview New Riders books for classroom use. Email should include your name, title, school, department, address, phone number, office days/hours, text in use, and enrollment, along with your request for desk/examination copies and/or additional information.
- For members of the media who are interested in reviewing copies of New Riders books. Send your name, mailing address, and email address, along with the name of the publication or Web site you work for.

BULK PURCHASES/CORPORATE SALES

If you are interested in buying 10 or more copies of a title or want to set up an account for your company to purchase directly from the publisher at a substantial discount, contact us at 800-382-3419 or email your contact information to corpsales@pearsontechgroup.com. A sales representative will contact you with more information.

WRITE TO US

New Riders Publishing
201 W. 103rd St.
Indianapolis, IN 46290-1097

CALL US

Toll-free (800) 571-5840 + 9 + 7477
If outside U.S. (317) 581-3500. Ask for New Riders.

FAX US

(317) 581-4663

New Riders

Solutions from experts you know and trust.

www.informit.com

- OPERATING SYSTEMS
- WEB DEVELOPMENT
- PROGRAMMING
- NETWORKING
- CERTIFICATION
- AND MORE...

Expert Access.
Free Content.

New Riders has partnered with **InformIT.com** to bring technical information to your desktop. Drawing on New Riders authors and reviewers to provide additional information on topics you're interested in, **InformIT.com** has free, in-depth information you won't find anywhere else.

- **Master the skills you need, when you need them**

- **Call on resources from some of the best minds in the industry**

- **Get answers when you need them, using InformIT's comprehensive library or live experts online**

- **Go above and beyond what you find in New Riders books, extending your knowledge**

As an **InformIT** partner, **New Riders** has shared the wisdom and knowledge of our authors with you online. Visit **InformIT.com** to see what you're missing.

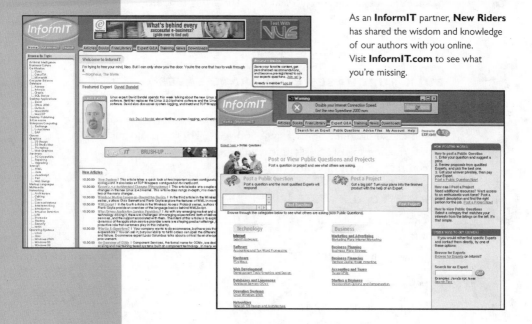

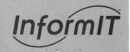